More Tax Tips and Tax Dodges

More Tax Tips
and Tax Dodges

What You Should and Shouldn't Do to Cut Your Taxes

Edited by Frederick Andrews

DOW JONES BOOKS
CHICOPEE, MASS.

Introduction

IF you're looking for a routine guide to the 1040 Form, this isn't it. This book doesn't recite the standard categories of exemptions or itemized deductions. It has no tables of tax rates. You won't find the answer as to whether you should file Schedule C. Answers to black-and-white tax questions are available elsewhere.

Instead, this book is about the gray area of tax law. It is about real conflict over taxes—actual borderline cases where taxpayers have cut their tax bills by contesting the Internal Revenue Service in court.

The book, if used properly, should help you cut your tax bill. It will enable you to look at the law and the IRS with a new degree of sophistication. Tax law is continually re-interpreted and in flux. The book will alert you to tax possibilities you'll never find in an IRS instruction booklet—mainly because the IRS is still resisting them in court. Some of these may fit your situation and save you money.

Unlike many tax guides, this book doesn't merely outline hypothetical tax situations. The book gives the specifics of real legal cases that have been tested in the crucible of the courts. In addition to legal decisions, the book also provides the latest interpretations by the Internal Revenue Service of many particular tax questions.

The selections are drawn from "Tax Report," the popular Page One column published weekly in The Wall Street Journal, the national business daily. It contains the best and most significant of the thousands of Tax Report items over the past five years.

Introduction

The book has a two-fold purpose. The first is to tell you about tax developments that may save you money by answering questions like these:

—If you're audited, the IRS agent follows confidential guidelines in negotiating with you. Can you find out what these are?

—You work at home evenings, but you aren't required to. May you take deductions for your "office" at home? If so, how much?

—If you get married, will your taxes go down?

—You are at odds with the IRS. Can you fight it in court without incurring expensive legal fees?

—You are a tax cheat, and the IRS has caught up with you. Should you cooperate?

The book is also intended to deepen your understanding of what the tax system is and how it really works. It may even amuse you in the telling. In fiscal 1972, the Internal Revenue Service collected no less than $209,855,737,000. The great bulk of this sum came from individuals and businesses who voluntarily paid what was due under the law. As every IRS Commissioner sooner or later reminds us, our willing compliance is an essential part of the tax system. But at the same time, hundreds of thousands of highly trained lawyers, accountants and tax advisers make a handsome living counseling clients how to avoid (at times, how to evade) the tax bite. That's part of our tax system, too.

Taxes are more than the government's prime means of raising revenue. They seep into every corner of our life. The IRS is an enormous bureaucracy; and like other institutions, it is undergoing unprecedented and demanding public scrutiny. Today perhaps no tax development is more significant than the effort to open up the traditional secrecy of the IRS to "audit" its procedures and decisions.

Taxes are also the end-product of a continual struggle not to pay them—or, rather, to have some groups pay more and others less. Not all classes, industries, interests, or areas are equal in this struggle, or equally well represented when tax laws are made (or, for that matter, interpreted in confidential rulings by the IRS). Too often the average taxpayer has no determined advocate at the table. The Internal Revenue Code may perhaps be classed among the wonders of the modern world. It combines some of the most complex formulations of the human mind with elemental avarice.

As stressed above, this book offers tax tips, not exhaustive answers. It deals with novel and unsettled tax questions. Many (perhaps most) tax matters are well-settled and thus underrepresented in this book.

This is a revised and enlarged edition of a book first published in 1971. The selections were printed in the Tax Report during 1969-73. We have excluded items that later developments have made clearly out-of-date. Of those included, however, only rarely have items been reworded merely to reflect the passing of time.

This revised edition differs from the first by an even greater stress on items of immediate, practical benefit to the reader. Dozens and dozens of new items have been added, as well as a couple of new chapters. These changes have expanded the book's scope and deepened its coverage.

We give the original date with every item. With most items, we also give a citation to the underlying court decisions or IRS ruling. We urge you to follow these citations to the full texts. These brief tax summaries are as accurate as we can make them, but they necessarily omit many details. One of the omissions may be a detail that makes the precedent unsuited to your circumstances.

A decision that stands as we go to press may later be reversed by a higher court or overridden by a new tax law. The citation should help you check whether an item is still up-to-date. When a substantial amount of money is involved, there's no substitute for professional tax advice.

The abbreviations "T.C." and "T.C. Memo." refer to the regular and memorandum decision of the United States Tax Court. The full text of these decisions can be found in *Tax Court Reporter* and *Tax Court Memorandum Decisions,* two legal series published by Commerce Clearing House, Inc. Decisions of other federal courts appear in *U.S. Tax Cases,* also published by Commerce Clearing House. Similar legal publications carry IRS Rulings, which can also be checked at IRS offices.

During 1969-71, I edited The Tax Report. Since early 1972, David McClintock has handled the column, and many fine examples of his work appear in this revised edition. I am grateful for the opportunity to include them.

—FREDERICK ANDREWS

Contents

Life Is Very Taxing These Days (I) 1

Marriage and Joint Returns 2

Claiming a Dependent 7

Taxes and Alimony 16

Is It Income? 22

. . . Or a Capital Gain? 44

Is It a Medical Expense? 49

Finding Tax Shelter at Home 59

A Few Points on Moving 66

Tax Aspects of Giving 69

Cutting Your Losses 81

Deducting Travel and Schooling 91

Is It a Business Expense? 99

The Business Traveler 117

Deductions for Business Entertainment? . . . 127

Deductions for Employment Fees? 133

Life Is Very Taxing These Days (II) 137

The Private Tax People 138

Dealing With the IRS 141

Your Day in Tax Court 157

Our "Voluntary" Tax System? 164

How Much Did He Really Earn? 171

Is It Fraud? 177

What Are a Taxpayer's Rights? 185

Breaking Down IRS Secrecy 205

Tactics for the Taxpayer 210

Life Is Very Taxing These Days (III) 223

A Few Shelters and Loopholes 224

You Can't Take It With You 242

Law in Flux on Life Insurance 256

Of Interest and Debts 265

If You Live Abroad 271

Salting a Little Something Away 278

When Doctors and Lawyers Incorporate . . . 286

Life Is Very Taxing These Days (IV) 291

Some Tax-Exempt Groups 292

Small Business Matters 307

The Much-Criticized Property Tax 315

And in Those Days 323

More Tax Tips
and Tax Dodges

Life Is Very Taxing
These Days (I)

An IRS chicken: Would you believe a "self-constructed egg-making machine"?

Uncle Sam lost a tax case but it's on appeal. The case involved a big chicken operator in Mississippi and how it carried its chickens on its books. The main business was selling eggs, but after the hens had given their all, they were dispatched to a meat-processing plant. (After a chicken becomes a laying hen at age 24 or 26 weeks, she has, on average, about 12 months of commercial output in her.)

The taxpayer inventoried his flocks at the price they fetched at the meat processor's. The IRS contended, however, the chickens shouldn't be inventoried at all. It argued that because the taxpayer was mainly selling eggs, the laying hens should be construed as "self-constructed production equipment ('egg-making machines')." The IRS would have the unsuspecting birds capitalized and amortized.

To the Tax Court, the whole thing smacked of which comes first—the chicken or the egg? Obviously, the taxpayer was selling both, the court decided, and the meat processor's price was a fair measure for depleted hens. The court saw no fowl play in the taxpayer's book.

(Garth v. Commissioner, 56 T.C. No. 50.)
11/17/71

Marriage and Joint Returns

Wages of sin? A working couple is taxed less unwed than wed, a study says.

"If you must work, don't marry; if you must marry, don't work." That's the conclusion of an article in Taxes magazine that spells out the impact of "tax reform" changes on a man and wife who both work. The author, Britt Richards, contends that raising the standard deduction and personal exemption and lowering rates on single persons results in a hefty "marriage penalty" on a working couple.

In 1970, he says, if husband and wife earn $14,000 apiece, together they will pay $360 more in Federal income taxes than a similar couple without benefit of wedlock. By 1972, as tax changes are phased in, the difference will rise to $972. Even if one partner's earnings are much greater than the other's, a similar (though smaller) penalty results. In the view of Mr. Richards, who is married, the notion of the joint return is rooted in inequity. It allows a husband and wife to split their income, but it really benefits only the single-income family, he contends.

"It assumes that marriage takes only one form," he asserts. "The husband goes off to work, kisses his wife at the door, and returns in the evening to hear about her day's activities with the garden club."

5/6/70

◦◁▷◦

"Sign it or I'll kill you," said Sid to Rebecca. She did, so he didn't.

Wives are difficult sometimes. According to Rebecca's testimony before a federal court, her husband, Sid, one year wanted her to sign a blank joint return. She said, "Of course not." He said: " 'If not, I'll break your head open and smash your face in.' " Rebecca still demurred, so Sid signed her name himself. The next year was worse. Questioned about the events of April 15, Rebecca testified:

". . . it was a day of terror. It started as early as we got up in the morning and proceeded all day long. 'You sign it or I will break your head open; you sign it or I will smash your face in.' " Rebecca finally gave in. "While my husband and Millie together stood outside, I opened the door just a crack, still keeping the door on the chain, just enough so he could shove the tax return in to me just about two inches, just enough to obtain my signature on the bottom line; and as soon as he obtained this signature he pulled it right back and said: 'Now I've got you.' "

The court extract didn't say who Millie was or tell how the drama ended. The issue before the court was whether Rebecca had intended to file joint returns with Sid those two years. The court decided she hadn't.

(Gaynes v. U.S.A., U.S. Ct. of Appeals, 5th Cir., 1972.)
2/9/72

Check, Check-Mate: A domestic drama in two acts:

A married taxpayer filed a joint return for 1965 without his wife's knowledge. (All the income on the return was his.) Then, in 1968, the IRS sent the couple a notice of deficiency for $2,154. The man petitioned the Tax Court in protest, but he also sent the IRS a check for an additional $954. The IRS records, however, didn't show that he owed anything for 1965 (apparently because the deficiency claim was still pending), so the IRS returned the $954 as a refund.

By this time, the couple was divorced, and the $954

refund check went to the ex-wife's address. She cashed
the check, after endorsing it with both her former husband's name and her own. The man protested that he
never received the refund, but the Tax Court ruled he
did. It cited the wife's testimony that she telephoned
him about the check, but he told her he didn't want to
be bothered with her and she should keep it. The ex-
husband never challenged this testimony, the Tax
Court said.

His statement "might reasonably be interpreted"
as an authorization to sign his name and cash the
check, the Tax Court decided. Thus, the man construc-
tively received the refund, it ruled.

(Wiener v. Commissioner, T.C. Memo. 1971-56.)
4/7/71

◦━━◦

No fraud results merely because a husband doesn't
tell all about a joint return.

That's the latest Tax Court decision in a painful,
difficult case. Back in 1968, it ruled, reluctantly, that
because a woman signed a joint return, she was liable
for taxes due on $100,000 her husband embezzled (with-
out her knowledge). Last year an appeals court disagreed. It ordered the Tax Court to look at the circumstances of her signing the return. It ruled that some
factors—duress, signing by mistake, trickery or fraud
—could wipe out the signature.

The Tax Court took a second look, but found no ex-
tenuating circumstances. The husband never threatened or forced her to sign, or even said the returns were
accurate. He didn't bother to forge her name because he
knew she would sign. (She felt she ought to "mind her
husband," she said.) In this context, the court held that
his keeping mum about not reporting the embezzled
funds wasn't fraud.

"To hold that such nondisclosure rises to the level

of fraud would open a Pandora's box to avoidance of liability on joint returns," the court declared.

(Huelsman v. Commissioner, 54 T.C. No. 135.)
7/8/70

०○○।

A 1971 law shields an innocent wife from being held
accountable for her husband's tax frauds. In one case,
because a woman had signed a joint return, she was
held liable for taxes due on $100,000 her husband em-
bezzled. Law now provides that a spouse who isn't a
party to fraudulent omission of income from a tax return won't be liable. The provision won't be applied,
however, unless the omission is more than 25% of the
total income reported.

1/20/71

०○○।

Wedlocked: In several cases, women who signed
joint returns were later dunned for taxes on money
their husbands stole, though they had no part in it. Now
a wife has been ruled liable for taxes the IRS couldn't
extract from her spouse on money he earned abroad.
The couple originally filed a joint return. They assumed
the $10,150 he earned in Vietnam would be tax-exempt
but he re-entered the U.S. too soon. The Tax Court
wouldn't allow the wife to file an amended separate return. This ruling created "unfairness, (but) we see no
escape from this unfortunate result."

(Wilson v. Commissioner, T.C. Memo. 1970-105.)
5/13/70

०○○।

A Montana man filed a joint return, but his wife
never signed it. Instead, the husband jotted on the return, "Wife away caring for ailing mother." The IRS
contended the return wasn't a joint return, and it
dunned the husband at higher single-taxpayer rates.

The Tax Court disagreed. If both spouses show that they meant a return to be joint when it was filed, then the lack of one signature doesn't matter, the court said.

(Hill v. Commissioner, T.C. Memo. 1971-127.)
6/16/71

Claiming a Dependent

Fine points in claiming a parent as a dependent come out in a Tax Court case.

To claim a dependent, one must provide more than half of his or her support. A Texas man met this test for his elderly grandmother, even though she received $942 in old-age benefits and $70 in Medicare-Medicaid premiums from the state of Texas. The IRS claimed that this $1,012 total exceeded the $915 that the grandson said he provided in food, lodging, utilities, laundry and transportation.

The Tax Court nevertheless ruled for the grandson because not everything the grandmother got from the state was spent on her support. She spent $19 on burial insurance and gave $60 more to her son—neither item considered "support." That narrowed the gap between the state's contribution and her grandson's to $18. And he provided more transportation, and she gave away a few more dollars than was precisely claimed, the court decided. These items tipped the scales for the grandson.

This was another case in which a taxpayer represented himself before the Tax Court. "Petitioner was forthright and truthful. We find no reason to doubt him," the court said.

(Carter v. Commissioner, 55 T.C. No. 13.)
11/4/70

o〇o

The IRS "defies logic" in a dependency case, the Tax Court says.

Ernest Mehringer lived with his 78-year-old mother in her house in a shabby section of South Chicago. The place needed constant repair, and Ernest did the work. One year, Ernest contributed $2,606 to his mother's support. Her Social Security payments came to $1,391. So it appeared Ernest had given more than half her support and was entitled to claim his mother as a dependent.

But the IRS contended that in addition to Social Security the mother's contribution to her support included the rental value of the house. That would have made her share more than half, the IRS figured, and would have ruled out Ernest's deduction. But the Tax Court approved the deduction. It pointed out the house was in such bad shape it couldn't have been rented under Chicago rent rules. So it hadn't any rental value.

Furthermore, the court said, Ernest as much as owned the house in the first place. He guaranteed the mortgage, would get title to the place upon his mother's death and was solely responsible through his repairs for its being habitable. Thus, if the place had any value, it was Ernest's contribution rather than his mother's.

(Mehringer v. Commissioner, T.C. Memo. 1973-41.)
2/28/73

◦───◦

The IRS proposes new rules for divorced parents in claiming dependents.

To claim a child as a dependent, one must provide more than half his support. In divorces or separations, that's often hard to prove, especially when the parents are at odds. So the IRS proposed new regulations to implement a 1967 law. They generally assume that the parent with custody of the child may claim him or her as a dependent, but they propose two important exceptions.

First, if the divorce decree provides, or the parents agree, that the "noncustodial" parent (usually the father) may claim the dependent, the IRS will accept that as long as he gives at least $600 a year in support. Secondly, whatever the divorce terms, if the noncustodial parent pays $1,200 or more in support his outlays will be presumed to provide more than half unless the custodial parent (the mother) clearly shows otherwise.

The IRS would also entitle either parent to get from the other an itemized statement of the support that parent provides. The parent asking the itemization must give a similar statement in exchange.

(Notice of Proposed Rule Making, Federal Register, Sept. 12, 1970.)
9/23/70

❦

The IRS reverses itself on a key aspect of child support in divorces.

If one parent gets custody of the children, the other parent still can claim them as dependents providing he contributes at least $1,200 a year to their support and the parent with custody doesn't show she provided over half the support. That's relatively simple until the custodial parent remarries. Then the decision can ride on whether the new husband's contributions to them are counted as part of her own, in comparison to her former husband's share.

The IRS historically has ruled that a new spouse's contribution can't be counted as part of a parent's share of support. But the Tax Court decided just the opposite in one case, and the IRS has reversed its position.

Rev. Rul. 73-175)
4/25/73

❦

Divorced parents may be affected by a decision on claiming a child as a dependent.

According to the law, if a "noncustodial" parent (usually the father) provides at least $1,200 a year in support for a child, he is presumed to provide more than half the child's support and thus entitled to claim the dependent. The "custodial" parent (usually the mother) can overcome this presumption, however, if she "clearly demonstrates" that she provides more.

The Fifth Circuit appeals court interpreted that requirement in a way that makes it easier for the mother. The father had argued that the mother had to meet the strict legal standard of "clear and *convincing* evidence." But the appeals court affirmed the Tax Court and ruled that the requirement simply means "by a clear preponderance of the evidence," a much less demanding standard.

The IRS has amended its proposed regulations on the subject to make them consistent with the courts' interpretation.

(Labay v. Commissioner, U.S. Ct. of Appeals, 5th Cir., 1971.)
11/17/71

◦⟨⟩◦

You can claim Nancy Sue but not Addie Lou, the Tax Court tells Jack.

He met Addie Lou one night in the bus terminal in Tallahassee, Fla. After two days together, they rented an apartment and "took up housekeeping." Addie Lou's six-year-old daughter, Nancy Sue, lived with them. The arrangement continued for a little over a year, until Jack and Addie Lou had a "falling-out" and Jack sent her and Nancy Sue home to Georgia.

As Jack had supported Addie Lou and her daughter, he claimed them both as tax dependents for the time they lived with him. But the IRS and Tax Court objected. The court said Jack's nonmarital relationship with Addie Lou violated local law where they lived; a dependent can't be claimed unless her relationship to the taxpayer conforms to local law. Addie Lou's and Jack's relationship was "on a day-to-day basis without the sanctity even approaching that of a common-law marriage," the court asserted.

Jack was allowed to claim Nancy Sue, however. Local laws apparently didn't cover her status.

(Martin v. Commissioner, T.C. Memo. 1973-136.)
7/11/73

Another court rules that head-of-household means more than token occupancy.

The Fourth Circuit has reversed a lower court decision that gave head-of-household tax status to an unmarried South Carolina man. The man supported his two elderly sisters, who lived in the old home place. The taxpayer kept a room and a few things there, but actually lived in a nearby town. The district court said he had always considered the old place "one of his homes," and "token or implied occupancy" was enough.

But the Fourth Circuit disagreed. It quotes legislative history specifying that the household be the taxpayer's "actual place of abode." (This doesn't apply to taxpayers who maintain homes for their parents.) The household needn't be his principal place of abode, but "it must be his home, where he and the other members of the household live together for a substantial part of the time," the circuit court said.

The decision accords with previous decisions in the Fifth and Seventh circuits. But the Ninth Circuit has ruled otherwise.

(Muse v. U.S.A., U.S. Ct. of Appeals, 4th Cir., 1970).
11/25/70

०⟨⟩०

The IRS modifies its stance on counting public assistance as support.

Sometimes a person will help support a relative who is also getting public assistance. To claim that relative as a dependent at tax time, the taxpayer must prove he provided more than one-half of his or her support. In the past, the IRS has counted the entire public assistance as support from another source.

But the IRS has announced it will no longer make this presumption. The use of the assistance benefits will become a factual matter. Only the portion the recipient actually spends on his support will be counted as such. Certain expenditures—life insurance premiums or buying a car—normally aren't considered as going for "support."

10/27/71

Supporting a parent in a rest home or home for the aged may become less expensive. An IRS ruling has conceded that an unmarried taxpayer who furnishes such support qualifies for head-of-household tax rates. Normally a single taxpayer who pays more than half the costs of his parent's household is a head-of-household, but the IRS has long argued that a room in a rest home doesn't amount to a household. Both the Tax Court and a circuit court have rejected this argument.

(Rev. Ruling 70-279.)
6/19/70

Foster children may be claimed as dependents under the same rules that apply to natural and adopted children, according to proposed IRS regulations. They define a foster child as one "in the care of a person or persons (other than parents or adopted parents) who care for the child as their own." The proposed regulations implement the Tax Reform Act.

4/22/70

Barring proof to the contrary, financial support of a family from an outsider—say a divorced father —has been treated for tax purposes as if it were distributed equally among the family members. But the IRS now says it will let a taxpayer designate different amounts for different recipients simply by noting the intended breakdown on his check. This makes it easier in many cases to establish dependency deductions.

(Rev. Rul. 72-591.)
1/10/73

When the law says "written," it means "written." That was made painfully clear to a divorced Kentucky man who tried to claim his children as dependents. They lived with his former wife. The law okays dependency deductions for the "noncustodial" parent if he pays at least $600 a year for each child, and a written agreement with his ex-wife gives him the deductions. The Kentucky father paid the $600. But the only evidence of an agreement was a court transcript of an oral agreement. The Tax Court said that wasn't enough.

(Sheeley v. Commissioner, 59 T.C. No. 51)
2/7/73

The Tax Court has ruled that U.S. savings bonds a divorced father bought for his two children didn't constitute support of the children. The bonds weren't cashed or otherwise used for support during the year under review, the court noted.

(Leslie v. Commissioner, T.C. Memo. 1972-151)
7/26/72

Maybe Uncle Sam can claim this deduction: When a California man underwent surgery, his illness cost his son $2,400 in medical bills, but the younger man gained no tax relief. He couldn't deduct the medical outlays because his father wasn't his dependent. And that was because the elderly man also received $3,000 from Social Security and government welfare agencies. The son argued vainly before the Tax Court that such nontaxable income shouldn't count. In plain English, a dependent must get "over half of his support from the taxpayer," the court recited.

(Beck v. Commissioner, T.C. Memo. 1970-153.)
6/24/70

Living proof: A divorced woman won the right to claim her four children, ages 8 to 15, as dependents even though her former husband gave $3,900 a year toward their support. The woman demonstrated that she provided more than half their support. She submitted a table of annual expenses that totaled $8,670, including $600 or $700 a child for food. "Although the amounts estimated for food seem a little high," the Tax Court said, "we had occasion to observe the boys at trial. Their size attests to the hearty appetites"—and the food costs.

(Herbert v. Commissioner, T.C. Memo. 1970-216.)
8/5/70

"Mens sana in corpore sano," the Tax Court declared in a camp opinion: A sound mind in a sound body. That dictum popped up in a dispute over who could claim a young boy as a dependent. His divorced mother had provided more than half his support if $917 for eight weeks at summer camp in Maine was counted. The IRS found the fee "preposterous" and argued that "support" meant the "necessities of life." But the court "completely disagreed" with so narrow a definition. Camp benefited the boy's development, it said.

(Shapiro v. Commissioner, 54 T.C. No. 31.)
3/4/70

Child care expenses, within limits, may be deducted by a woman or a widower, provided the purpose is to allow the taxpayer to be gainfully employed. But a twist in the law often denies a mother the deduction if she is divorced. For example, the Tax Court ruled against a divorcee who claimed a $709 child-care deduction. To qualify, the court said, the children must be her dependents, and—as is frequently the case—her former husband's support payments entitled him, not her, to claim the dependents.

(Bosher v. Commissioner, T.C. Memo. 1971-10.)
1/27/71

A divorced woman raised a novel tax claim. She argued that the IRS violated the Ninth Amendment by checking whether she (rather than her former husband) could claim their children as dependents. The amendment states that the enumeration of certain constitutional rights shouldn't be construed as denying the existence of others. The IRS violated her privacy by intruding into "unpleasant personal, domestic affairs," she said. A sincere plea, but "legally unsound," the Tax Court ruled.

(Campbell v. Commissioner, T.C. Memo. 1971-51.)
3/31/71

٥◇٥

A child who lives only momentarily after birth can be claimed as a tax dependent if state or local law considers the baby to have been born alive and if a birth certificate is issued, the IRS says.

(Rev. Rul. 73-156)

Taxes and Alimony

A liberated idea of support for a former wife is taxed as plain ol' alimony.

In Texas, a divorced woman didn't ask "alimony," but her former husband agreed to pay her way through law school to help her become self-supporting. The woman claimed he was discharging "a moral obligation" because she had worked while he went to school. And under Texas law, she contended, he wasn't obliged to educate his former wife.

But the IRS called it alimony and taxed it as such. The Tax Court recently agreed. If the former husband undertook a legal obligation to make payments, and the obligation had all the earmarks of alimony, then the alimony tax rules apply, the court said. It made no difference that he did more than the law required.

(Kern v. Commisioner, 55 T.C. No. 40.)
12/16/70

◑〰◐

In a divorce, fees for tax advice may be readily deductible, the IRS says.

Normally legal fees in a divorce or separation are nondeductible personal expenses. If such fees include tax advice, however, they may be deductible in part, provided a relatively simple test is met. The key element, the IRS says, is the existence of "a reasonable basis" for deciding what portion of the total fees was for tax advice. That portion may be included in the taxpayer's itemized deductions.

What is "a reasonable basis?" As an example, the

IRS ruling cites a taxpayer who retained an attorney to handle all aspects of his divorce, including advice on claiming his children as dependents after the divorce was granted. The lawyer's bill allocated his fee between tax and non-tax matters "based primarily on the time attributable to each, the fee customarily charged for similar services, and the results obtained in the divorce negotiations." That rationale was acceptable to the IRS.

In another instance, a taxpayer retained a law firm specializing solely in tax practice to advise him on the tax consequences of a property settlement. That fee was clearly deductible.

(Rev. Rul. 72-545)
11/22/72

One man's payments to his niece and nephew count as alimony to his ex-wife.

Melvin and Marie took custody of her brother's children because they weren't getting proper care in their own home. Later Melvin and Marie were divorced and agreed that Melvin, in addition to paying regular alimony to Marie, would pay the kids' education expenses until they finished college. Marie, however, felt she had an obligation to contribute half the education money. So, as she wasn't able to do so directly, Melvin gave half his contribution to her to turn over to the children.

Melvin took a tax deduction for the part he paid through Marie, just as if it were part of the alimony. But the IRS barred the arrangement, contending that in substance the money didn't go to Marie but to the children. The Tax Court, however, said the obligation she had assumed to provide half the education support was legitimate, and insofar as the money from Melvin allowed her to meet that obligation, it constituted an economic benefit to her.

Thus, the money amounted to alimony and Melvin could deduct it, the court ruled.

(Christiansen v. Commissioner, 60 T.C. No. 49.)
6/27/73

०─○

Some marriages are made in Heaven, but others aren't.

Here's an odd one for you: A twice-married woman was collecting $23,000 a year in alimony from Husband No. 2. Somehow Husband No. 2 wasn't invited to wedding No. 3, perhaps because he was entitled to cut off the gravy if his former wife remarried. Husband No. 3 later testified that keeping things quiet was his wife's idea; she claimed it was his. In any event, she collected an extra $23,000 before Husband No. 2 caught on. He obtained a judgment that she pay it back as "unjust enrichment."

The couple also neglected to mention the $23,000 to the IRS. Later, Husband No. 3 contended the sum wasn't taxable as alimony because No. 2 hadn't been legally obliged to pay it. The money must have been a tax-free gift or loan. The Tax Court thought that calling it a gift was stretching things. In addition, it said, the wife's obligation to repay the sum didn't mean it wasn't income. Her obligation, it declared, was "not in substance different" from an embezzler's, whose embezzlement is taxable even though the law requires that he pay the money back.

By the time the case reached court, Husband No. 3 was simply Former No. 3. But the court held him liable for taxes on the entire $23,000 because he knew of the omission when he signed the joint return.

(Joss v. Commissioner, 56 T.C. No. 27.)
6/2/71

Tax-free alimony was upheld by a U.S. circuit court. The ruling concerned a woman who benefited from an alimony trust set up by her former husband. Normally alimony is taxable, but part of the trust holdings was tax-exempt bonds. The court ruled that a like portion of her payments were tax-exempt. Under standard "conduit" rules applied to trusts, income keeps its original exempt character in the hands of a beneficiary.

(Ellis v. U.S.A., U.S. Ct. of Appeals, 6th Cir., 1969.)
10/22/69

A deal's a deal, an appeals court says, and it upholds a good-faith compromise.

In 1944, a GI divorced his wife, who had left him, and she soon married again. He heard nothing more for 20 years, until he was about to sell some land for $322,-350. The buyer questioned the original divorce and required that the woman sign a release. This she happily did—for $40,000 in cash and land. She claimed the sum was paid for release of her dower rights, but the IRS and the Tax Court called it taxable income. If the divorce was valid—and they weren't convinced it wasn't —she had no dower rights to give up, they said.

The Fifth Circuit Appeals Court toppled that decision and sided with the woman. The key point, it said, wasn't whether the divorce was valid, but rather whether the woman had good reason to think it wasn't and entered a "good faith compromise" of her rights. Society has a stake in the peaceful settlement of disputes, the court said, and thus "there are strong policy reasons for taking at face value compromises based on claims made in good faith."

Nor had the woman waited too long to question the

divorce. No one had been clearly injured by the delay, the court said.

(Howard v. Commissioner, U.S. Ct. of Appeals, 5th Cir., 1971.)
6/16/71

○◇○

Insurance premiums as alimony payments are clarified by an IRS ruling.

The ruling concerned a divorced man who took out two policies on his life. The first he irrevocably assigned to his ex-wife, with her as beneficiary and their children as beneficiaries in the event of her death. The second policy named the children as beneficiaries and the former wife as next in line.

Premiums on the first policy qualified as alimony deductions and were income for the woman, the IRS ruled. That's because the arrangement was part of a court-approved settlement, and the man signed over the policy for good. The second policy, however, was voluntary, and he retained control of it. Thus it was neither alimony nor otherwise deductible.

(Rev. Ruling 70-218.)
5/13/70

○◇○

An Illinois woman didn't have to pay taxes on support payments from her former husband, the Tax Court rules. Federal law says a divorced woman's gross income includes payments received under "a legal obligation . . . imposed on or incurred by the husband." But in this case, the woman married again, and even though her first husband continued to pay her support, he had no legal obligation under Illinois law to do so.

(Hoffman v. Commissioner, 54 T.C. No. 156.)
8/19/70

○◇○

Free ride: A Florida man wasn't allowed to deduct as alimony the mortgage payments and maintenance he paid on the house where his former wife and their children lived. He had put the house in trust for his children and thus the payments benefited them, the Tax Court ruled. It was incidental that his ex-wife also lived there free.

(Isaacson v. Commissioner, 58 T.C. No. 67)
8/2/72

Bridget and Howard split up but weren't immediately divorced. They signed an agreement providing for Howard to pay certain of Bridget's expenses. Under a separation agreement, such payments would have been taxable income to her. But she claimed they weren't taxable because their agreement didn't specifically mention separation. The Tax Court, though, ruled it amounted to a separation agreement, even though the word wasn't used.

(Bogard v. Commissioner, 59 T.C. No. 6)
10/25/72

Is It Income?...

Ford leases bargain Continentals to Congressmen —but is the bargain taxable?

United Press International detailed how Ford Motor Co. leases its luxury cars to at least 19 ranking Congressmen for $750 a year. You or I would have to pay about $3,480 to lease similar splendor. Ford says the preferential arrangement is part of a policy of putting its cars in the hands of prestigious drivers. But tax lawyers say there's some question whether the $2,730 saving is a tax-free gift or taxable income for the Congressmen.

The IRS says it hasn't ruled on the point. But back in 1962, Ford provided Paul Hornung, the football star, with free use of a Thunderbird. The Tax Court ruled Hornung had to pay taxes on its $600 rental value. It said Ford enjoyed "the intangible benefits of (Hornung's) implied personal endorsement." A gift springs from "detached and disinterested generosity . . . affection, admiration (or) charity."

Maybe Ford feels that way about football stars and Congressmen. In Hornung's case, "it seems more likely that (Ford) believed football stars would (help) the sales image of Thunderbirds," the court said.

(Hornung v. Commissioner, 47 T.C. No. 42.)
8/5/70

◦⟨⟩◦

"Oh fiddlesticks!" Sen. Cotton says: It'd be "absurd" to tax his bargain auto lease.

Congressmen and Senators who enjoy slashed-rate leases on Continentals say it never entered their heads that their saving could be considered taxable income. Many say the only tax treatment they give the matter is to deduct their $750 rental as a business expense—and not all of them do that. Sen. Cotton disputes the $3,480 quoted as the normal cost of leasing a Continental for a year. "You'd have to be an awful simpleton to pay that amount."

A number of lawmakers say the preferential leases have gone on for years without being questioned. "I'm a former Internal Revenue man, and it isn't a gift," Rep. Dulski (D., N.Y.) asserts. "It's a contract between Ford and myself. A deductible item. I checked with IRS."

8/5/70

०───◒

Here's how a doctor gave his office to his kids and got a nice tax break.

After he transferred the property, he got a court to appoint him as his children's guardian. As their guardian, he collected rent in their behalf from himself on the office he'd given them. He deducted the rent as a business expense. And in his role as guardian, he used the rent to pay the kids' private school tuition, insurance premiums, swimming lesson fees and other expenses.

The IRS rejected the rent deduction. It contended the property gift hadn't any "business purpose," but was merely an effort to avoid taxes. The IRS also said the law requires that when a guardianship's income—the doctor's rent payments in this case—are used to pay expenses for which the guardian is legally responsible —e.g. child support, the guardian must pay taxes on that income.

But the Ninth Circuit appeals court has okayed the entire deal. It ruled the transaction had "economic reality" and didn't require a specific business purpose. Moreover, the court found the child's expenses for which the guardianship's income was being used went beyond those the guardian was legally responsible for like food and lodging. So the requirement that such income be taxed personally to the guardian didn't apply, the court said. It further ruled the deal met other requirements for such gift/lease-back transactions.

One judge strongly dissented and some observers expect the IRS to appeal.

(Brooke v. U.S.A., U.S. Ct. of Appeals, 9th Cir., 1972)
8/23/72

o⊂⊃o

Financial counseling fees a firm pays for executives are taxable income to them.

As fringe benefits, more and more companies are hiring financial counseling firms to give personal financial advice to the companies' top executives. At one company, the IRS says, the service included counseling on investments, insurance, real estate, tax planning, preparation of tax returns, retirement benefits and estate planning. The cost to the company for one executive was $3,000.

The IRS says the cost of such aid is taxable compensation just like the executive's regular salary. But there's a significant ameliorating factor: The cost of investment counseling, and of tax counseling and return preparation, are tax deductible. So the executive is actually being taxed only on the other services.

(Rev. Rul. 73-13)
1/24/73

o⊂⊃o

The IRS stiffens its line on scholarship aid tied to future employment.

In fields where qualified people are scarce, a public agency will sometimes give college scholarships to students who promise to work for the agency after graduation. Such aid hasn't been considered taxable income for the recipient. Now, however, the IRS says it will no longer abide by the leading precedent on the point, a

1960 Tax Court decision involving a girl who went through nursing school under such an arrangement with the State of Tennessee.

The IRS is basing its turnabout on a Supreme Court decision in 1969. The High Court ruled that what Westinghouse paid an employe on leave of absence in graduate school was taxable income. (He had agreed to return to Westinghouse for at least two years.) Prior employment with the donor really doesn't matter, the IRS contends. The key point is whether a stipend is "granted to return for the quid pro quo of a promise to render future services."

(Rev. Ruling 70-283.)
6/17/70

o⟨⟩o

Rare case: A doctor gets a tax break on government research grants.

Educational stipends are taxable if they constitute compensation for service or obligate the recipient to future service. Perhaps more than any other taxpayers, doctors clash frequently with the IRS on this point. Most physicians, between formal schooling and full-time private practice, pass through a period of advanced training when they may be living primarily on grants but still be obligated to serve the source of the aid, e.g. care for a hospital's patients. A doctor claims the pay is a nontaxable fellowship. The IRS, usually with court backing, claims it is taxable.

In one case, the IRS tried to tax the pay of a doctor at a University of Texas hospital. He was doing research financed by a grant from the National Institutes of Health. The IRS said the doctor's situation was similar to others in which pay was found to be taxable, but the Tax Court discerned some key differences.

The man spent less than a quarter of his time caring for patients, his research didn't uniquely benefit the

Texas hospital, and he wasn't obligated to work for the hospital after the research was completed. So, no tax.

(Bieberdorf v. Commissioner, 60 T.C. No. 14)
5/2/73

○══○»

By judge or jury? Two similar tax disputes are resolved very differently.

A taxpayer who disagrees with the IRS may go to Tax Court, where a judge will decide his case. Or he may pay what the IRS says he owes, then sue for a refund in a U.S. district court or the Court of Claims. Two resident physicians at the University of Arkansas Medical Center not only went to district court, but also had their cases decided by a jury. At issue was their pay: Was it ordinary income or a fellowship grant—up to $3,600 a year of which goes tax-free?

The jury said their pay indeed qualified as a tax-free grant. That was just the opposite of what the Tax Court told another doctor, a resident in psychiatry at two hospitals in Texas. If a "grant" is really pay for employment services or primarily benefits the grantor, then it is taxable—and that's the way it was in the Texas doctor's case, the Tax Court said. He provided "essentially the same regular patient care" as a staff doctor. If the hospitals hadn't had the residents, they would have had to hire more staff.

The Tax Court considered it immaterial that the resident was seeking training. Nothing says pay should go tax-free "merely because the recipient is learning a trade," it declared.

(Leathers v. U.S.A., U.S. Dist. Ct., East Dist. Ark., 1971, and
Emory v. Commissioner, T.C. Memo. 1971-191)
8/25/71

○══○»

A research grant is ruled deductible over the IRS's objections.

A scholarship or fellowship can be kept out of taxable income up to $300 a month only if it principally benefits the recipient rather than the giver. If a grant is in any way a payment for past, present, or further service, it is taxable.

Louis Vaccaro was awarded a post-doctoral grant by the University of Oregon to enable him to continue studies in educational administration. He considered the money a fellowship and excluded a $300-a-month portion when he reported taxable income. The IRS objected. It pointed out the money came from a federal government fund intended to be used as salaries for university staff members working on projects of benefit to the school. That's right, the Tax Court acknowledged. But Vaccaro didn't happen to be working on university projects; his course work and other activities mainly benefited him personally. So the tax break was allowed.

(Vaccaro v. Commissioner, 58 T.C. No. 72)
8/9/72

◑━◐

Medicare benefits aren't income, but they may count as support, the IRS says.

Basic Medicare benefits—financed by payroll taxes and open to almost all elderly persons—are legally the same as Social Security, the IRS says, and thus not taxable. Supplementary Medicare, which covers only those who enroll and pay a monthly premium, isn't taxable, either, but for a different reason: It's treated like proceeds from private health and accident insurance, which generally aren't considered income.

But Medicare may affect an elderly person's status as a dependent, the IRS says. To claim someone as a dependent, a taxpayer must provide over half his total support. Basic Medicare benefits will be counted as support the recipient provides himself. The supplementary benefits won't constitute support, the IRS says, but the premiums paid will be support provided by whoever pays them.

The IRS also says that Medicare benefits aren't included in computing the limit on the income tax credit elderly persons already enjoy on retirement income.

(Rev. Ruling 70-341.)
7/15/70

A gift isn't really a gift if the giver is mentally incompetent, a court says.

An elderly San Francisco man gave a friend $290,783 in cash. At least that's what the friend told the IRS. Had the tax agency believed him, he wouldn't have had to pay any tax; gifts generally are tax-free to the recipient. But the IRS did a little checking and found the elderly man had a history of amnesia and other mental problems and had been declared incompetent to handle his financial affairs.

In fact, the IRS discovered, he wasn't handling his financial affairs. The friend to whom he supposedly had given the money was. In deciding the case, the Tax Court implied the friend had taken the money improperly. The court pointed out a gift is legitimate only if the giver is mentally competent to give it. Otherwise, the recipient has to pay ordinary income taxes on it.

(Bader v. Commissioner, T.C. Memo. 1973-16)
8/15/73

An executive died, and his company wanted to "do something" for his widow.

It was a young company, and the man was the first of its principals to die. The firm voted to give his widow $25,000 plus her late husband's company car. Was all this a gift or income? A jury decided the transfer was a tax-free gift. The IRS asked an appeals court to set the verdict aside, but the court refused.

In theory, a gift is motivated by "detached and disinterested generosity." There are so many shadings in practice, however, that "each case must be treated individually," the court declared. For instance, a payment to express gratitude for an employe's services, without regard for his widow's needs, is considered income. So is a payment mainly intended to assure surviving executives that the company is a good place to work. In the present case, the company's only possible self-serving motive would be to show that it "takes care of its own," the court said.

Had it been the jury, the court declared, it would have ruled for the IRS. But it decided "reasonable people" could have found that "natural sympathy and concern" were the firm's motive. Thus the court let the verdict stand.

(Grinstead v. U.S.A., U.S. Ct. of Appeals, 7th Cir., 1971.)
8/11/71

०⊂⊃०

Foiled again! The Second Circuit steps in to protect a widow from the IRS.

When a loyal employe dies, his firm often pays his widow something, and this frequently produces a tax dispute: Is the sum income for the widow, or a tax-free gift? Of late, the Tax Court has consistently ruled the sums income, on the ground that the firm gets an economic benefit, if only greater loyalty from employes. Also, higher courts have hesitated to second-guess a lower court's overall sense of the situation.

The Second Circuit appeals court overcame this reluctance and reversed the Tax Court. When a long-time employe of Salomon Bros. died, the firm paid his widow $60,131, the amount he would have earned, had he lived out the year. In the circumstances, the appeals court decided the sum was a genuine gift.

The court was perturbed that the Tax Court almost invariably held such sums income, but U.S. district courts have consistently called them gifts. The outcome shouldn't depend on which court you go to, the higher court said.

(Estate of Carter v. Commissioner,
U.S. Ct. of Appeals, 2nd Cir., 1971)
1/12/72

◐——◑

It all started when the Virgin of Guadalupe gave Jose Diaz a lottery tip.

Life hadn't been kind to Jose. He lived in Juarez, Mexico, and ran errands for $12 a week. His vision was bad and he limped. But he had strong religious faith. Once a year he went to Mexico City to pay homage to the Virgin of Guadalupe, the patron saint of Mexicans. And one night in a dream, Jose later recounted, the Virgin advised him to buy ticket number 37281 in the Mexican National Lottery.

Jose hadn't had much experience with such things. So he consulted his nephew, Alfonso Diaz, an American citizen who lived across the border in El Paso and had taken courses in finance. Using Jose's money, Alfonso bought all lottery tickets numbered 37281 (75 tickets) and had them sent to Jose. The Virgin knew what she was talking about. Number 37281 was the big winner and Jose collected $3 million.

Jose asked Alfonso to manage the money. Most of it was put in a bank and, for a time, Alfonso had signatory power over it. At tax time, the IRS claimed that because Alfonso had played an influential role in the situation all along, he in effect had won the money himself and, being a U.S. citizen, was liable for U.S. taxes on the winnings.

The Tax Court said the decision could go either way based on the "objective facts." But, citing a "consistent thread of testimony" from the Diaz family, it ruled Jose owned the tickets and the IRS should get nothing.

(Diaz v. Commissioner, 58 T.C. No. 57)
7/12/72

◦───◦

The nurse gets $75,000; the nephew gets nothing; Merrill Lynch gets ignored.

An elderly woman hired a nurse to care for her during recovery from surgery. They became fast friends, and the nurse stayed on permanently at a weekly salary. Nearly two years after the surgery, the woman gave the nurse a $75,000 check as a gift. But Chase Manhattan Bank refused to honor the check; the signature was "irregular." That was because the lady's advancing age made her hand unsteady. So the bank sent two tellers to witness the writing of another check.

But Chase didn't cash that check either because in the meantime the old woman's nephew had filed suit to have her declared incompetent. (He had designs on her money himself.) A court found her competent, however, and she told her Merrill Lynch broker to sell most of her stock so she could cover the check. The broker implored her to keep her money. But she persisted and the nurse finally got the $75,000. Enter the IRS: It said the money wasn't a gift but was taxable pay for the nurse's services. The IRS alleged the woman had agreed to give the nurse the money in exchange for care for the rest of the woman's life (two more years as it turned out).

But the Tax Court decided the money was a legitimate gift. It denounced the "apparently greedy nephew" and said it believed the nurse's story that there hadn't been any agreement that the money was payment for future service.

(Johnson v. Commissioner, T.C. Memo. 1972-180)
9/13/72

The tax court guts some strained IRS reasoning in a damage case.

A company president was fired by the firm's directors. A legal squabble followed and the deposed president got some unfavorable publicity. Rather than press litigation, the parties agreed on a settlement under which the ex-official got a year's salary plus $45,000 to cover embarrassment, mental strain and other "damages" caused by the publicity.

Personal injury settlements usually aren't taxable, but the IRS tried anyway. It said the man failed to prove any injury for which he could recover damages. But, citing a host of precedents, the Tax Court said he didn't have to prove the claim was valid; he had to show only that the settlement he actually received stemmed from an injury claim. The IRS contended the lawyer who negotiated the settlement for the company didn't have the authority to allocate a portion to personal damages. The Tax Court showed he clearly did. The IRS claimed a letter delineating the settlement was a device for avoiding taxes by designating part for damages. The Tax Court said the letter only confirmed the agreed-on allocation.

Finally, the IRS said embarrassment isn't a damage exempt from tax, and as the damage part of the settlement wasn't allocated between embarrassment and other damages, the whole amount was taxable. The court held embarrassment was incidental to the other injuries and exempted the entire $45,000.

(Seay v. Commissioner, 58 T.C. No. 3)
4/19/72

∞

Tip income causes problems for some wage earners.

There's no question that tips are taxable payment for services and not gifts, but this hasn't prevented all sorts of tax difficulties for waiters and others who fail to keep an accurate record of such income.

In one case, a San Francisco beautician reported receiving $575 in tips during 1965. But on the basis of the employer's records, the IRS figured the man's average tip was 8% for his services which raised the amount of tips to $2,250. Since the beautician kept no records of his own, the Tax Court agreed that he should ante up another $741 in taxes. It was a bit harder for the IRS to figure the tax deficiencies for three Salt Lake City waitresses who didn't keep records but reported tip income equal to about 3% of their total checks during the year. After studying the operation of the restaurant, the Revenue Service figured the average tip was 11%, but adjusted that to 8% since some 25% of patrons didn't tip at all and part of the tip money was passed along to bus boys.

The Tax Court went a little easier on the waitresses. It agreed with the IRS' method of computing their income but decided the average tip was only 8%. This lowered the adjusted tip income to 5¾% of sales.

(Becerra v. Commissioner, T.C. Memo. 1969-22
Hills et al. v. Commissioner, T.C. Memo. 1968-293.)
2/12/69

Maury Wills claims artistry in stealing bases, but an appeals court cuts him down.

It upheld a Tax Court decision that dealt with awards Wills won in 1962, the year the Dodger star smashed all base-stealing records. The appeals court ruled that Wills had to pay taxes on the $1,700 MG he won as "most popular Dodger" and the S. Rae Hickok belt, worth about $8,000, as outstanding pro athlete of 1962. By law, prizes are normally taxed, but there are exceptions for "artistic, literary or civic achievement." But the circuit court turned an umpire's eye to Wills' contention that his base-line thefts qualified for the exception.

The court also denied the ballplayer's claim that the Hickok belt shouldn't be taxed because it was a trophy, rather than a useful prize like the car. The belt could be sold, the court noted, and thus was the equivalent of cash.

"The law requires the foregoing conclusion," the court added with distaste. "We are convinced that it is an inequitable result. The next step would be to tax the gold and silver in Olympic medals."

(Wills v. Commissioner, U.S. Ct. of Apeals, 9th Cir., 1969.)
5/28/69

◊⟨⟩◊

There's no quid pro quo in a football scholarship—or so the Tax Court says.

Back in 1965, James Heidel, a University of Mississippi football star, was given a $50,000 bonus when he signed with the St. Louis Cardinals. Later, Heidel was in Tax Court, claiming the right to average his 1965 income, including the $50,000, over 1961-65. The IRS had balked, contending that he hadn't provided 50% or more of his own support each year during the five-year period, as tax law normally requires. At issue was 1961, when Heidel earned $716, his parents provided $964, and $657 came from an Ole Miss football scholarship.

Heidel said the $657 was support he provided for himself because he had to play football to keep the scholarship. But the Tax Court wouldn't go along. If Ole Miss required services in return, the grant would have to be taxable income, the court declared. It would be "more consistent with the ordinary understanding" of an athletic scholarship to rule the $657 wasn't support Heidel provided for himself, the court concluded.

Heidel also argued the $50,000 was attributable to

"work" performed in 1963 and 1964. But the court said he was paid to sign, not to reward him for his play.

(Heidel v. Commissioner, 56 T.C. No. 10.)
4/28/71

०●○०।

Miss America finds a court unimpressed by her efforts to win the crown.

Deborah Bryant Wilson, Miss America of 1966, lost her claim to average her hefty title-year earnings over five years for tax purposes. To qualify for averaging under the special "major accomplishment" rule, she had to show that more than half of her 1965-66 income was attributable to work done in at least two previous years. She contended it was because she had entered beauty contests and taken courses in modeling and dramatics, all with an eye to the Miss America crown.

Such efforts may have made her Miss America, a district court conceded, but they weren't what the tax code meant by work. Winning the Miss America title merely gave her the chance to make some money, the court said; the actual income came from appearances for pageant sponsors like Oldsmobile. All that was done in her reign, not before.

(Wilson v. U.S.A., U.S. Dist. Ct., Dist. Kansas, 1971.)
2/10/71

०●○०।

The salad days of the Great Salad Oil Swindle left an incredible tax tangle.

A lot of cash changed hands before the bubble burst in 1963 for Allied Crude Vegetable Oil Refining Corp. Ever since, the IRS has been trying to figure who owed taxes on what. One court case involves Lillian Pascarelli, who "lived as husband and wife" with Anthony DeAngelis, the Tax Court found. (DeAngelis was convicted in 1965 of interstate transportation of forged warehouse receipts.)

The case involved $202,000 Mrs. Pascarelli received

from DeAngelis over five years, plus $32,406 he put into a commodity account in her name. Mrs. Pascarelli claimed she merely held the assets for DeAngelis, despite a documented record of expenditures of her own. The IRS argued that the money was pay for services rendered in helping DeAngelis to entertain business friends. If that wasn't so, the IRS said, then the transfers were gifts.

The Tax Court found the money was indeed a gift, prompted by "love and affection and disinterested generosity." But it held Mrs. Pascarelli liable for gift taxes because DeAngelis hadn't paid them.

(Pascarelli v. Commissioner, 55 T.C. No. 100.)
3/31/71

◦⟨⟩◦

An embezzler on a binge wasn't too drunk to enjoy the money, the Tax Court says.

After working 10 months for a Tulsa armored car service, Bob Riddell came in on a Sunday near the end of December one year, took $133,753 from the vault, and did $685 worth of damage to the premises. Then he flew to Los Angeles and lived it up for three weeks. In late January he flew back to Tulsa, returned about $121,000 to his employer and surrendered to authorities. Bob received a five-year suspended sentence after agreeing to pay back the $13,000 or so he hadn't already returned. But the worse financial trouble started when the IRS said he had to declare the whole amount he had taken as income the year he took it and pay $73,265 in taxes on it.

Embezzled funds generally are considered taxable income, but under some circumstances embezzlers have escaped taxes. A few months ago the Tax Court ruled that money a man embezzled could be treated as a loan rather than income because the same year he took it he signed a pledge to repay it. But in the Riddell case, the Tax Court backed the IRS.

The court noted Riddell hadn't made repayment arrangements until the year after he took the money. It also rejected his contention that he hadn't "received unrestricted use of the money" in the few remaining days of the year he took it because of "excessive use of alcohol."

(Riddell v. Commissioner, T.C. Memo. 1972-227)
11/15/72

○◁▷○

Sometimes it pays to be small-fry: A court concludes that a rake-off was meager.

Two Massachusetts lawyers (Richard C. Simmers and Richard K. Gordon) were convicted of larceny in a 1960 conspiracy with officials of Foundation Co., New York, to pay a $150,000 bribe in connection with the firm's contract to build a parking garage under Boston Common. Fake legal fees, a dummy corporation and other devices were part of the scheme, during which the two men received $174,000 from Foundation Co. On investigation, the IRS ruled the entire sum was taxable to them.

But the Tax Court accepted the lawyers' protest that they were mere go-betweens in handling $140,000 of the money. The court said they were "small town lawyers," unlikely to receive so large a fee either for legal services or for peddling their non-existent influence. It found that "payment for their services" had been limited to $34,000.

The court conceded that the stories the men related differed from what they had told the IRS earlier. But it decided they had been lying previously, to avoid self-incrimination or reprisals.

(Nunez v. Commissioner, T.C. Memo. 1969-216.)
10/22/69

Was the apartment John Mecom provided for a gossip columnist taxable income?

More than a decade ago, the wealthy Texas businessman and his wife became close friends of Maxine Mesinger and her husband, Emil. Maxine writes a column called "Big City Beat" in the Houston Chronicle. The couples socialized a lot, took trips together and spent weekends at the Mecom ranch. Maxine and Emil were divorced in the early 1960s, and Maxine subsequently had some financial difficulties. So the Mecoms provided Maxine and her son an apartment rent-free at Lamar Tower, a building partly owned by Mecom in an exclusive section of Houston.

The IRS said the rental value of the apartment was taxable income to Maxine. It claimed the real motive for letting her use the place was to induce her to mention Lamar Tower in her column and thereby attract more renters. During the years in question, the column mentioned Lamar Tower 113 times.

But the Tax Court didn't agree. It pointed out that during the same period Maxine's column mentioned the Shamrock Hilton Hotel 434 times and the Warwick Hotel 637 times. The court decided the apartment was a nontaxable gift, stemming simply from the Mecom's "generosity and friendship."

(Mesinger v. Commissioner, T.C. Memo. 1972-229)
11/29/72

◖━━◗

The IRS gives examples of when an employer could provide meals for employes without it counting as income for them. Such meals must be served on the employer's premises and for his convenience. Some employes were served at their desks so they could remain on duty, and others were on call in the dining room. Both instances met the IRS requirements. But other employes were free to leave the premises during lunch hour. This suggested to the IRS that they weren't urgently needed, and their meals weren't for the employer's convenience.

(Rev. Rul. 71-411)
9/29/71

◦━━◦

The IRS approves a plan under which a corporation's directors could choose to defer their fees and not be taxed on such earnings until the sums were actually paid. The plan provided that the deferred fees, plus interest, be paid in installments when a director left office. The key point, the IRS said, was that the plan wasn't funded, covered by a note, or secured in any way. "A mere promise to pay" isn't considered income until it's actually paid.

(Rev. Rul. 71-419)
9/29/71

◦━━◦

Note-worthy: A California man served as a financial adviser to a wealthy man, who on one occasion lent him $25,000. The debt was evidenced by a demand note, bearing no interest, on which the lender scribbled, "In case of my death . . . tear up. It's all yours." The lender later died, and his estate acknowledged it had no claim to the sum. The IRS promptly held the $25,000 was income because the estate had forgiven the debt. But the Tax Court ruled the lender had made a gift, even though he could have called the note before he died.

(Bosse v. Commissioner, T.C. Memo. 1970-355.)
1/20/71

◦━━◦

Too exclusive: A family-owned corporation voted to pay the medical expenses of all its officers not already covered by insurance. In effect, this meant only its founder-president, as the others had just taken out coverage at their own expense. When he suffered a stroke, the company paid his bills, as much as $39,000 a year. But the Tax Court ruled the payments taxable income for him. To be tax-free, such payments must be part of a health plan "for employes," not just for the president.

(American Foundry v. Commissioner, 59 T.C. No. 23)
11/22/72

◖◁▷◗

They laughed when they searched the piano but oh, when they started to pay! An Ohio couple paid $15 for an aged piano, then seven years later found $4,467 in greenbacks inside. The couple paid an $857 income tax on their find, but promptly sued for a refund. Any tax owed was due the year they acquired the piano-and-cash, they argued, and the statute of limitations had since expired. Not so, a U.S. district court ruled. Possession began with discovery, and the sum was taxable that year.

(Cesarini v. U.S.A., U.S. Dist. Ct., No. Dist. Ohio, 1969.)
3/26/69

◖◁▷◗

Bank giveaways to long-term depositors are interest income and fully taxable in the year received, the IRS rules. Some banks have claimed that gifts like autos and boats, offered in lieu of interest, should be treated as a return of capital and the tax on interest spread over a number of years. But the IRS says the merchandise is interest, taxable when received at its fair market value.

(IRS News Release No. 1032, 1970.)
4/15/70

◖◁▷◗

A Pan Am pilot claimed that $3,500 of his 1968 pay should be tax-free as combat pay because he flew 20 missions in Vietnam, ferrying troops or supplies. Once his airplane was hit by small-arms fire. The Tax Court shot him down. It ruled that the exclusion was limited to persons on active service with the Armed Forces. Whatever the danger, the pilot didn't qualify.

(Fagerland v. Commissioner, T.C. Memo. 1971-134.)
6/16/71

◐━▷

An award paid to the widow of a naval officer killed when Israeli airplanes fired on the U.S.S. Liberty in June 1967, during the Mideast outbreak, didn't have to be included in her income for tax purposes, the IRS held. The award resulted from a claim submitted to the Israeli government by the State Department.

(Rev. Ruling 68-649.)
1/8/69

◐━▷

Payments stemming from violation of civil rights are taxable, the IRS rules. The U.S. sued a company for discriminating against certain employes by paying them less than other employes doing the same work. The company finally agreed to make up the difference in a lump sum. The IRS ruled it was taxable because it amounted simply to payment of back wages.

(Rev. Rul. 72-341)
7/19/72

◐━▷

A bronze sculpture caught the eye of an Ohio couple, who bought it with $7,000 from the funds of their wholly owned small business. The work of art was carried as an investment on the company's books but actually it graced the couple's living room. The couple said they were just holding it, but the Tax Court ruled it a $7,000 dividend. The business never controlled the sculpture, charged them for its use, or invested in any other art.

(Proskauer v. Commisioner, T.C. Memo. 1971-174.)
7/28/71

◐━▷

Nurses in a hospital's anesthetist training program don't have to pay taxes on their stipends, the IRS rules. The nurses don't provide any service to the hospital during their training and aren't obligated to take jobs there on completion of the course. Thus, their grants comply with the rule that nontaxable financial aid can't be payment for past, present or future service.

(Rev. Rul. 72-568)
12/13/72

◦⟨⟩◦

A Jewish cantor deserves the same tax advantage as any other clergyman.

So ruled a federal appeals court in a Minneapolis case. A dispute had arisen because of a tax law that permits "ministers of the gospel" to receive tax-free the part of their salary they spend for rent. The IRS says the law covers only "ordained" clergymen. It contended the cantor hadn't been ordained and wasn't authorized to perform all Jewish ecclesiastical duties.

But the court said the cantor qualified for the special treatment. It was enough, the court held, that he participated prominently with the rabbi in religious services, weddings, funerals and other functions. The ordination requirement doesn't apply for Jewish clergymen because the Jewish religion doesn't formally ordain rabbis and cantors as other denominations ordain ministers, the court ruled.

(Silverman v. Commissioner, U.S. Ct. of Appeals, 8th Cir., 1973)
7/25/73

◦⟨⟩◦

Render unto Caesar: A minister was buying a new house, and it occurred to him to ease the burden by having his entire pay designated a "rental allowance," which by law is tax-free for ministers. It didn't work. The tax-free portion of his pay is limited to the "fair rental value" of his home, plus utilities, the IRS said.

(Rev. Ruling 71-280.)
7/14/71

Sweeter-smelling roses: Foundation grants to creative writers can't be excluded from taxable income as gifts, awards or prizes (many of which are excludable), the IRS says. But the grants can be treated as scholarships (which generally are excludable, too) if they're primarily for the recipient's benefit and aren't compensation for services.

4/19/72

No bull: In its report on the 1969 Tax Reform Act, the Ways and Means Committee also commented on "an erroneous interpretation of present law." It seems that some cattle-raisers speed the building up of breeding herds by trading off unwanted male calves for female calves in a tax-free "like kind" exchange. That's not what Congress meant by "like kind," the committee said. "The male animals are not held for breeding and, in fact, are not of a 'like kind' with females," it observed.

8/27/69

...Or a Capital Gain?

Many a tax fight is waged over whether a deal qualifies as a capital gain.

The gain on the sale of a capital asset held for six months is taxed at lower rates, but the IRS may have a narrow view of what constitutes a capital asset. Back in the Fifties, a group paid $1.6 million for a tanker subject to a charter. That pact bound it to haul for a particular charterer at a fixed rate. Not long after, the tanker was lost in a collision. Its owners collected $1.3 million insurance, and they sold the charter for another $1.3 million.

The IRS claimed the profits from the charter sale were taxable as ordinary income. It contended the owners were selling merely the right to earn future income —and that's not capital gain. The Tax Court disagreed. The charter's value didn't depend on its projected income (which was fixed), it noted. Rather, the value was tied to current rates for ocean charters, which fluctuate widely with world events. When current rates fell below the charter's fixed rate, it became a valuable item.

Thus the gain, the court said, was "due purely to the action of market forces. This is precisely the type of profit for which capital gain treatment is intended."

(Estate of Shea v. Commissioner, 57 T.C. No. 3)
10/13/71

◦⟷◦

Two taxpayers best the IRS in a tax game that's played frequently.

The cases were complex but the question in both was simple: Was a financial gain to be taxed as ordinary income, or at the lower capital gains rate? A fellow convinced Cities Service Co. to participate with him in developing and building a gas processing plant. Later, however, he withdrew from the deal and sold his interest to Cities Service for $50,000. He claimed that was just like selling a piece of property so the money was a capital gain. But the IRS said the $50,000 actually was payment for the man's service in initiating the project, and thus was taxable as ordinary income.

In the other case, a California construction company received $33,520 from cancellation of a lease on some property. The company said the cancellation amounted to selling the lease; the proceeds were a capital gain. The IRS contended the lease arrangement was a guise for paying the company for constructing a building. That would make the money ordinary income.

The Tax Court backed the taxpayers in both cases.

*(Crisp v. Commissioner, T.C. Memo. 1973-6,
and Modiano-Schneider Inc. v. Commissioner, T.C. Memo. 1973-5)
1/24/73*

ı○—◇○ı

What new partners pay to join a practice may qualify as capital gain.

The IRS has backed away from a previous position it took despite some court decisions to the contrary. It had held that when a lawyer, doctor or other professional admitted a new partner to his firm, the newcomer was buying a share in the firm's future earnings. Thus what he paid was taxable as ordinary income to the original partner or partners.

The Revenue Service refused to recognize any part of the sum as a payment for goodwill. It argued that unless the firm changed hands entirely, the original partners, remaining in practice, continued to benefit from goodwill. Now, however, it concedes that a partial transfer of goodwill may in fact be involved when a new partner enters a firm. A payment for such goodwill is a capital gain for the seller.

The IRS says such transactions "will be carefully scrutinized to assure that goodwill in fact exists." The new ruling doesn't give details on the criteria to be applied.

(Rev. Ruling 70-45.)
2/11/70

A real estate broker gets a tax break on a land deal over IRS objections.

Deciding whether to tax a real estate broker's profits at full income tax rates or at the lower capital gains rates occasionally can be tricky. There sometimes is a fine line between his dealings in land in the normal course of business, profits from which are fully taxable, and selling a piece of land he bought as a long-term investment. Profits on long-term investments, of course, are capital gains for tax purposes.

A New Jersey real estate company bought a plot of land which it divided into home sites. But to get the land it had to agree to buy an adjoining plot it didn't really want because it was steep, marshy and unsuitable for homes. Later the company sold the unwanted land to another real estate developer at a profit and performed certain brokerage services for the buyer. The IRS contended the profit was fully taxable as income but the Tax Court disagreed.

It pointed out the purchase wasn't part of the broker's normal real estate development business. The company bought the land only because it was forced to and got rid of it at its first good opportunity. So the court decided the profit should be given capital gains treatment as an investment profit would be.

(Frank H. Taylor & Son v. Commissioner, T.C. Memo. 1973-82)
4/25/73

A dealer's hand didn't spoil a capital gain for fellow real estate investors.

A real estate dealer organized a group of individual investors to join him in buying an interest in an unimproved tract. When the dealer subsequently sold his share to another group member, his profit was taxed as ordinary income, because of his dealer status. Later, the remaining participants sold the property. The Treasury sought to tax their gain as ordinary income, too.

In this case, a U.S. Court of Appeals demurred. Teaming up with a dealer didn't necessarily transform his partners into pros, the court said. Not all who take part in a joint venture need have the same intent and purpose. For some, the court noted, the transaction may be a routine step in their business; but for others, merely a single investment opportunity with a view to ultimate profit. The individual investors' profits were capital gains, the court ruled.

(Riddell v. Scales, U.S. Ct. of Appeals, 9th Cir., 1969.)
2/26/69

◦⟨⟩•

Sol C. Siegel, the movie producer, failed to produce a capital gain. His production company was guaranteed $300,000 by Loew's Inc. for making two movies in a joint venture with Loew's. After making the movies but before being paid, the company liquidated and assigned Siegel and his wife the right to collect the $300,-000. This, they claimed, was a capital gain for them. But a circuit court ruled the production company had fully earned the sum and had to pay taxes on it as ordinary income.

(Siegel v. U.S.A., U.S. Ct. of Appeals, 9th Cir., 1972)
8/2/72

◦⟨⟩•

An insurance man was paid $50,000 to terminate his exclusive general agency contract. He claimed the sum was a capital gain, but a U.S. Circuit Court disagreed. He was giving up the chance to earn commissions, which are taxed as ordinary income. Thus the money he got was also ordinary income, the court held.

(Elliott v. U.S.A. Ct. of Appeals, 10th Cir., 1970.)
9/2/70

◦━━◦

Horse feathers, said a circuit court to a taxpayer who claimed long-term capital gains treatment for insurance proceeds on a colt that died five days after birth. The claimant, who raised racing horses, argued he acquired a property interest in the foal when it was conceived—which, in the nature of things, was more than six months before. He noted he could insure the unborn foal, which he said presumed an insurable interest existed. But an unborn colt wasn't useful property, the appeals court said. The holding period began with birth.

(Greer v. U.S.A., U.S. Ct. of Appeals, 6th Cir., 1969.)
4/2/69

Is It a Medical Expense?

An invalid at home raises a factual question about what's a medical expense.

When someone is hired to care for an invalid at home, there isn't any hard-and-fast rule about what portion of the expense is deductible as a medical outlay. The tax situation may be especially uncertain when the hired help has no special medical training. The Tax Court recently allowed a Missouri couple a bigger medical deduction than the IRS did, but provided no explicit rationale for doing so.

The man's wife had suffered a series of strokes, which left her unable to wash, dress or feed herself or walk unassisted. The husband hired several people in turn to care for her while he worked, but they also did the family cooking and light housework. The IRS conceded that the woman needed someone to stay with her and that services directly affecting her wellbeing were deductible as medical costs. But it disallowed 40% of the $2,785 deduction as simply payment for routine housework.

The Tax Court decided that the employes did spend "a majority of their time" performing medical services. It then raised the deductible portion to 75% from 60%.

(Frier v. Commissioner, T.C. Memo. 1971-84.)
5/12/71

❦

A Montana farmer bests the IRS in a home medical care deduction case.

The cost of hiring someone to do housework so a sick person can rest isn't deductible. But direct medical

49

care at home is. Confusion often arises when the same person provides both services. In the farmer's case, hospital authorities told him his mentally ill wife, Catherine, could live at home only if he hired someone to look after her. So he asked his Canadian niece and her seven children to move to his farm. In return for caring for Catherine and helping with chores, the niece's family was to receive room and board and, after the first year, a share of the farm's profits.

The farmer deducted the room and lodging costs as a medical expense. The IRS disallowed the deduction on the ground the niece and her kids did farm and house work in addition to caring for Catherine. But the Tax Court went along with the farmer. He incurred the costs mainly to obtain care for his wife that otherwise the hospital would have performed; the chores were incidental, the court ruled.

The judge added sympathetically that hiring the niece was a last resort; the farmer had tried unsuccessfully to find a nurse.

(Bye v. Commissioner, T.C. Memo. 1972-57)
3/8/72

○◁▷●

School costs as medical expenses are mainly a factual issue, the Tax Court says.

Under tax regulations, if a child goes to a special school principally to overcome physical or mental handicaps, the entire costs are deductible medical expenses. But if the school isn't "special," only outlays specifically for medical care are deductible.

One case involved an emotionally troubled girl sent to a school for children with "special learning disabilities." The staff was well-trained in psychology and kept up-to-date through workshops. Psychiatrists were on call as consultants. Classes were small, flexible and ungraded. Children were allowed to set their own pace, and their programs were individually tailored for them. The Tax Court said the school readily qualified as special.

(Greisdorf v. Commissioner, 54 T.C. No. 167.)
10/7/70

0⟨◯⟩◗

A new ruling slightly eases the burden for parents of a retarded child.

Upon advice by a physician, they put their mentally retarded son in a special school run by a religious order. The main reason was availability of resources there to alleviate his handicap. The school was licensed by the state, which also gave the parents financial help by paying part of the tuition, room and board.

The IRS ruling was favorable to the parents. It held that the payments from the state were a scholarship. Thus they weren't taken into account in figuring whether the parents had provided more than one-half their son's support and could claim him as an exemption. The IRS so ruled the part the parents paid was a deductible medical expense.

(Rev. Ruling 71-347.)
8/4/71

0⟨◯⟩◗

Homes for the aged: It's tough but not impossible to deduct their fees.

A circuit court affirmed, without opinion, a previous Tax Court decision on whether room and board at a home for the elderly was deductible as a medical expense. The Tax Court had conceded that such costs "at an institution other than a hospital might constitute medical care." It's "a factual question," the court said. It depends "not upon the nature of the institution but the condition of the person and the care he receives."

In one case, the court had allowed a deduction for an elderly person who was totally unable to care for himself and relied on professional nursing at the home.

But in this most recent case, the court refused the deduction because no medical care was received. The taxpayer's father was in good health and clear of mind. It didn't matter that, according to one witness, the old man couldn't have lived alone "with dignity" because he couldn't feed or dress himself properly.

That's not enough, the court said. "The general happiness and dignity with which a person lives is not the criteria."

(Robinson v. Commissioner, U.S. Ct. of Appeals,
9th Cir., 1970, affirming 52 T.C. 520.)
3/25/70

Food and lodging as a medical deduction is allowed by an appeals court.

Back in the Fifties, Congress became concerned about people deducting the cost of a Florida vacation as taken on doctor's orders. It tightened the tax law to rule out a medical deduction for meals and lodging while away from home for medical treatment. However, the Seventh Circuit appeals court reversed the Tax Court and refused to find an "absolute" bar against such a deduction.

The case involved a Milwaukee man who was stricken with appendicitis while in New York City. The hospital was crowded, and he had to give up his room before he was ready to travel. Thus his doctor had him stay a week at a nearby hotel. Under these circumstances, his $184 hotel bill was "a true medical cost," the court said.

(Kelly v. Commissioner, U.S. Ct. of Appeals, 7th Cir., 1971.)
3/31/71

Medical travel deduction allows non-transport costs, says a circuit court.

The court backed the Tax Court in allowing a Kentucky couple to deduct $162 spent on food and lodging while traveling to the Mayo Clinic for the wife's medical treatment. The higher court brushed aside an IRS objection that living costs while being treated at a medical center away from home aren't deductible. The IRS would have held the couple's deduction to the bare cost of transportation.

The circuit court demurred. Congress had written the restriction on living expenses into the law because too many people were having their doctors prescribe a stay in Florida for their health. But the lawmakers didn't disturb the traditional medical deduction for travel.

(Montgomery v. Commissioner, U.S. Ct. of Appeals, 6th Cir., 1970.)
6/24/70

<><

Doctor's orders: The Tax Court accepts driving as deductible medical therapy.

The courts have been dubious about recognizing activities such as golf or dancing lessons as medical expenses, even when prescribed by a physician. Such pursuits are personal expenses, the courts have held. But now the Tax Court has accepted ordinary driving costs as deductible in a case involving a woman whose face had been mutilated in an auto accident.

The woman's doctor insisted she drive, both to alleviate her fears after the accident and to avoid the stares on public transportation. Her husband therefore bought a new Chrysler, which she drove extensively, as well as to and from the doctor's office. The IRS would allow only the mileage to medical appointments as a deduction, but the Tax Court was willing to accept "all the driving (she) did directly to alleviate her mental condition."

The court drew the line there, however. It wouldn't allow a deduction for the cost of her car as well.

(Bordas v. Commissioner, T.C. Memo. 1970-97.)
3/13/70

The costs of donating a kidney are deductible medical expenses whether or not the kidney is actually donated, the IRS says. It ruled in the case of a mother who had traveled from out of town and undergone lab tests only to discover her kidney couldn't be used by her son who needed a new one. His brother then came from another city and gave one of his kidneys. The IRS says both the mother's and brother's expenses are deductible.

(Rev. Rul. 73-189)
5/2/73

If you drive to the doctor's or use your car in rendering a service to a charity, your out-of-pocket expenses are deductible medical expenses or charitable gifts. These can be itemized, but since 1964 the IRS has also allowed a flat rate, which in October 1970, it raised to six cents a mile. It has never pinpointed exactly what that six cents a mile was meant to cover, however. It has now ruled that tolls and parking fees can be claimed on top of the flat mileage rate.

(Rev. Procedure 70-12.)
4/29/70

Brain-damage therapy can be deductible, even though administered by a layman. In "patterning," brain-damaged children are helped through normal motions like crawling in hopes that undamaged portions of the brain will pick up the pattern and assume control of such motions. The therapy requires several people to help, and most parents rely on volunteers. But if someone is paid, the IRS says that is a deductible medical expense. "Medical care" depends on the services rendered, not on who renders them.

(Rev. Ruling 70-170.)
4/22/70

Medical deductions for the cost of educating a mentally retarded child were expanded by a recent IRS ruling. It involved a boy who attended a regular school 25 miles from home because it had a special curriculum for the "educable mentally handicapped," while nearby schools did not. The IRS said the curriculum made the school the equivalent of a special school (where charges are routinely deductible), and its facilities were "a principal reason" for the child going there.

(Rev. Ruling 70-285.)
6/17/70

Medical deductions were broadened a bit by an IRS ruling to explicitly include some capital outlays. The ruling involved a man who suffered from arthritis and a severe heart condition. On advice from a doctor, he had a shower stall built on the first floor of his house. The IRS ruled the plumbing costs were deductible because their primary purpose was medical care.

(Rev. Ruling 70-395.)
8/12/70

Alcoholics' treatment costs at a therapeutic center are deductible as medical expenses, the IRS rules. The deductible items include room and board. In issuing the new ruling, the IRS reminds taxpayers that expenses of attending meetings of Alcoholics Anonymous also are deductible.

(Rev. Rul. 73-325)
8/15/73

Tax handicap: A New York woman, burdened with an artificial limb, could get to work only by driving her own car. She sought to deduct the costs, either as medical or business expenses. The Tax Court conceded that the tax laws "bear heavily on the physically handicapped" who must incur extra expenses, but it denied the deduction. She hadn't shown that she worked or used her car because her physician told her to do so as a form of therapy.

(Coopersmith v. Commissioner, T.C. Memo. 1971-280)
11/10/71

◦⟷◦

If you're a drug addict, or one of your dependents is, you can deduct the cost of treatment in a therapeutic facility, including lodging and meals. So ruled the IRS. It referred to a Supreme Court decision that narcotics addicts should be considered "proper subjects for medical treatment."

(Rev. Rul. 72-226)
5/17/72

◦⟷◦

Legal fees to have someone committed to a mental institution are deductible as medical expenses, the IRS rules. The IRS hadn't allowed such a deduction, but it recently reversed its position in line with a 1969 court decision. In that case, doctors had advised commitment of a woman with a history of violent behavior and alcoholism. The court found "a direct or proximate relationship" between the legal fees and medical treatment.

(Rev. Ruling 71-281.)
7/14/71

◦⟷◦

China policy? Acupuncture payments qualify for medical expense deduction, the IRS says.

(Rev. Rul. 72-593)
12/27/72

◦⟷◦

A live-in maid is a help but hardly medicinal, a U.S. court of appeals ruled. The case involved a heart-attack patient who lived alone. His doctor advised hiring a housekeeper to take his household chores off his hands and also to summon help if he were stricken again. The patient claimed a medical deduction for her salary, but the court said no. Her job was just to call for help, not to give medical aid, and relieving him of his chores bore no "direct and proximate therapeutic relation" to his health, it said.

(Borgmann v. Commissioner, U.S. Ct. of Appeals, 9th Cir., 1971.)
3/17/71

◀▭▶

A wheelchair patient bought a specially equipped automobile, at a $1,500 premium over the $4,500 price of a standard car. The special design included exit and entry ramps, a higher roof, special doors, and locks to hold wheelchairs in place. All this made the outlay deductible as a medical expense, the IRS ruled, but only the extra $1,500.

(Rev. Ruling 70-605.)
12/16/70

◀▭▶

The Tax Court denied a Los Angeles doctor, suffering from emphysema, a medical deduction for the cost of travel to and from a golf course for play. His physician had recommended the exercise. Light exercise might be desirable, the court said, but he could walk without golfing and could swing a club without swinging it on a course. The court was unmoved by his plea that exercise within Los Angeles was impossible because of smog and pollutants.

(Altman v. Commissioner, 53 T.C. No. 47.)
1/21/70

◀▭▶

A staff doctor at a Veterans Administration hospital enjoyed the normal "professional courtesy" under which doctors don't bill one another for services rendered. He couldn't reciprocate or refer patients, so he bought $120 in gift certificates and gave them to seven doctors. The Tax Court refused him a medical deduction, however. He wasn't expected to pay, it said, and the $120 was simply a tangible, but token, expression of appreciation.

(O'Hare v. Commissioner, 54 T.C. No. 84.)
5/6/70

∘⊂⊃∘

Social Security taxes keep going up, and Prentice-Hall Inc. offers a tip on shaving the tax bite. If an employer pays his employes while they are out sick, he should do so under a definite sick-pay plan because such payments aren't subject to Social Security. As the taxable wage base goes up, more workers will find their entire pay subject to Social Security tax. Thus a switch to sick pay from wages will yield a saving.

7/28/71

Finding Tax Shelter at Home

An office at home may be deducted more easily under a circuit court decision.

When an employe keeps an office at home, the IRS has restricted any deduction for its cost to someone whose employer required him to do so. However, the Second Circuit ruled in favor of a television time salesman for ABC who deducted part of his rent, cleaning expenses and electric bill. He used a small study every evening to plan his rounds and watch ads on ABC and competing networks.

The IRS denied the deduction because ABC didn't require the study. If the salesman wanted to work late, the IRS said, the ABC office was open and little more than 20 blocks away. But the circuit court said no law restricts a business expense to an outlay required by one's employer. It was enough for the expense to be "appropriate and helpful" in one's work. The salesman had to see as much TV as he could, the court said, and what better place than "in the isolation of his study den"?

The salesman originally deducted one-fourth the expenses of a four-room apartment. But a lower court cut the deduction to 20% because the study was so small.

(Newi v. Commissioner, U.S. Ct. of Appeals, 2nd Cir., 1970.)
11/11/70

◦⟨⟩◦

The IRS's formula for office-at-home deductions is liberalized by a court.

The deduction involves a double calculation. First, you must determine what portion of total home expense is accounted for by the room used for business. Then you have to figure how much time the room is used as an office. In the latter calculation, the IRS determines what portion of a 24-hour day the room is used for business and allows deduction only of that percentage of the room's total expense.

But the Tax Court ruled that the basis for figuring the percentage, rather than total hours in the day, should be the total hours out of 24 that the room is actually used for any purpose. In the case of a school-teaching couple, the court permitted deduction of two-eighths of the cost of maintaining a home office. They used it for school work two hours a day out of eight hours of total use. (The court reasoned it wasn't used during the eight hours they were away at school and the eight hours they slept.)

The IRS wanted to allow only 2/24 of the cost.

(Gino v. Commissioner, 60 T.C. No. 37)
6/13/73

An office at home is ruled deductible for an insurance man over IRS objections.

The IRS still sticks pretty close to its traditional view that an employed person can't deduct an office in his home unless his employer requires him to have one. But, fortunately for people who work at home and know enough to challenge the IRS, the Tax Court isn't so rigid. It says only that a home-office must be "appropriate and helpful under the circumstances."

The sales supervisor for an insurance company worked most weekday evenings in one room of his home. He read reports and sometimes interviewed prospective salesmen. The IRS contended the room duplicated the man's regular office at his company's district headquarters and he could just as well have worked there.

But the Tax Court allowed him to deduct 80% of the cost of his home office.

(Gillis v. Commissioner, T.C. Memo. 1973-96)
5/9/73

०**<>**०

Here's an instance of when an office at home is a deductible business expense.

The courts have allowed a deduction in less clear-cut circumstances, but a Tax Court decision was almost a textbook case. It involved an airline pilot, who used the office for outside business pursuits as well as for paper work relating to his job. These included an unsuccessful stint selling for a family firm, real estate interests, and union activities.

The pilot put aside a room for exclusive use as an office, and he furnished it appropriately. It contained all his records, and at times he used it for meetings with union members. The court ruled that all this clearly established a need for the office, and the pilot's $338 deduction for depreciation, utilities and insurance was reasonable.

(Bailey v. Commissioner, T.C. Memo. 1971-107.)
6/2/71

०**<>**०

A house for sale was also for rent, so the owner got a tax break.

The law says you can't depreciate a home for tax purposes or deduct the cost of maintaining it unless you use it "for the production of income," e.g. rent it out instead of live there yourself. Thus, the IRS balked when a California CPA deducted maintenance and depreciation on his home for a period prior to selling it.

The man moved from the house two years before its sale. He put it on the market when he moved out. It didn't sell, so 90 days later he offered it for rent also. Still no takers. He finally sold it only after chopping the asking price. The IRS rejected his deductions on grounds the rental offer was incidental to the attempt to sell and wasn't a "bona fide" effort to produce income. But the Tax Court sided with the owner.

Even though he never actually rented the place, his motive clearly was "to turn an expense 'eater' into an income-producing asset," at least until he could sell, the Court said.

(Sherlock v. Commissioner, T.C. Memo. 1972-97)
5/10/72

◐━━◑

Selling a house: Are the costs of holding it for later sale deductible?

The law gives a tax deduction for expenses connected with "property held for the production of income," and some taxpayers have claimed the deduction in selling their home. A Tax Court case involved a Pine Bluff, Ark., couple who moved out of a home that cost $71,000. They asked $70,000 for it—considerably more than its market value. It was finally sold 14 months later for $50,000.

The couple claimed it was held for income (a possibly higher price) and wanted to deduct $3,750 for expenses and depreciation while the house was vacant. The Tax Court disagreed. If a homeowner merely wanted to recoup his investment, it was "difficult" to consider the house held for income, it said. Putting it on the market immediately was also "strong evidence" the owner didn't intend to hold it. An owner would have to show he expected the house would become more valuable than it was when he moved out.

Half a dozen Tax Court judges concurred in the denial of the deduction. They felt, however, a taxpayer needn't prove he was out to make a profit over his cost.

(Newcombe v. Commissioner, 54 T.C. No. 123.)
6/24/70

A homeowner trips over a law governing buying and selling houses.

If you sell your house at a profit, you can avoid tax to the extent that you reinvest the proceeds in another home and occupy it within a set period of time (one year if you buy an existing house, 18 months if you have a new one built). This rule is enforced strictly, and Nelson Elam found the courts wouldn't bend it to fit his particular circumstances.

Elam sold his old home for $93,000, $45,000 of which was profit. He reinvested $83,000 in new land and construction of a main house and guest house on it. But only the guest house was completed and occupied in 18 months; the main house still was under construction. So, sticking to the letter of the law, the Sixth Circuit appeals court allowed only the cost of the land and the guest house (totaling less than a third of the $83,000) to be counted as part of the reinvested funds.

That meant that Elam owed more tax on the profit from his old house than he would have if the main house on his new property had been finished and occupied before the deadline imposed by the law.

(Elam v. Commissioner, U.S. Ct. of Appeals, 6th Cir., 1973)
6/6/73

0⊂⊃0

Mortgage 'points' may be deductible as interest, the IRS rules.

With mortgage money under feverish demand, many lenders are extracting from borrowers a special, one-time charge—or "points"—in addition to a stated annual interest. Often this form is chosen to skirt state ceilings on interest rates. A charge of three points (or $3 on each $100 of mortgage principal) boosts to 7.4% the actual interest rate on $10,000 borrowed for 20 years ostensibly at 7%.

Until recently, the tax treatment of points has been

in doubt. Now the IRS has said that points may be deductible as interest. A key part of the ruling: "By whatever name called, (interest) must be compensation for the use or forbearance of money per se." If points represent payment to a lender for services, such as checking an applicant's credit, they won't be deductible interest, the ruling indicated.

(Rev. Ruling 69-188.)
4/30/69

o⊂===o

Mortgage points can be fully deducted in the year they are paid, the IRS says.

Earlier, the Revenue Service ruled that points were deductible as interest when they were in fact a payment "solely for the use or forbearance of money" (and not for services, such as checking the borrower's credit). Points are usually paid as a lump sum, however, and the IRS left unclear whether that sum was immediately deductible or had to be pro-rated over the life of the mortgage.

Now, in an advisory ruling, the tax service has concluded that pro-rating isn't required. The ruling concerned a $1,200 "loan processing fee" paid on a $20,000 mortgage, in addition to annual interest of 8%. The points didn't have to be pro-rated, the IRS said, because deducting them in the year paid wouldn't cause "a material distortion" of income for that year.

(Rev. Ruling 69-582.)
12/3/69

o⊂===o

A court rebuffs an effort to mix business with pleasure.

It's estimated that Americans are building second homes at better than 150,000 a year. But the Tax Court rejected one effort to ease the expense of a home-away-from-home. A couple owned a $75,000 "cottage" at Sea Island, Ga., which they used four months a year and offered for rent the other eight. Rents never matched cash expenses plus depreciation, however, and they tried to deduct the difference from taxable income. (They only included expenses for the eight months.)

The Tax Court refused the deduction. It said the couple failed to show any intent to make a profit, rather than simply defray expenses. It noted that over 12 years, actual rentals averaged one month a year. But the court ducked the tougher question of whether a property could be used for pleasure part of a year and genuinely run for profit during the remainder.

(Carkhuff v. Commissioner, T.C. Memo. 1969-66)
4/23/69

◦⟨⟩◦

Oh give me a home: The IRS Commissioner's annual report shows how home ownership fits into the tax scheme of things. Itemized deduction for 1970 (the latest figure available) came to $88.2 billion. Of that, $24.5 billion, or 28%, was directly related to home ownership; $11.6 billion for real estate taxes and $12.9 billion for interest on home mortgages. By comparison, $12.9 billion was deducted for charitable gifts and $10.6 billion for medical or dental expenses.

(Rev. 9/73)
5/12/71

A Few Points on Moving

When IBM covers an employe's "loss" on his home, that's income, a court rules.

The initials IBM stand for "I've been moved," some long-time employes of International Business Machines Corp. say ruefully. With so many transfers, the giant company is relatively thorough in cushioning the financial burden of moving. Under its "home guarantee policy," the company paid an employe the $2,000 difference between the $58,000 appraised value of his home and the $56,000 he sold it for.

The taxpayer argued that the $2,000 was simply part of the sales proceeds, and as his new house cost much more than the old, there was no gain to tax. This argument impressed neither the IRS nor the Tax Court. A circuit court also ruled the sum was ordinary income for the taxpayer.

The new Tax Reform Act counts reimbursed moving costs as income, but it then allows most taxpayers to deduct certain costs in selling their house and buying a new one. But the deductible costs don't include any such paper "loss" on a home.

(Lull v. Commissioner, U.S. Ct. of Appeals, 9th Cir., 1970.)
12/9/70

◦━━◦

The IRS denies a deduction for the cost of moving new furniture.

Normally, a taxpayer who moves to a new job site is entitled to deduct the cost of moving his furniture (and certain other outlays). However, the IRS denied a deduction to a taxpayer who moved from England to Colorado but bought new furniture in Massachusetts en route. The deduction doesn't apply to new furniture, the IRS said.

The law doesn't require that furniture come directly from the old residence to the new. It could come out of storage, the IRS said, as long as it had been used before. The cost of moving used household goods from a place other than the former residence is deductible to the extent it doesn't exceed what it would have cost for a move from the former residence.

The IRS ruling doesn't specify how long it takes "new" furniture to become "used." According to Tax Coordinator, an advisory service, elsewhere in the tax law where use is required for a reduction, even one day is technically sufficient.

(Rev. Ruling 70-625.)
12/23/70

◦⟷◦

Moving expenses, under the Tax Reform Act, must be included in gross income if they are reimbursed or paid (directly or indirectly) by one's employer. Normally the employe can offset that income by also deducting the expenses, provided they meet certain tests. Last week the IRS recognized this wash-out effect. It ruled that the employer's payment isn't subject to withholding "if it is reasonable to believe at the time of payment that a corresponding deduction is allowable."

(Rev. Ruling 70-482.)
9/23/70

◦⟷◦

Moving season: Of the 14.5 million working people who moved in 1970, about one million were eligible for tax deductions for moving expenses, the IRS says. (If an employer reimburses the expenses, such payments count as income, which is then offset with appropriate deductions.) Now, employers must give their employes a new IRS Form 4782 detailing moving expenses paid on their behalf.

(IRS News Release IR-1154, 1971.)
7/28/71

◦⊂⊃◦

Citizen soldier: A serviceman moved his family overseas to his new post, even though it was against the rules at his new station for his family to come along. The IRS ruled that as long as the soldier met normal tax law rules about moving expenses in connection with a new place of work, he was entitled to deduct his family's moving costs. His violation of the Army's housing preferences didn't cut any ice.

(Rev. Ruling 70-520.)
10/21/70

◦⊂⊃◦

Moving expenses, when job-related, are normally deductible, and that includes travel by car from the old residence to the new one. In such instances, taxpayers may deduct a flat six cents a mile in lieu of keeping detailed travel expense records, the IRS ruled. Parking and tolls are deducted separately.

(Rev. Procedure 71-2.)
1/21/71

◦⊂⊃◦

Three years too soon: In denying a California couple's deduction of certain moving expenses in 1967, the Tax Court noted that most costs of their move would have been deductible under the 1969 reform act. Most transferred employes and self-employed persons moving to new job locations can now deduct basic expenses of selling a house and buying a new one, settling an unexpired lease, and living up to 30 days while house-hunting at a new location.

(Kay v. Commissioner, T.C. Memo. 1970-202.)
7/22/70

Tax Aspects of Giving

A gift plan, with something for everyone but the IRS, is upheld by an appeals court.

The plan was devised by Rensselaer Polytechnic Institute to induce one of its alumni, Philip Grove, to contribute to the school. Grove agreed to give RPI shares of stock in his engineering company. The gift wasn't to include dividends from the stock; the right to receive them remained with Grove. The plan mightn't have raised IRS eyebrows if it had been that simple in practice. But it wasn't.

Grove's company didn't pay dividends on its stock. So if RPI had held onto the stock Grove gave, he wouldn't have received any continuing benefit from it. But instead of holding the shares, RPI redeemed them for cash from Grove's company. Then it invested the cash in other securities, and paid the dividends and interest from those securities to Grove. The reinvestments were made on the advice of Grove's personal investment adviser.

Grove paid taxes on the dividends and interest he received, but the IRS said the proceeds from RPI's redemption of his company's stock also was taxable income to Grove. It was used to replace securities that didn't pay him income with securities that did. That amounted to Grove's "manipulating" funds from his company "to produce income for his benefit," the IRS said.

But in a two-to-one ruling, the second U.S. appeals

court upheld the deal as nothing more or less than astute but legal tax planning.

(Grove v. Commissioner, U.S. Ct. of Appeals, 2nd Cir., 1973)
8/8/73

Willie and Joe, the dogface heroes of World War II,
survive a tax battle.

The Smithsonian Institution repeatedly urged
prize-winning cartoonist Bill Mauldin to donate to it
several of the few surviving originals of his famous
Stars and Stripes cartoons. In 1966, Mauldin gave the
Smithsonian a set of six, including the first and last of
the Willie and Joe drawings. To appraise the gift, the
Smithsonian brought in no less than the official biogra-
pher of Gen. George C. Marshall, who put a $15,000
value on the cartoons. When Mauldin deducted the
$15,000 as a charitable contribution, the IRS objected
that Willie and Joe were worth a mere $450 tops.

The Tax Court found the IRS figure "hardly worthy of comment." Mauldin, the court said, was "perhaps
the greatest World War II artist and cartoonist."
Though the Smithsonian's estimate wasn't binding, the
court relied on it heavily and allowed the full $15,000.
(Since 1969, tax law changes have curbed the deduction
for such gifts.)

Mauldin fared less well with a gift of manuscripts
to the Library of Congress. The Library had appraised
them conservatively at $3,740. The Tax Court allowed
only $5,000 of the $14,500 Mauldin originally deducted.

(Mauldin v. Commissioners, 60 T.C. No. 78)
9/5/73

Give until it hurts: Tax treatment eases the pain of
large gifts, fund-raisers say.

Professional fund-raisers argue that tougher tax
treatment of large charitable gifts may cripple university and hospital campaigns to raise capital funds.

"Eighty-five per cent of your money comes from 15% of your donors," says A. C. Barnett of Tamblyn & Brown Inc. Very large gifts are "totally and completely all-important," declares Robert L. Conway of John Price Jones Co. He says a $20 million campaign typically must garner at least one $5 million gift, two of $2 million and three of $1 million. A recent survey found some 112 schools seeking $4 billion in capital funds.

Fund-raisers contend that tax angles rarely move people to give. "I've never had anyone say, 'What the hell, it won't cost me much. Who can I give it to?'" claims Austin V. McClain of Marts & Lundy Inc. Attorney Conrad Teitell agrees—but "once you do believe in Olde Ivy, taxes become very important." Barnett recalls one would-be donor of $50,000 who was shown how to raise his to $500,000 by giving away appreciated land. "It cost him practically nothing," Barnett says.

Philanthropist Louis Schweitzer says he gives away as much as tax law permits him to deduct. "There's no question" the law encourages giving, he says.

4/16/69

◦━━◦

A minister's word prevails in Tax Court over IRS legal objections.

In many Tax Court cases, taxpayers represent themselves and at times rely on simple fairness, unadorned by legal niceties. Over the years, the court has shown itself remarkably open to their pleas. One case concerned a New Mexico man, a minister in the Word of Life Church, whose flock had dwindled to his family and four or five friends. The minister said he tithed scrupulously, handled the church's money and paid its bills. But he kept no records at all.

The IRS disallowed his $727 contributions deduction as unsubstantiated. Further, it argued, the church lacked a charter, hadn't shown it merited an exemption, and amounted to the parson's personal venture. But the court accepted testimony that there really was an active group, albeit a small one, that pursued a religious purpose. It also believed the minister made the donations he claimed.

(Blake v. Commissioner, T.C. Memo. 1970-117.)
5/27/70

◦━━◦

Legal fees a donor paid to defend a park from highways are ruled deductible.

In 1924, the late Anne Archbold gave the U.S. land that became part of Glover-Archbold Park in the District of Columbia. Three decades later, a highway was proposed that would have destroyed half the park. Mrs. Archbold hired a law firm to resist the plan, and it was shelved. Similar encroachments were threatened in the early 1960s, and Mrs. Archbold paid a total of $30,-000 in legal fees. Along the way, Congress passed a five-year freeze on highways through the park.

The Court of Claims ruled that Mrs. Archbold was entitled to deduct her legal fees as a gift "for the use of" the U.S. This applied even though "elements" of the government (the Interior Department for one) were the target of her suits. That made the case "slightly thorny," the court said, but Congress had accepted the original gift, and its voice was crucial in approving or disapproving Mrs. Archbold's later efforts. The court interpreted the freeze on construction as conveying congressional approval.

That didn't mean the public-at-large could get a similar deduction. A donor "enjoys a continuing relationship to his gift which others don't have," the court said.

(Archbold v. U.S., U.S. Ct. of Claims, 1971)
7/28/71

The IRS allows a deduction for expenses in a project to help unwed mothers.

Normally the IRS won't allow a deduction for contributions made directly to an individual, no matter how worthy. Similarly, gifts to a charity aren't deductible if they are earmarked for a particular person. However, the IRS has found its way to allow such outlays by one family, even though they were spent to help a particular girl.

Under the program, a pregnant woman was taken into the home of the volunteer family, which was expected to treat her as a member of the household. The family was to provide proper diet and clothing and a small weekly allowance. The woman, in turn, was expected to lend a hand with household chores, but she wasn't to be considered an employe. In this context, the IRS ruled the family was helping the sponsoring charity carry out its program, and its expenses were contributions.

But the IRS ruled out a deduction for expenses the family would have incurred anyway, such as rent and utilities.

(Rev. Ruling 69-473.)
9/17/69

o⊂⊃o

An adoption fee isn't a gift, even though based on income, the Tax Court rules.

In recent years, most adoption agencies have moved from asking adoptive parents for a donation to charging a fee for professional services rendered. The fees are nevertheless commonly based on income and ability to pay. In one typical case, the Talbot Perkins Adoption Service in New York charged $1,750—that is, 10% of the adoptive father's income.

The adoptive parents sought to deduct the payment as a charitable gift. They noted that it was tied to income, rather than to services rendered, and in addition it wasn't mandatory—it was waived if a couple couldn't afford it. But the Tax Court nevertheless found it a fee for "a significant and direct benefit to them." If a great discrepancy existed between the fee and what the services were worth, the payment could be part fee and part gift, the court said. But no discrepancy was shown.

(Murphy v. Commissioner, 54 T.C. No. 22.)
2/25/70

◦⟷◦

She provided a place for homeless teen-agers, but the refuge wasn't deductible.

As new needs emerge, charitable giving changes its face, but not all giving is tax-sheltered. In California, a social worker provided food and shelter for teen-agers who had been turned out by their parents or left home. She said her religious beliefs wouldn't allow her "to turn a youngster into the street and not feed him," so the stray teen-agers were welcome to stay with her and her family. The young people drifted in and out; over a year, she spent $2,400 on their support.

The California woman sought to deduct those expenses on her tax return, but the Tax Court said no. Tax law doesn't permit a deduction for contributions to individuals, no matter how worthy. The court managed to turn up a degree of tax relief, however. It noted that one teen-ager had lived with her family the entire year. She could claim him as her dependent.

Actually the boy had been gone two months "when he was really out of his head and was in the streets." But the court ruled that was an absence "by reason of illness," which doesn't count as breaching the entire-year rule.

(Dollar v. Commissioner, T.C. Memo. 1971-177.)
8/4/71

Some skiers find a tax deduction to ease their runs down the slopes.

If a taxpayer works for a charitable cause, his out-of-pocket outlays are normally deductible. Many of the 22,000 members of the National Ski Patrol System Inc. are taking advantage of the provision to defray the hefty costs of the sport. The patrol volunteers serve as safety monitors and offer first aid at about 750 ski areas, mostly in the U.S.

Normally the patrolmen's expense for food, lodging and transportation qualify. One New Yorker commutes weekends to Vermont by small plane and deducts part of the plane's upkeep. Special ski gear used for patrol duties can usually be claimed. "It's something you do, but you do it with discretion," says a Wall Street broker and patrol skier. Linda Curtis of New York City, a patrol member for four years, says the deduction is "obviously a side benefit" but a substantial one.

Patrol members must meet tough standards, prowl long hours over ski runs, and perform many nonskiing duties. "Anyone who does it for the tax break has got to be out of his mind," says Edward L. Ericson of National Ski Patrol.

1/28/70

"Cardiac Capers," a film of a hospital staff's musical comedy show, was ruled a deductible charitable contribution to the hospital from the film maker. The Tax Court rejected an IRS contention that the film was a nondeductible service and that the producer hadn't satisfactorily established its value. Although service in the form of the producer's labors did go into making the film, the final product was tangible property the man could have sold, the court said.

(Holmes v. Commissioner, 57 T.C. No. 44)
1/19/72

If you write an essay and give it to a charity, it's deductible. So said the Tax Court in the case of an Arkansas economist who wrote two essays on economic opportunities for low income groups and donated them to the National Council for Negro Women. He deducted $1,500, claiming that was the essays' value. The IRS said the essays constitute service, which isn't deductible. But the Tax Court said the essays were property. It set their value, however, at only $500.

(Goss v. Commissioner, 59 T.C. No. 58)
2/14/73

◀▭▶

A gift to a retirement home wasn't really a gift and thus isn't deductible, the IRS says. The home "requests" a gift from everyone admitted who can afford it. The size of apartment a resident gets depends partly on the size of his gift. The IRS pointed out that gifts, to be deductible, must be given without expectation of a return benefit.

(Rev. Rul. 72-506)
11/1/72

◀▭▶

Larger deductions for charitable donations may be sustained if you take it to court. One taxpayer recently claimed $600 in church contributions, but the IRS chopped that to a nominal $52 for lack of proof. The Tax Court, however, found reasonable his testimony that he went to church every Sunday and put at least $10 in the plate each time. The court restored $540 of the $600.

(Grinis v. Commissioner, T.C. Memo. 1970-94.)
5/13/70

◀▭▶

We shall return, but the return isn't deductible. That's what the Tax Court ruled concerning a pilgrimage to the Philippines by a survivor of the Bataan Death March. The old soldier returned in 1967 with fellow members of the American Defenders of Bataan and Corregidor Inc. The taxpayer claimed his travel expenses were a charitable contribution to the veterans group. The Tax Court found his patriotism "praiseworthy," but the travel outlays were nondeductible personal expenses.

(Wood v. Commissioner, 57 T.C. No. 20)
11/17/71

Avery Brundage, president of the International Olympic Committee, bested the IRS in a tax tangle. It concerned the gift in 1963 of his renowned Asian art collection to San Francisco for the de Young Memorial Museum. A taxpayer could then deduct up to 30% of his income as a gift to "educational organizations" (currently, it's 50%), but only 20% to ordinary charities. The IRS argued the museum wasn't an educational organization, but Brundage convinced the Tax Court it was.

(Brundage v. Commissioner, 54 T.C. No. 139.)
7/15/70

Gosh, Sarge, you never appreciated me: A U.S. district court jury in Connecticut concluded that 1,055 original Beetle Bailey cartoons were worth $28,000 when they were donated to Syracuse University. The decision means that Mort Walker, who draws the woeful soldier, will be able to claim a charitable contribution of that amount for income tax purposes.

(Walker v. U.S.A., U.S. Dist. Ct., Dist. Conn. 1969.)
7/2/69

By the book: James L. Robertson, Federal Reserve Board vice chairman, wanted to give Uncle Sam the royalties from his book "What Generation Gap???" but "absolutely amazing" Treasury red tape deterred him, he says. To keep the donated proceeds from being taxed as income would have required: A ruling from the Internal Revenue Commissioner, assignment of copyright to the Treasury and at least three other legal steps that "just weren't worth my time," Mr. Robertson says. A college will get the royalties.

2/4/70

⊶

The septic tanks in a low-lying Houston suburb never worked, so about 40 homeowners chipped in $1,-560 each to put in a water and sewage system. They turned the system over to their village, which had agreed to maintain it. One homeowner sought to deduct the $1,560 as a charitable gift, but the IRS balked. So did the Tax Court, even though the man said he expected nothing in return for his outlay. Maintenance by the village was "an anticipated benefit of an economic nature," the court said.

(Wolfe v. Commissioner, 54 T.C. No. 170.)
8/16/70

⊶

No gift: The Tax Court recently held that C. F. Mueller Co., a pasta maker owned by a voting trust for the benefit of New York University School of Law, couldn't deduct $445,000 in "contributions" to the Law Center Foundation at NYU. The sum would have to come out of after-tax earnings, the court said. Otherwise, the arrangement would get around a law that if a tax-exempt group owns an ordinary business, it must pay taxes on what it earns.

(C.F. Mueller Co. v. Commissioner, 55 T.C. No. 28.)
11/18/70

⊶

Some gift: The Tax Court denied an Oregon man a $2,757 charitable deduction for giving 700 pounds of suppositories to an old people's home. They had been

left in his basement by the prior occupant, a drug salesman, and they ended up in the county dump.

(Goodman v. Commissioner, T.C. Memo. 1970-122.)
5/27/70

o⟨⟩o

A big game hunter brought down a clean kill in
darkest Texas. A U.S. district court jury decided he
could deduct as a charitable gift the cost of a safari trip
to Kenya. It accepted his claim that the hunt was arranged to bag specimens for an American museum. The
court ordered a $6,700 tax refund.

(Jersis v. U.S.A., U.S. Dist. Ct., West Dist. Texas, 1968)
4/16/69

o⟨⟩o

The Irish sweeps is officially a wager, the Tax
Court decides. It's hard to see how the matter could
have been in doubt, but one winner claimed she bought
her tickets as a charitable contribution to the Irish hospitals that benefit from the sweepstakes. The court
found her motives irrelevant. It ruled her $139,555 win-
nings were "wagering income" and thus ineligible for
income-averaging.

(Stevens v. Commissioner, 56 T.C. No. 86)
9/22/71

o⟨⟩o

A Bas Mitzvah wasn't deductible, the Tax Court
told a California couple. The court disallowed a deduction of $567 the couple paid their temple for their
daughter's event. "This is not a charitable contribution,
just as the cost of a wedding is not a charitable contribution," the court said. "Although each occasion has religious significance, it is primarily a social event."

(Feistman v. Commissioner, T.C. Memo. 1971-137.)
6/30/71

o⟨⟩o

A private school levied a certain tuition fee but also
required each pupil's family to make a "donation" of

twice that amount. The IRS refused to grant a tax deduction to cushion the burden, however. A donation, it said, is "a voluntary transfer" made with donative intent and not for consideration. In this case, there was consideration—enrollment in the school—and the "donation" wasn't deductible as a charitable contribution, the IRS said.

(Rev. Ruling 71-112.)
3/10/71

A farmer's tenants paid him rent in grain instead of cash. He didn't include the grain's value in his taxable income. But he donated the grain to his church and deducted it as a charitable contribution. An appeals court okayed the deduction but said the man first had to add the grain to his taxable income, just as he would rent in cash.

(Parmer v. Commissioner, U.S. Ct. of Appeals, 10th Cir., 1972)
11/15/72

Cutting Your Losses

Ice storm losses are deductible, but more storms may brew over how much.

The IRS should absorb some of the losses from an ice storm that downed trees and glazed much of the Northeast. Storm damage, if uninsured, is deductible as a casualty loss, to the extent it exceeds $100. The rub comes, however, in establishing the dollar amount. Contrary to some expectations, the loss isn't measured by what it costs to repair or replace the property. The loss is the difference in property's value before the storm and after.

Ornamental trees and shrubbery are "an integral part of the real property," the IRS has said in a similar context. Thus the loss is the "actual decrease in the value of the property as a whole." Replacement costs don't decide the issue, but they are acceptable "as evidence of decrease in value." In one case where expensive boxwoods were damaged the court gave their replacement cost "some secondary weight," but it determined the loss by the overall-value rule.

Courts have accepted the cost of cleaning up storm debris as a storm loss and also the cost of removing a limb from a storm-damaged tree.

12/16/70

◦◦◦

Another home in California slides in value without incurring a casualty loss.

The Tax Court decided another case growing out of the 1965 slides in Pacific Palisades, when a great many lovely homes overlooking the Pacific almost ended up in it. The controversial tax point is that while most homes suffered minor physical damage or none, property values tumbled in the entire area. In this case, the home was worth $65,000 before the slide, but only $42,000 afterwards. The owners simply moved out, sacrificing their $21,094 equity in the property.

The taxpayers claimed a $21,094 casualty loss, but the Tax Court agreed with the IRS in denying the claim. The court found the loss in value was attributable mainly to "general buyer resistance" and "only to a minor degree" to post-slide cracks that appeared in the property. Physical damage or destruction is "an inherent prerequisite" of a casualty loss, it said. Thus when the owners moved out in early 1966, they incurred a nondeductible personal loss, not a casualty loss, because they chose to dispose of the home while its value was down.

The court chopped their casualty loss to $1,000, which it concluded was the actual damage the slide inflicted.

(Kamanski v. Commissioner, T.C. Memo. 1970-352.)
1/20/71

❦

A Maryland couple beats the IRS in the elusive task of calculating a loss.

In tax law, the measure of a casualty loss is simply the difference in the fair market value of the property immediately before and immediately after the casualty. But how do you set the fair market value of goods that were never meant to be sold? The couple were burned out of their home, and the entire contents of the house destroyed. They hired an adjuster, who said the goods had been worth $42,521: their $55,568 cost, less $13,047 in depreciation.

By contrast, the IRS claimed their things had been worth a mere $15,304, but the Tax Court threw that figure out. The IRS had tried to prove what the goods would have fetched "if hawked off by a secondhand dealer or at a forced sale." That wouldn't do, the court said, because it wasn't a reasonable measure of the "actual value" to the couple. The method the taxpayers relied on—original cost less 20% or 25% for depreciation —struck the court as "fair and reasonable."

For one thing, the court said, insurance companies also used the couple's method. And they obviously had no interest in inflating loss figures.

(Cornelius v. Commissioner, 56 T.C. No. 77.)
8/19/71

◦⟨═⟩◦

How and how not to prove the value of your stamp collection and jewelry.

After their home was burglarized, Max and Lillian Engel settled hastily with their insurance company for only about half what they thought the stolen property was worth. They claimed they were under "great stress" at the time. Max was under federal indictment (later dismissed). Lillian was suffering from hypertension and diabetes following an auto accident.

The Engels tried to deduct the portion of their claimed loss the insurance company wouldn't pay. The IRS objected, but the Tax Court said okay on the stamp collection. A stamp dealer, who previously had appraised the collection, testified it was worth what the Engels claimed. But the court balked at their valuation of the jewelry. It seemed the Engels had bought some of it from "Mr. Blatt," a man who gave big discounts, dealt only in cash and refused to give receipts. The court refused to accept this explanation as proof of the jewels' value.

(Engel v. Commissioner, T.C. Memo. 1972-246)
12/27/72

A lawyer tries to salvage a tax deduction from his daughter's broken marriage.

She had paid all her and her husband's expenses during the few months they were married, so the separation agreement called for the husband to repay to her the $4,200 she had spent on him. (Her father had given her much of the money originally.) The same day the separation agreement was signed the wife transferred the right to receive the husband's payments from herself to her father. In exchange, he agreed to pay her rent for a year.

The husband, who was unemployed and didn't own any property, didn't pay the debt, and the father eventually got a default judgment against him. He collected nothing, so he deducted the $4,200 as a bad debt. The Tax Court balked. It ruled the money the wife contributed to her husband's support was a gift rather than a loan. But even if it had been a loan, the court said, the obligation obviously was worthless when the separation agreement was signed because of the husband's lack of assets and a job.

You can't take a bad-debt deduction for an obligation that is obviously worthless when it is made. As a financially astute lawyer, the father must have known that, the court noted. So the deduction appeared to have been only a ploy to salvage something from his original gift to his daughter.

(Johnson v. Commissioner, T.C. Memo. 1973-159)
8/8/73

◦⟨⟩◦

A weather-beaten driveway is deductible as a casualty, a court rules.

Rather than install a reinforced asphalt driveway like their neighbors', the O'Connells simply laid two parallel two-inch-thick concrete strips from their garage to the street. Everything was fine until the rains came to Northern California in January 1967. It was much colder and rainier than usual for the next four months. The driveways slowly broke up.

The IRS and the courts generally define "casualty" as a sudden calamity. Slow deterioration doesn't qualify. Nor do losses resulting from faulty construction. The IRS disallowed the O'Connells' deduction of their loss, saying the damage hadn't been sudden enough and had stemmed partly from the driveway's "substandard construction." "The question isn't free from doubt," a district court said. But it disagreed with the IRS on both counts and complimented Mrs. O'Connell, who argued the case herself, for an "able job" of persuasion.

(O'Connell v. U.S.A., U.S. Dist. Ct., No. Dist. Calif., 1972)
4/5/72

◦◁▷◦

A doctor kills his lawn inadvertently and the loss is deductible.

An Idaho physician wanted to kill the weeds in his large lawn. A local seed store recommended a spray called Cytrol, and the doctor sprayed up a storm. The spray killed the weeds. But it also did in the entire lawn, 13 trees and several evergreens. The Cytrol cans carried a warning against using the product on lawns, and the store claimed the doctor had said he only planned to spray around the edges. The doctor asserted he hadn't seen the warning on the can. He filed a big claim with the store's insurance company, but only collected a small amount. So on his tax return he claimed a casualty deduction of $6,900.

The tax law defines a deductible casualty as a sudden calamity such as a fire or storm that causes property damage. The IRS barred the doctor's deduction. It contended he either "willfully" applied the spray, knowing it would kill the lawn, or was "grossly negligent." But the Tax Court upheld the doctor, finding no evidence of "wanton conduct."

(Farber v. Commissioner, 57 T.C. No. 72)
3/15/72

The footprint caper. Or: How not to prove you lost money at the track.

There was this cab driver who liked to bet on horses. He went to various tracks several times a week, sometimes hitting one in the afternoon and another at night. He won sometimes and lost sometimes. But once, he hit the daily double for $21,854. When he filed his tax return for that year, he somehow came up with more than enough losing tickets ($23,680) to balance that one windfall and wipe out any tax obligation for it. (He didn't report any other winnings.)

A skeptical Tax Court judge examined the losing tickets and found that several had "unmistakable heel marks" on them. The judge didn't make any bald accusations, but he hinted that the cabbie just might have supplemented his loss record by collecting losing tickets other players had discarded on the ground.

The man "failed to offer a satisfactory explanation" of why some tickets bore footprints, the judge said. He denied all but $2,000 of the loss claims.

(Green v. Commissioner, T.C. Memo. 1972-131)
6/28/72

A $2,355 fee paid to adjusters to appraise fire damage to an apartment was ruled deductible by the Tax Court. The court decided the appraisal wasn't directly connected with an insurance claim; its purpose was substantiating a casualty loss deduction. Thus, the fee was deductible like any other expense incurred in figuring income tax liability.

(Stein v. Commissioner, T.C. Memo. 1972-140)
7/12/72

Some home mishaps are deductible, the IRS agrees. When a husband accidentally slammed a car door on his wife's hand, her 1.38 carat diamond popped from its setting, never to be seen again. At tax time, the couple claimed a $1,200 casualty loss, but the IRS demurred. It considered their misfortune an ordinary household mishap, like a boy tearing his new pants. But the Tax Court judged it a true casualty loss, caused by a sudden, unexpected, violent event. The IRS recently acquiesced in the ruling.

(White v. Commissioner, 48 T.C. No. 42.)
6/11/69

◦⟨⟩◦

Stealing money or getting it through fradulent misrepresentation amounts to the same thing, the IRS rules. It allowed a New Jersey man to deduct as a theft loss a loan he made to a company on the basis of financial data that a court later found false and misleading. (The firm went bankrupt, and the taxpayer never saw his money again.) The IRS said that "theft" might vary according to local law, but tax law uses the term to cover "any criminal appropriation of another's property."

(Rev. Rul. 71-381)
9/22/71

◦⟨⟩◦

With a little help from his postmaster, a collector of new-issue stamps proves his collection, which had been stolen from his home, was worth $50,000. The IRS wouldn't allow any theft loss deduction; it said the collector couldn't substantiate the amount of the loss. But the postmaster, also a collector, testified he had been in the theft victim's home and seen his collection. "If anyone would be competent to estimate the worth of . . . stamps, it would be a postmaster," the Tax Court said in upholding most of the man's claim.

(Whiteman v. Commissioner, T.C. Memo. 1973-124)
6/27/73

◦⟨⟩◦

If there's a good chance you'll recover some of a casualty loss, you must await the results of your

damage claim before deducting the remaining loss.
That's the gist of a Tax Court ruling. Some furniture
was destroyed in a moving van fire, and the taxpayer
sued the moving company. Six years later he won a partial settlement. He was a lawyer with a good record of
winning damage claim cases. Thus, the Tax Court said,
his chances of winning his own case were good. So he
couldn't deduct the unrecovered portion of the loss
until the year of the settlement.

(Chandler v. Commisisoner, T.C. Memo. 1972-193)
9/20/72

◦⟨⟩◦

An ice fisherman's car took an unexpected swim,
but the IRS accepted the plunge as a casualty loss and
allowed a tax deduction. The car, which was uninsured,
was parked on an ice-covered lake, where the owner was
fishing. The ice suddenly gave way, and the car sank to
the bottom, a total loss.

(Rev. Ruling 69-88.)
3/12/69

◦⟨⟩◦

IRS washout: Unusually heavy rain and snow
one winter washed away the soil supporting one corner
of a Seattle couple's house. Things gave way, and the
couple sought to deduct $2,136 in damages as a casualty
loss. The IRS demurred. A casualty loss, it said, must be
from some "sudden, unexpected or unusual cause," and
the washing away didn't qualify. The Tax Court concluded the IRS was being too narrow, however. The
washout led to a sudden movement of earth, which at
least to the people involved was "cataclysmic in character."

(Klawitter v. Commissioner, T.C. Memo. 1971-289)
12/1/71

◦⟨⟩◦

A casualty loss, to be deductible, must be due to a
sudden, unexpected or unusual cause. Slow death

doesn't qualify, the Tax Court recently ruled. A couple paid a premium price for a wooded lot, graced by beeches and maples. A month later, the lot was graded improperly, and fill dirt blocked aeration of the trees' roots. The inept grading doomed the trees, but the court said their death was from "progressive deterioration," a gradual suffocation over 16 months.

(Miller v. Commissioner, T.C. Memo. 1970-167.)
7/8/70

Shock of recognition: A Virginia couple discovered $2,729 in termite damage, even though exterminators had found "no visible evidence" of termites when the couple bought their house about four months before. The Tax Court wouldn't allow a casualty loss, however. A "casualty" must be sudden, it said, and the termites had been chewing away for years. (Previous owners had known this.) The court sympathized with the couple's "catastrophic shock," but their "sudden realization" doesn't make the damage sudden.

(Sahkul v. Commissioner, T.C. Memo. 1970-60.)
3/25/70

Totaled: A Maryland couple gave their 20-year-old son $1,000 to buy a car. He bought a used Austin-Healey roadster, which was registered in his name. Even before he acquired collision coverage, one of his friends smashed up the car. At tax time, the parents claimed a casualty loss, but the Tax Court turned them down. They had given the $1,000 to their son, and the casualty loss was his.

(Oman v. Commissioner, T.C. Memo. 1971-183.)
8/4/71

In a burglary it can be tough to prove the value of items stolen from you, or that you ever owned them at all. In one recent case, a Brooklyn man claimed he lost

$434 in cash, a TV set, and two diamond rings, but the IRS recognized no theft loss whatsoever. He appealed to the Tax Court, which proved less sticky. He argued his own case, and the Tax Court believed him. It cut the estimated loss to $1,209 from $1,489, however.

(Farrior v. Commissioner, T.C. Memo. 1970-312.)
11/25/70

◦⟨⟩◦

Communist Rumania confiscated an art collection after the war, but the owner couldn't claim a theft deduction for the loss, a court of appeals recently ruled. Taking private property "under color of governmental action" isn't theft. The widow of the last pre-war U.S. Minister to Rumania lodged the claim.

(Farcasanu v. Commissioner, U.S. Ct. of Appeals, D.C. Cir., 1970)
9/2/70

◦⟨⟩◦

Gem lode: The Tax Court accepted a taxpayer's unlikely and unsupported claim that he had lost some diamonds when his garage burned down. It seems he hid them there to keep them out of his estranged wife's hands.

(Williams v. Commissioner, T.C. Memo. 1970-143.)
6/17/70

◦⟨⟩◦

Theft loss claims again fare better in Tax Court than with the IRS. The law allows a casualty deduction for the portion of theft losses that exceeds $100, but the IRS can be very sticky about proof that the theft occurred. In one recent case, the IRS entirely disallowed a taxpayer's $2,285 claim for a coin collection, some cash stashed away, a TV set and other personal goods. The Tax Court allowed the deduction but it cut the amount in half.

(Pharr v. Commissioner, T.C. Memo. 1971-28.)
3/3/71

Deducting Travel and Schooling

Summer travel: The Tax Court draws some lines on when the costs are deductible.

A New York City man and wife, both high school teachers, took a charter flight to Europe, rented a car and toured France. The IRS claimed their expenses weren't deductible because the trip wasn't "primarily undertaken" to maintain or improve job skills. But the court said it was enough that "the major portion" of the travel was directly related to such skills. On this basis, it ruled the wife's expenses were deductible, but her husband's weren't.

The husband taught Latin, and the court found "only a tenuous relationship" between visiting two Roman sites in France and his work. His wife, however, taught world civilization, and their itinerary clearly centered on places of importance in her instruction. It was "significant," the court said, that the couple shunned a group tour for the flexibility of going their own way. The trip helped the wife give a more "stimulating presentation" of her course.

The entire car rental and gasoline costs were deductible (because the wife wouldn't have paid less had she traveled alone) but only her share of other outlays.

(Marlin v. Commissioner, 54 T.C. No. 49.)
4/1/70

Another professor wins a deduction for summer travel to Europe.

Anyone may claim a deduction for far-ranging travel—provided he can show "the major portion" of his travel activities "directly" maintained or improved skills required in his job. In practice, teachers and scholars tend to do the best job of beating the IRS on this one.

In one Tax Court case, a Rutgers professor of management clearly established his claim to the deduction. During his trip, he spent eight hours a day touring European auto plants or interviewing personnel. Much of what he gathered went directly into his courses. His wife went along and took notes, but that's where the Tax Court drew the line: It disallowed her share of the expenses as personal.

(Steinmann v. Commissioner, T.C. Memo. 1971-295)
12/8/71

◦⟷◦

A young lawyer won his claim to deduct the cost of getting a master's degree.

It isn't easy to justify a deduction for graduate study, but he managed. The law allows a deduction for education undertaken to maintain or improve skills required in a taxpayer's trade or business. There's no deduction, however, for schooling to meet the minimum education required to enter the field, or for schooling that's part of a program that leads to qualifying for a new field.

One case involved a young man who passed the Georgia bar in his third year of law school. The following summer, he worked for an Atlanta firm, then entered a master's program at Harvard Law. He tried to deduct all the education expenses he incurred after passing the bar, but the Tax Court drew a line. His final two quarters at law school weren't deductible because they were part of the program qualifying him to practice law. But the court allowed a deduction for his work at Harvard, mainly because the IRS conceded that if he had been a lawyer before he entered Harvard, his expenses would be deductible.

The court said he had clearly worked as a lawyer for the Atlanta firm. It also implied the IRS conceded too much in limiting its case to that point.

(Ruehmann v. Commissioner, T.C. Memo. 1971-157.)
7/14/71

◦⬦○

A Baptist preacher gets to deduct college costs over the IRS's objections.

John Glasgow was ordained a Baptist minister when he was 19 years old. Over the next several years he went to college off and on, and deducted some of his education expenses. The law allows such deductions if the education "improves or maintains" a person's job skills (but not if it equips him for a new field). The cost of an undergraduate education seldom qualifies, and the IRS wouldn't allow the Rev. Glasgow's deductions.

He took child psychology, teaching methods and humanities among other things, and argued they would help him in his ministry. The Tax Court agreed. It said the courses clearly were relevant to his work. It also ruled the man hadn't prepared himself for a new field; he had been ordained early in college and remained in the ministry after he finished.

Rev. Glasgow also made a good personal impression on the court. "He was an excellent witness for himself," it said.

(Glasgow v. Commissioner, T.C. Memo. 1971-77)
4/5/72

◦⬦○

School's out: It's still tough to justify education costs as business expenses.

An IRS agent sought to deduct the cost of graduate courses at a business school. The Tax Court found, however, that the schooling wasn't intended to maintain or improve skills required in his present job, but to qualify him for a better post. That's not deductible, it said. In another case, a high school teacher and his wife, a guidance counselor, toured the world for five months on sabbatical leave at half-pay. But they failed to persuade the court the trip was taken to maintain or improve their teaching skills. The tour was merely of general cultural value, the court said.

(Menas v. Commissioner, T.C. Memo. 1969-114.)

◦⟨⟩◦

Another taxpayer's petition was denied because his schooling was too closely related to his work. An IBM engineer claimed the salary IBM paid him while it sent him to graduate school was a non-taxable fellowship. But the court noted that IBM passed on his choice of school and his research topic.

"Participants in the program were obviously viewed by IBM as undertaking regular job assignments," it said.

6/18/69

◦⟨⟩◦

A teaching assistant flunks the Tax Court's tests for a business deduction.

As fellowship money becomes scarcer, more graduate students rely on jobs as teaching assistants. The Tax Court decided a test case on whether a teaching assistant could deduct tuition and fees as a business expense. The taxpayer, an assistant in the zoology department at the University of Minnesota, contended that the university required him to be enrolled to retain his job. Further, he argued, he had already satisfied the minimum education to obtain the job (a bachelor's degree).

The Tax Court ruled against him. For one thing, it said, he had to be a student to obtain—not retain—his job. The post was temporary, and having it one year didn't mean he would have it again the next. (Educational expenses to obtain a position aren't deductible.) Beyond that, the court said, his real goal was to become a college professor, and he was still working on the Ph.D. required for that.

Two concurring judges would have given the claim even shorter shrift. "Petitioner worked because he studied," they said. "He did not study because he worked."

(Jungreis v. Commissioner, 55 T.C. No. 58.)
1/6/71

Working wife: A federal district court ruled Fraser Wilkins, a former State Department Inspector General, can deduct as a business expense the cost of taking his wife on two foreign trips. For one thing, she gathered information he might have missed, the court said.

11/1/72

A tax victory turns to defeat for a first-grade teacher who circled the world.

When the Tax Court ruled last year that Marion Krist could deduct 80% of the $1,764 it cost her to visit 15 countries during a sabbatical, it was a pleasant surprise for teachers in general. Making a case for deducting foreign travel isn't easy; a teacher must convince the IRS the trip relates directly to specific job skills.

Mrs. Krist taught her first-graders about life abroad, concentrating on Switzerland and Japan. And in giving her bulk of the deduction she sought, the Tax Court was impressed that she had visited schools and homes in those countries and had brought back pictures and other items to aid in her teaching. But the Second U.S. Circuit Court of Appeals, to which the IRS appealed the Tax Court's ruling, denied the deduction.

It concluded Mrs. Krist had spent most of her time abroad vacationing rather than improving her teaching skills. She visited schools on only five days during the six-month trip, the court found. It said a "general cultural broadening" isn't enough to support the deduction.

(Krist v. Commissioner, U.S. Ct. of Appeals, 2nd Circuit, 1973.)
9/19/73

❯❮❯❮

Aphrodite's trip doesn't stimulate the Tax Court. With her employer's approval, Aphrodite Thanos, a high school librarian, substituted a trip to Europe for required attendance at summer school. She visited historical sites, collected books, pamphlets and pictures for library use, and deducted the cost of the trip as an educational expense. The Tax Court upheld the IRS disallowance of the deduction. The court ruled the trip might have made the librarian generally more capable but didn't directly maintain or improve her prime skills as the deduction rules required.

(Thanos v. Commissioner, T.C. Memo. 1970-193.)
7/22/70

❯❮❯❮

Study abroad proved deductible in part for a Brooklyn, N.Y., junior high school teacher. The Tax Court allowed her to deduct $1,582 for a five-week summer course at Sophia University in Tokyo. The course was directly relevant to her teaching. The court, however, denied a $406 deduction for her return via South Asia, the Middle East and Rome. That was mainly for pleasure, the court decided.

(Weiman v. Commissioner, T.C. Memo. 1971-92.)
5/5/71

❯❮❯❮

A teacher's plight shows the difficulty of deducting law school expenses. The cost of education that prepares one for a new line of work isn't deductible. But the teacher thought he had avoided that restriction; he claimed he didn't intend to practice law but was only trying to boost his teaching salary, which rose as he accumulated graduate school credits. In barring the deduction, the Tax Court stressed that the point isn't whether one plans to enter a new profession, but whether, as in the teacher's case, the education prepares him to do so.

(Wright v. Commissioner, T.C. Memo. 1973-8)
1/24/73

◦⟷◦

School expenses to qualify a taxpayer for a new trade aren't deductible, but one fellow who went to television-repair school tried a new twist. He sought to deduct what the final six months of a two-year program cost him. That portion dealt with color TV and solid-state circuitry, he said, and his earlier lessons had already qualified him to fix black-and-white sets. Thus the final six months were to improve existing job skills, he claimed, not to enter a new trade. The Tax Court found the two portions inseparable and entirely nondeductible.

(Betz v. Commissioner, T.C. Memo. 1971-29.)
2/17/71

◦⟷◦

Shot down: A reserve officer in the Air Force sought to deduct the cost of completing his college degree, but the Tax Court refused. The officer argued that without a degree, he couldn't get a regular commission; and without that, he would have to retire after 20 years. The court decided he was trying to better his status, rather than maintain it, and while the Air Force encouraged a college education, it didn't expressly require it.

(Kinch v. Commissioner, T.C. Memo. 1971-117.)
6/7/71

Grossinger's, the Catskills resort, had a fellow to entertain guests with "the art and science of hypnosis." He lacked formal training, so the management, fearful of being sued, ordered him to get some qualifications. That was in 1957. By 1966, he was a Ph.D. in psychology and almost a licensed psychologist. He tried to deduct his schooling, but the Tax Court wasn't entranced. His education "far exceeded" what Grossinger's, his employer, required, it said.

(Fleischer v. Commissioner, T.C. Memo. 1971-163.)
7/21/71

Is It a Business Expense?

A fish story? A monger claims he had to make payments to customers' help.

When frozen fish came on the market, things turned rotten for New Amsterdam Fish Inc. and other New York City purveyors of fresh fish. Not only was the competing frozen product cheaper. In addition, the kitchen help at restaurants and hotels disliked fresh fish, which had to be "scaled, gutted, cleaned, deheaded, deveined, and portioned" before cooking, the Tax Court recited. Thus, the fresh-fish sellers worked out a system of cash "compensation" to relieve the kitchen help's distaste.

New Amsterdam claimed it regularly paid fishhandlers in its clients' kitchens 2% to 10% of their employers' monthly purchases. The firm said it routinely stuffed the cash in brown envelopes, which its salesmen distributed as they made their rounds. The sums came to $205,317 over four years and were debited to "sales commissions." The IRS smelled something fishy, however. It doubted the firm ever made such payments—or suspected the salesmen simply pocketed the money. But the Tax Court concluded the payouts were customary, the salesmen honest, and the payments real.

And if substantiated, the court said, there was no question they were deductible business expenses.

(New Amsterdam Fish Inc. v. Commissioner, T.C. Memo. 1971-17.)
1/27/71

○⊂⊃○

The Cuban scene was a banker's Bay of Pigs, but Uncle Sam proved understanding.

An investment banker urged customers, family and friends to invest in a plant that would make wallboard in Cuba. When the enterprise ran short of cash, the banker felt obliged to bail it out by arranging a bank loan. The loan was formally guaranteed by a closed corporation the banker and his brother owned, but in fact it rested on the banker's pledge that the debt wouldn't sour. When the infusion of money proved insufficient, the banker lent more, this time from his personal funds.

Along came Castro, who seized the business and lit his cigars with its IOUs. As good as his word, the banker ponied up to pay off the bank note the family corporation had backed. Then at tax time, he sought to deduct the payments as business expenses and the other money he lost as a business bad debt. The IRS balked; the personal loan wasn't part of investment banking, it said nor was the banker liable for the corporation's guarantee.

The Tax Court was more sympathetic and allowed both deductions. The banker could reasonably believe that failure of the venture he had touted would hurt his own business, the court said. And by absorbing the bank note, the investment banker was protecting his reputation for business integrity.

(Milbank v. Commissioner, 51 T.C. No. 79.)
3/5/69

◦⟨◯⟩◦

A business doesn't become a hobby just because you enjoy it a lot, the Tax Court says.

Thomas Jackson bought a 65-foot yacht in 1958, and over the next several years looked into the chartering business. He remodeled the boat, moved it to the Virgin Islands and in 1965 took in $30,000 and cleared a small profit from chartering. Former TV host Hugh Downs chartered the yacht for an extended jaunt to the South Pacific. But bad weather and damage to the boat delayed the party's return and most charters for 1966 had to be canceled. Jackson still deducted business expenses and claimed depreciation for that year, however.

The IRS disallowed the expenses and depreciation. It said the yacht was more a hobby than a business. (An activity must be operated for profit to qualify for business expense deductions.) But the Tax Court ruled for Jackson. It pointed out he had outfitted the boat for charter passengers, advertised the service, made a profit in 1965 and used the boat personally only a little.

The court noted Jackson's pleasure in operating the yacht didn't make it a hobby. "Suffering has never been made a prerequisite to deductibility," the court said.

(Jackson v. Commissioner, 59 T.C. No. 31)
12/6/72

His bull went sterile. He lost money on tobacco and feeder cattle.

And very little else went right for former U.S. Ambassador to Uruguay Jefferson Patterson on his farm in Maryland. Patterson, a 37-year State Department veteran, failed to show a profit every year but one since he bought the farm in the 1930s. He tried to deduct losses from the place, but the IRS said no. It maintained the long string of deficits showed Patterson's "indifference to profit." (For losses to be deductible, an enterprise must be operated mainly for profit, not pleasure.)

But the Court of Claims has upheld its commissioners' finding that the losses are deductible after all. The court was impressed that Patterson had hired experts to run the farm, marketed the corn and hay the cattle didn't eat, consulted with a county agricultural agent for advice, and kept good records.

The court conceded Patterson mightn't have operated the farm "in the most efficient manner possible."

But it said his "good faith effort" to make money was
the key to the tax write-off.

(Patterson v. U.S., U.S. Ct. of Claims, 1972)
5/31/72

◐━◗

IRS Waterloo: A father and son trounce the tax
men in a horse matter.

Back in the 1950s, the father began raising shet-
land ponies on some land near Waterloo, Iowa, where he
practiced dental surgery. Several years later, his son,
also a dental surgeon, started a herd of Tennessee Walk-
ing Horses—known for their distinctive gaits. Both men
considered themselves to be in the business of selling
and showing horses; they deducted as business expenses
the considerable costs of maintaining their herds.

But the IRS said the horses were a hobby, expenses
of which aren't deductible. It pointed out the doctors
had made little if any money from the horses; for expenses to be deductible, a business must be motivated by
profit.

The Tax Court upheld the doctors. It said they legitimately tried to make money: They devoted a lot of
time to the horses, hired expert help and kept good financial records.

(Foster v. Commissioner, T.C. Memo. 1973-13)
1/31/73

◐━◗

James B. Carey, the longtime Electrical Workers
president, loses a Tax Court case.

The issue was whether Carey could deduct, as ordinary and necessary business expenses, about $16,000 he
spent in his losing bid for reelection in 1964. The Tax
Court said no, in part because it doubted that "common
understanding in the ordinary affairs of life" would
consider such outlays business expenses. It also leaned
heavily on a Supreme Court case that denied a deduction to a state judge seeking reelection. "Powerful con-

siderations of public policy" were invoked against the deduction.

The Tax Court decided the presidency of a large union involves "a comparable public policy element," but not all the court's judges agreed. Six would have denied the deduction but without getting into "public policy." Five others dissented. Carey, they said, was clearly "in the trade or business of being a labor leader," and campaign expenses were ordinary and necessary. "We must be realistic," the dissent declared. "Election expenditures are frequently the sine qua non of winning."

The courts have allowed a taxpayer to deduct the expenses of a corporate proxy fight, the dissent said. It considered that a better comparison than the case of the state judge.

(Carey v. Commissioner, 56 T.C. No. 36.)
6/23/71

A public official, fighting to hold his job, merits a deduction, the IRS says.

The costs of running for public office or for reelection aren't deductible as business expenses (or otherwise), the courts have ruled. The expenses of seeking election as a judge, for instance, aren't part of a transaction entered for profit or incurred in the production of income, the Supreme Court has said.

But now the IRS has conceded something of an exception to this. Its ruling involved a taxpayer who was elected to public office and shortly thereafter faced a recall campaign. He waged a vigorous defense and defeated the recall. The IRS ruled his campaign expenses deductible because he was "merely defending his position," not seeking a new one.

(Rev. Rul. 71-470)
11/3/71

How Leroy Gillis maintained his image, kept peace and got a tax deduction.

When the company LeRoy worked for opened new quarters, it put new furniture in every office but LeRoy's. He got an old metal desk and a worn chair. The origin of the problem, it seemed, was a personality clash between LeRoy and the man in charge of the furnishings. So, rather than go over the man's head, LeRoy spruced up his office with $332 out of his own pocket. He installed draperies, a walnut desk and a Naugahyde sofa, and had his chair reupholstered.

The IRS refused to allow LeRoy to depreciate the new furnishings on his tax return, but the Tax Court backed him. Noting the "unusual circumstances," the court said LeRoy exercised a "tolerable degree of employe prudence" in refraining from complaining about his furniture. That, plus the necessity of maintaining his "image as a successful manager," justified the expenses and favorable tax treatment, the court asserted.

(Gillis v. Commissioner, T.C. Memo. 1973-96)
5/9/73

⚬⟷⚬

The Big Board takes care of its own, and the IRS rules it's deductible.

Since 1873, the New York Stock Exchange has maintained a "gratuity fund" to pay a death benefit to the family of a deceased member. The payment was doubled to $20,000 in 1930, and it hasn't been changed since.

A throwback to when the exchange was run as a private club, the fund is financed through nominally voluntary gifts. The exchange's 1,366 members pay $15 on joining and pledge to pay $15 more whenever a member dies. The IRS ruled that whatever the payments were called, they were deductible business expenses. A member "is bound to make such 'gifts' to maintain his standing," it said.

(Rev. Ruling 70-342.)
7/15/70

◦⟨⟩◦

A brokerage firm gets to deduct a charitable contribution as a business expense.

The firm gave 6% of its brokerage commissions to a group organized to reduce tensions and combat deterioration in the neighborhood where the firm was situated. The concern mentioned the gifts in its advertising, hoping to woo customers who might otherwise trade through other brokers.

The community organization had been recognized as a charity by the IRS. But corporations aren't allowed to deduct more than 5% of their taxable income as charitable contributions. However, the IRS ruled the payments could reasonably be expected to "further" the brokerage firm's business. So it allowed their deduction in full as business expenses.

(Rev. Rul. 72-314)
7/12/72

◦⟨⟩◦

Questionable stock trading spawns a fat tax deduction for an executive.

Nathan Cummings, executive committee chairman of Consolidated Foods, made a $53,870 profit trading in MGM stock within a six-month period. He was a director of MGM, and directors and other insiders are barred by law from such short-term trading. Any profits must be paid to the company issuing the stock. When MGM informed Cummings he might have violated the law, he claimed the infraction was inadvertent and immediately paid MGM the money. That meant the company didn't have to disclose the problem in its proxy statement.

Later, Cummings' financial adviser informed him

that, as the violation was inadvertent, he mightn't have been required to pay MGM after all. So Cummings asked MGM officials to give the money back. They didn't. As a last resort, therefore, he deducted the payment as a business loss. Cummings figured that by keeping the matter off MGM's proxy statement he was guarding against public disclosure and thus protecting his business reputation. The cost of doing that is a legitimate business expense and thus deductible, he felt.

The IRS wouldn't go along. It said the payment was a long-term capital loss, less advantageous in tax terms than a straight deduction. But the Tax Court upheld Cummings.

(Cummings v. Commissioner, 60 T.C. No. 11)
5/2/73

◦⟨⟩◦

A lawyer claims politicking helps business, but the Tax Court is unimpressed.

Lawyers can't advertise, so they often go into politics instead. According to Martin Mayer's "The Lawyers," the neophyte who fails to run for office "may be suspect in the eyes of his colleagues—what other, sinister way does he have to find clients?" In a Tax Court case, a Florida attorney ran for the state senate and lost. He then tried to deduct about $7,200 in campaign outlays as ordinary and necessary business expenses.

Not only was it his duty to run for office, the attorney said, but the bar also urged its members to do so "as a practical means of 'advertising.' " But the Tax Court said his expenses were entirely personal. "He has not pointed to a single client obtained or a single fee received . . . as the result of his campaigning." It found only a "vague relationship" between the campaigning and his law practice.

(Maness v. Commissioner, 54 T.C. No. 155.)
8/19/70

Good government can merit an investment, a court says in a gift-tax case.

A decade ago, Mrs. Edith Rosenwald Stern, a wealthy Louisiana resident, gave $60,850 to support reform slates in New Orleans and statewide elections. She and her fellow contributors said they were disturbed by the state's lagging economy and considered the state's politics responsible. The money went for campaign literature and advertising. The IRS claimed the sums were gifts, however, and dunned her for $35,908 in taxes and interest.

Mrs. Stern contended she got full value for her money because she had a stake in better government. The tax law presumes that a transfer in the ordinary course of business is made for adequate consideration (and thus isn't a gift) if it's bona fide, at arm's length and free from donative intent. That's fine, the IRS said, but it denied the transfer was made in the course of "an actual business carried on by Mrs. Stern."

The Fifth Circuit appeals court said the IRS construed the law too narrowly. "The transfers were permeated with commercial and economic factors," it said. "In a very real sense, Mrs. Stern was making an economic investment."

(Stern v. U.S.A., U.S. Ct. of Appeals, 5th Cir., 1971.)
2/10/71

◦⊂⊃◦

A law firm can't expense legal fees it foots for some clients, the Tax Court says.

The case involved a California firm that specialized in personal injury cases, which it usually accepted for a share of any recovery won for the client. The law firm claimed that fierce competition for such cases forced it to bear many litigation costs (such as witness fees) itself—subject to repayment only if the client won the case and a monetary award. On its tax returns, the firm treated such outlays as expenses when incurred and as income if and when repaid.

The Tax Court sided with the IRS in denying that such costs were ordinary business expenses. The expectation of repayment meant the outlays were "in the nature of loans," the court said. It noted the firm's care in screening the clients it would accept on such a basis and also the firm's "good hopes" of being paid back. (Of the $6,925 the firm advanced in 1960, it recovered $6,233 within two years.)

The court also refused to allow a bad debt reserve in connection with cases still pending. It ruled that an "unconditional obligation" to repay didn't take effect until the cases were closed. If the money then proved uncollectible, the firm could make normal bad-debt deductions, the court said.

(Canelo v. Commissioner, 53 T.C. No. 23.)
11/19/69

Legal fees to fend off a suit weren't deductible, the Tax Court decides.

A case involving a wealthy Charlotte, N.C., woman concerned whether legal fees were deductible as expenses "for the management, conservation, or maintenance of property held for the production of income." The woman's home was burglarized, and she was attacked. She identified a suspect, who was indicted for burglary and rape. He was acquitted, however, and promptly sued her for malicious prosecution, asking $2 million in damages. The suit was thrown out, but the woman's legal bill came to $46,000.

The woman contended that if the suit were lost, then she would have lost most of her property, mainly stocks and bonds. Thus the outlay conserved property held for the production of income, she argued. But the Tax Court disagreed. Relying on a Supreme Court ruling, it said the deduction depended on whether the expenses were "in connection with the taxpayer's profit-seeking activities."

"It is perfectly clear," the Tax Court said, "that the circumstances which engendered the expenditures . . . were personal in nature."

(Brooks v. Commissioner, T.C. Memo. 1971-152.)
6/30/71

∘⊂⊃∘

Payments to a pollution control fund are deductible as business expenses.

So says the IRS in the case of a retailer which, along with other stores, lost business after oil leaking from an off-shore well damaged a resort city's tourist trade. The city council set up a fund to control the effects of oil pollution on the city's businesses. The fund is used for scientific research, physical preservation of beaches and advertising to counteract damaging publicity about the pollution.

In the retailer's case, the IRS said its payment to the fund was voluntary and was "reasonably calculated to improve the taxpayer's future business." Furthermore, the payment was "commensurate with the financial return" the company expected the fund to produce.

(Rev. Rul. 73-113)
3/14/73

∘⊂⊃∘

A coffee man's safaris were business trips but not grounds for deductions.

Dana W. Brown, former president of Manhattan Coffee Co., built up quite a reputation in coffee circles by showing movies he had taken on safaris to East Africa and other coffee-producing areas. The firm defrayed his expenses and built its advertising around his trips. But when Manhattan Co. changed hands, the new owners were less enthusiastic about the movies, which they felt mainly advertised Brown. He continued the safaris but paid for them himself.

The Tax Court ruled Brown couldn't deduct the outlays as ordinary and necessary business expenses. The trips were more than a hobby, it conceded, but they were "primarily" for enhancing his personal business reputation and "only incidentally" to boost Manhattan's sales. As such, the expenses were a capital outlay, akin to the costs of developing goodwill.

Normally the cost of capital assets is written off, and deducted, over their useful life. But there was no evidence that the useful life of his enhanced reputation could be ascertained, the court said. (On appeal, a circuit court was more direct: The trips couldn't be deducted as business expenses because Brown never proved they were necessary.)

(Brown v. Commissioner, T.C. Memo. 1970-253.)
9/16/70

○══◐

Amend, brother, the Tax Court rules out a deduction for spiritual harmony.

Fred W. Amend, whose company makes Chuckles candy, fell into consulting a Christian Scientist before making many personal and business decisions. This spiritual guidance helped so much that Amend had his company put the man on retainer for consultation on business affairs. In 1965-66, he was paid $11,700, but the IRS wouldn't let it deduct the sum as a business expense.

The Tax Court found the question "vexatious" and "convoluted," but it upheld the Revenue Service. Even though the arrangement clearly aided Amend, "some expenses are so inherently personal they simply cannot qualify" as deductible business outlays, the court said. And what Amend sought wasn't business advice. It was "a state of harmony," reconciling his business thinking with spiritual beliefs.

(Amend v. Commissioner, 55 T.C. No. 31.)
11/25/70

Physician, depreciate thyself: The IRS takes a new view of human "useful life."

For many years, the IRS has routinely and rigidly rebuffed professional athletes, actors and others who sought to take write-offs on the gradual deterioration of their physiques or faces and thus their earning power. Outright amortization of the human body remains anathema, IRS officials say, but they've taken a step in that direction. They are permitting a doctor to use his life expectancy as the period for amortizing a hospital fee.

The doctor paid the fee for life-time, nontransferable privileges of practicing in a hospital he and other doctors organized. The IRS ruled the fee a capital outlay, rather than an immediately-deductible business expense. It purchased an intangible asset with a useful life of more than one year. Thus, the IRS concludes, the fee is "recoverable through amortization deductions based on a useful life equal to the taxpayer's life expectancy."

A "shorter useful life" could possibly be justified, the IRS adds. That presumably, refers to retirement plans rather than to anticipation of an untimely demise.

(Rev. Ruling 70-171.)
4/22/70

◦━━◦

Little things mean a lot? A court won't quibble over small capital outlays.

Under the Internal Revenue Code, outlays on plant or equipment that last more than a year can't be deducted as current expenses. They must be capitalized and written off over the usual life of the asset. The code is hard and fast on this point, but businesses commonly ignore it for very small expenditures. The Treasury usually goes along, but there's no explicit statutory basis.

One Court of Claims decision may furnish some

basis in case law, however. The decision involved a railroad that followed the old Interstate Commerce Commission rule permitting it to expense capital outlays less than $100. But when the ICC raised that limit to $500 some years ago, the Treasury balked.

The Court of Claims backed the railroad. The code's rule against expensing capital outlays isn't overriding, it said. The $500 rule was consistent with generally accepted accounting principles, the ICC said it didn't distort income, and, in dollar terms, it didn't make much difference, the court summarized.

Over 17 years, the $500 rule gave the railroad $230,000 in deductions, compared with $176,000 the IRS way. In context, that difference was "so minute as to become unfathomable," the court said.

(Cincinnati, New Orleans & Texas Pacific Railway Co. v.
U.S., U.S. Ct. of Claims, 1970.)
4/29/70

◠◡◠

His first name is Walter. That was one of the disclosures when entertainer Liberace took the IRS to Tax Court. The principal issue was whether a corporation Liberace controlled could provide him with a $345,000 home and deduct the cost as a business expense. He lived there for a mere $300 a month, but the place also housed his production facilities, so the Tax Court more or less split the difference. It allowed one-half the corporation's claimed deduction, but it also ruled that Liberace had to include in his income one-half the home's fair rental value.

(International Artists Ltd. v. Commissioner, 55 T.C. No. 12.)
10/28/70

◠◡◠

The Tax Court wouldn't grant a teacher a deduction for books and radios he gave his pupils. But it allowed him to write off over five years a phonograph, TV set and other equipment he bought for use in class.

(Patterson v. Commissioner, T.C. Memo. 1971-234)
9/29/71

◦⟷◦

Bad debts in an illegal loan business are deductible as business losses, the Tax Court decided. As the debts stemmed from loans bearing illegally high interest, they weren't legally collectible and therefore weren't deductible as bad debts. But the law doesn't require the taxpayer's business to be legal to qualify for an ordinary loss deduction, the court rules.

(Tharp v. Commissioner, T.C. Memo. 1972-10)
1/19/72

◦⟷◦

A jury in a U.S. district court in Nebraska decided the IRS was wrong in disallowing an architectural firm's expenses in connection with its president's activities as head of a local civic organization. In doing so, the jury decided the president kept the company's name before the public by heading up the civic organization, and thus the expenses constituted "ordinary and necessary" business expenses.

(Leo Daly Co. v. Vinal, U.S. Dist. Ct., Dist. Nebr., 1968)
3/5/69

◦⟷◦

Downtown merchants get a boost from the IRS. The service advised it would permit merchants to deduct voluntary payments to city authorities to help develop public parking facilities near their businesses. The IRS promised similar treatment where merchants chipped in to remake a street. Their plans included ceramic tile sidewalks, a cobblestoned mall and continuous canopies. The city would own and maintain all the improvements.

(Rev. Rulings 69-85, 69-86, 69-90.)
3/12/69

A trade secret isn't depreciable unless a company can show what the secret's useful life is, the Tax Court says. A company that paid $200,000 for title to a secret manufacturing process wasn't allowed to deduct depreciation because, the court said recently, it failed to prove its claim that the useful life of the process was four years.

(Yates Industries v. Commissioner, 58 T.C. No. 93)
10/4/72

◐◐

A physician who raised 800 apple trees as a sideline was allowed by the Tax Court to deduct his losses on the operation even though the Revenue Service claimed that the trees may have had an aesthetic value but not a commercial value to him. The court said the size of the orchard suggested a business and agreed with the taxpayer's contention that "there's nothing aesthetic or pleasant about thousands of decaying apples on a 10-acre farm."

(Currie v. Commissioner, T.C. Memo. 1969-4.)
1/22/69

◐◐

No contest: A couple carried off a $10,000 Better Homes and Gardens prize by redoing their attic as a recreation room in the style of a Victorian ice cream parlor. But while their prize was taxable, a circuit court recently turned down their claim that the $9,800 they spent on the job was an off-setting deductible expense. The money produced a permanent improvement, the court said.

(Paxman v. Commissioner, U.S. Ct. of Appeals, 10th Cir., 1969.)
8/20/69

◐◐

What's news? Mahlon H. Elliott, a Methodist minister in Alexandria, Va., was in a tax audit when the IRS auditor questioned the books and magazines he had taken deductions for. Why The Wall Street Journal?

the IRS lady asked. Well, a clergyman has to know what's going on in the world, and the newspaper keeps him in touch, the minister said. The IRS lady denied the deduction. Mr. Elliott then asked about "Portnoy's Complaint," which the auditor allowed. Why the book but not the Journal? "'Portnoy's Complaint' has social relevance, and the Journal doesn't," the IRS lady replied.

3/24/71

❮◯❯

Fat chance: An overweight airline pilot sweated off 38 pounds in two months to land a job with United. He then sought to deduct $500 as a business expense, representing about two-thirds of what a new, slimmer wardrobe cost him. The Tax Court backed the IRS in refusing the deduction. It is well-settled, the court said, that only clothing required for employment but unsuitable for daily wear is deductible.

(Kennedy v. Commissioner, T.C. Memo. 1970-58.)
3/18/70

❮◯❯

Abe Saperstein, the late owner of the Harlem Globetrotters, was upheld in a Tax Court case. Back in the early 1960s, he tried to set up the American Basketball League and lent it $56,000 in a fruitless effort to keep it alive. The IRS claimed the debt was merely personal, but the court allowed his estate to deduct the sum as a business bad debt; Saperstein had had a falling-out with the National Basketball Association, and he hoped the new league would assure his Globetrotters competition and access to arenas.

(Estate of Saperstein v. Commissioner, T.C. Memo. 1970-209.)
8/12/70

❮◯❯

Back in the fifties, Consumers Power Co. of Michigan chipped in for an industry advertising campaign that extolled privately owned electric power companies over publicly owned. It also attacked the latter as "creeping socialism." But a circuit court denied Consumers Power a deduction for its outlays. They were an attempt to influence legislation, the court said, rather than an ordinary and necessary business expense.

(Consumers Power Co. v. U.S.A., U.S. Ct. of Appeals, 6th Cir., 1970.)
6/17/70

The Business Traveler

The overnight rule for deducting meal costs withstands a tough practical test.

Under its "overnight" rule, the IRS allows a business traveler to deduct the cost of meals only if his trip requires a stop for sleep or rest. The Supreme Court upheld the rule in 1969. The test seems even firmer now, following another decision in the Court of Appeals for the First Circuit. That case was interesting because it was brought by a taxpayer who put in extremely strenuous one-day travel but still failed to win a deduction.

The taxpayer, Frederick J. Barry, a consulting engineer, routinely left his home by 6:30 a.m. for business trips and didn't return until 10:30 p.m. or midnight. He ate all his meals on the road, and—for safety's sake, he said—normally pulled over for a refreshing nap before completing the drive home. But the circuit court upheld the Tax Court in deciding that a catnap wasn't what was meant by "sleep or rest." That required a stop long enough to entail "a significant increase in expenses."

The court didn't want to breach the clearcut overnight rule. "The tax involved is too small to warrant case by case haggling," it said.

(Barry v. Commissioner, U.S. Ct. of Appeals, 1st Cir., 1970.)
1/20/71

❦

The IRS boosts allowable travel outlays before detailed accounting is required.

It ruled that if an employe is reimbursed for not more than $36 a day for subsistence while away from home on business, the IRS will consider its requirements for substantiating such outlays automatically met. The tests will also be met if any employe is paid a per diem of not more than $36 instead of being reimbursed. These limits had been $31.25 since 1969. A similar limit of 15 cents a mile for transportation was left unchanged.

Meeting these limits spares an employe from documenting his expenses, but he still must show the time, place and business purpose of travel. The IRS requires his employer to maintain "adequate internal audit controls" over reimbursements (such as having someone approve expense accounts). An employer must also make sure that per diems are reasonable estimates of actual expenses.

The IRS says $36 for "subsistence" includes "meals and lodging, laundry, cleaning and pressing of clothing, and fees and tips for services." It doesn't include taxis, telegrams, phone calls or transportation to or from a destination.

(Rev. Rul. 71-412)
9/22/71

◄═►

The IRS eases its posture on when a taxpayer is away from home.

The taxpayer may deduct travel and living expenses while "away from home" on business, but that apparently simple phrase has spawned many disputes. The IRS contends that a taxpayer's "tax home" is his regular place of work. (If he chooses to live elsewhere, that's a nondeductible commute.) In some cases, however, the IRS argued that a taxpayer had no tax home at all because he worked at several sites rather than one. Thus he couldn't deduct expenses for being away.

But, the IRS backed down a bit by ruling that someone who lacks a "principal place of employment" may nevertheless have a tax home. The ruling concerned a construction worker who worked at sites over a 12-state area. Considering "all the facts and circumstances," the IRS said, the man's tax home was his residence, where his family lived and where he lived when he wasn't traveling.

The ruling carefully noted that his trips were long enough to require his stopping for "substantial sleep or rest." Normally, one isn't considered away from home on business unless the trip is at least overnight.

(Rev. Ruling 71-247.)
6/16/71

Does your "home" move around? A Second Circuit decision is raising doubts.

A taxpayer's expenses while "away from home" on business are deductible, but the matter isn't simple. The IRS argues that when a taxpayer takes a job at a new location for an indefinite period, the new job site becomes his fictional "tax home." He isn't "away from home," even though his residence hasn't changed. On this theory, a U.S. district court denied a deduction to Ethel Merman, the Broadway star. She claimed she was away from her Colorado home while playing in "Gypsy," a two-year Broadway run.

The Second Circuit appeals court told the district court to look again and ignore the "tax home" hocuspocus. What mattered was whether Miss Merman's expenses were compelled by her business affairs. The key question, the higher court said, was whether her New York stint was indefinite enough that "a reasonable person in her position would pull up stakes and make her permanent residence in New York." If it was, then keeping her residence in Colorado was a personal matter.

"When an assignment is truly temporary, it would be unreasonable to expect the taxpayer to move his home," the court said. His expenses are thus forced by "exigencies of business."

(Six v. U.S.A., U.S. Ct. of Appeals, 2nd Cir., 1971)
11/3/71

◦⊂⊃◦

Home is where you hang your hat? The Tax Court tries to find a consistent rule.

The court returned to a perennial issue and tried to clarify it. The issue is deciding when a taxpayer is temporarily away from home on business and thus entitled to deduct his living costs. The case involved a teacher who lived in Knoxville, Tenn., but couldn't find a job there. He taught a year in Georgia and then a semester in North Carolina, while his family remained in Tennessee.

The Tax Court decided the two stints weren't what the law meant by being away temporarily. Ultimately, it said, the issue turns on whether under all the circumstances, the taxpayer could reasonably be expected to move his residence to near his work. The court decided the teacher had no business ties to Knoxville. Considering how bleak the job prospects were there, he might well be expected to move his family to greener pastures. Thus living in Knoxville but working elsewhere was a personal choice, it said.

It wasn't the same, the court said, as a taxpayer whose employer sent him elsewhere temporarily, or whose work forced him to take jobs "of necessarily brief duration in disparate localities."

(Tucker v. Commissioner, 55 T.C. No. 82.)
3/3/71

◦⊂⊃◦

Business interests in two cities entitled an Ohio man to travel deductions.

After his retirement as a GM engineer, Francis Markey spent five days a week in Warren, Mich., doing consulting work for GM. But he spent weekends 250 miles away in Lewisburg, Ohio, where he maintained a home, owned farms, houses and apartments, and was secretary of a bank. He deducted the cost of making 50 round trips a year to Warren and living there during the week.

But the IRS ruled Markey's home for tax purposes was Warren and allowed him to deduct only 12 trips a year back to Lewisburg. Among other things, the IRS noted he derived most of his income from his work in Warren. The Tax Court, though, allowed his full deductions.

It stressed that even though Markey's activities in Lewisburg didn't produce a great deal of net income, his investments there were "considerable" and fully justified a trip every weekend.

(Markey v. Commissioner, T.C. Memo. 1972-154.)
8/9/72

⚬━▷◦

How long is "temporary"? The Tax Court upholds a taxpayer but ducks an answer.

If a person works away from his home temporarily, his traveling and living costs are deductible. The catch, however, is that if the new employment becomes more than temporary, the taxpayer's "tax home" is presumed to have moved to the new site, and living expenses become nondeductible personal outlays again. It isn't necessary for the new job to become permanent—indefinite is, enough.

The Tax Court had to decide whether a steam fitter's stint had slipped from temporary to indefinite. When construction work dried up in his home city, his union found him work elsewhere. In April 1967, he went to work on a nuclear power plant. He thought the job might last six months, but in fact it ran on for 31 months. On his 1967 return, the IRS disallowed his deduction of $2,562 in living and traveling expenses, but the Tax Court ruled for him. It noted that "complication after complication" had prolonged the thorny job.

The court didn't say how long "temporary" could be. It simply said that the job hadn't become indefinite by the end of 1967, the tax year involved in the litigation.

(Brown v. Commissioner, T.C. Memo. 1971-7.)
1/20/71

○⊂⊃○

Another decision on commuting continues the hard line of no deduction.

Few tax precepts are stricter than the rule that commuting isn't deductible. A Tax Court decision makes this rule even stiffer. It involved a Brooklyn, N.Y., consulting engineer who worked for two New York City firms that sold his services to still other companies. The man worked a 16-month stint at a Long Island company and eight months in Connecticut. He sought to deduct the expenses of his daily drive to the job.

The IRS denied the deduction because it claimed the jobs weren't temporary or far enough from home. The Tax Court went further and concluded that the engineer was simply a commuter. It said he worked for the New York firms "in form only." His job stints might be temporary, but that didn't transform his daily travel expenses into business transportation costs. "Commuting is commuting, regardless of the work, the distance traveled or the mode of transportation," the court said.

One judge dissented. He protested that the court was interpreting the law even more stiffly than the IRS.

(Turner v. Commissioner, 56 T.C. No. 3.)
4/28/71

○⊂⊃○

The tax court refuses to lighten the tax load of a Washington policeman.

His case turned on a recent Supreme Court ruling concerning commuters—carpenters, for instance—who have to carry bulky tools or other heavy materials back and forth to work. The High Court said a commuter shouldn't be allowed to deduct any load-related car expenses, unless the need to carry the load is his sole reason for driving and without the load he would take public transportation. Two circuit courts previously had given partial deductions to commuters who had to carry loads but would have driven in any case. But the Supreme Court said there isn't any rational way to make that type of allocation.

As this more lenient approach is closed off, it can be expected that many commuters will try to qualify for a deduction under the stricter Supreme Court formula, trying to make a case that they drive to work only because of their load. A Tax Court decision, however, indicates that won't be so easy as it may seem. A National Park Service policeman who patrols historic sites in the District of Columbia claimed he would have taken a bus to work if he hadn't had to carry 51 pounds of gear back and forth every day.

But a skeptical Tax Court denied his commuting deduction. The officer on some days would have spent two hours more commuting by bus than by car, the court figured. It didn't think it was plausible he would put up with that.

(Bradley v. Commissioner, T.C. Memo. 1973-163)
8/1/73

❀

A court tosses out the IRS one-year rule on withholding taxes from per diems.

The IRS has ruled that if "temporary" job assignments go on a year or more, then per-diem allowances for meals and such become wages subject to withholding. A Houston engineering firm contested the point, however, and the Fifth Circuit appeals court ruled in its favor. The Houston outfit paid employes a living allowance while they worked on a Bartlesville, Okla., project.

The job could be canceled on two weeks' notice, but it went on for four years.

The appeals court brushed aside the IRS ruling as "merely the opinion of a lawyer in the agency" and not binding. It also saw no basis for a one-year rule. "The payments are either wages or not from beginning to end." Wages are payment for services, the court recited, and it decided the living allowances weren't wages at all. The company paid employes the same allowance, whatever their base pay. It accounted for the payments separately, and it paid none to employes hired in Bartlesville.

Whether the payments were taxable income for the employes was another matter, the court said. But the company wasn't required to withhold taxes from them.

(Stubbs, Overbeck & Assoc. v. U.S.A.,
U.S. Ct. of Appeals, 5th Cir., 1971.)
7/21/71

No deduction for commuting expenses is one of the strictest tax rules, and apparently it will remain that way. The Supreme Court has declined to review a notable case denying a deduction to civilian employes at Vandenberg Air Force Base, Calif. They argued that because they were forced to live off base, at least part of their commute should be deductible. The lower courts found their hardships "no different than those confronting the many taxpayers who cannot find suitable housing close to their urban place of employment."

(Sanders v. U.S.A., U.S. Ct. of Appeals, 9th Cir., 1971)
10/27/71

Another decision allowing a deduction to a commuter was reversed. A U.S. district court in Seattle, bucking a trend in other courts, had allowed a business expense deduction to a man who had to drive about 70 miles roundtrip each day to his job at an atomic energy project. No one was allowed to live at the site, and the nearest town was 35 miles away. But an appeals court says his expenses, like nearly all commuters' costs, were personal, thus not deductible.

(Edmerson v. U.S.A., U.S. Ct. of Appeals, 9th Cir., 1972)
10/25/72

◦◁▷◦

The Supreme Court rules on a long-standing tax dispute. It denies a deduction to an automobile commuter who had to carry heavy materials back and forth to his job but would have commuted by car even if he hadn't had the load. Commuting costs generally aren't deductible, and the court said that as the man would have used his car in any case, it was impossible to rationally allocate part of his costs to business use of the car.

(Fausner v. Commissioner, U.S. Supreme Ct., 1973)
7/1/73

◦◁▷◦

No place like home? Normally traveling expenses while away from home on business are deductible, but a district court denied a salesman's claim. The court said the deduction was meant to spare business travelers the burden of double living expenses. But this salesman had no "sleep-in, eat-in home" that cost him anything on a regular basis. He kept a few things at his brother's in Brooklyn, but that cost him nothing, and he spent almost all his time on the road.

(Rosenspan v. U.S.A., U.S. Dist. Ct., East. Dist. New York, 1970.)
4/22/70

◦◁▷◦

Where's home? An employe can deduct living expenses incurred while working "away from home." The IRS argued that when a Boeing employe was assigned to Los Angeles for a year, that city became his home. (He had rented out his Seattle house and taken his family along.) But the Tax Court said a year's stint could be "temporary": It was long enough to bring the family but short enough to keep the house. And not selling the house was an important factor.

(Michaels v. Commissioner, 53 T.C. No. 28.)
11/26/69

✦

A carpenter sustained his claim to deduct living expenses while working "away from home," even though one of his job stints lasted 15 months. He couldn't find work in Colorado Springs, Colo., so he took jobs in nearby states. The Tax Court concluded that he maintained his home and personal ties in Colorado Springs, and all his jobs elsewhere qualified as "temporary."

(McGimsey v. Commissioner, T.C. Memo. 1971-124.)
6/2/71

✦

Lawyers say that anyone who represents himself has a fool for a client. But an elderly lady from Florida persuaded the Tax Court she deserved substantial deductions. A retired legal stenographer, she came to New York for seven months to find temporary work. It would be "highly unreasonable" to expect her to move her permanent home to New York, the court said. It let her deduct train fare and 32 weeks' lodging.

(Avery v. Commissioner, T.C. Memo. 1970-269.)
9/30/70

✦

Short haul: A St. Louis physician had his main office at home, from which he set forth on his rounds of calls and to a second office. The IRS claimed that the cost of driving to his first call, and back from his last, should be nondeductible commuting expenses. "We do not agree," the Tax Court said. "When (the doctor) makes his first business stop at his main office in his home . . . his commuting is not by automobile."

(St. John v. Commissioner, T.C. Memo. 1970-238.)
9/9/70

Deductions for Business Entertainment?

It may be easier to deduct entertainment as a business expense.

The Court of Appeals for the Second Circuit has ruled the IRS is too strict in its requirements for documenting such an outlay. According to the tax code, a taxpayer must substantiate the expense (1) by adequate records, or (2) by "sufficient evidence" corroborating his own testimony. The IRS has insisted that "sufficient evidence" means a written statement, but the circuit court says that isn't essential.

To demand something in writing is the same as requiring "adequate records," the court said, and that would make the two requirements mean the same thing. The taxpayer's alternative would mean nothing. The court ruled in a case involving a New York surgeon who always bought lunch for interns and residents assisting him. He offered no proof of what he spent except testimony from a cafeteria cashier. That wasn't enough for the Tax Court.

The Second Circuit ordered the case back to the Tax Court for more testimony on the meal costs. "Oral testimony, properly corroborated" would do, the higher court said.

(LaForge v. Commissioner, U.S. Ct. of Appeals, 2nd Cir., 1970.)
11/25/70

◦⟨⟩◦

An easier rule for deducting entertainment makes no difference in its first test.

The Second Circuit Court of Appeals caused a stir when it held the IRS too strict in requiring that business entertainment be documented to be deductible. By law, a taxpayer must substantiate such an outlay (1) by adequate records, or (2) by "sufficient evidence" corroborating his own testimony. If "sufficient evidence" had to be in writing, then the choice would be meaningless, the court said.

With this in mind, the Tax Court reconsidered another case where it denied a taxpayer a deduction, but the court stuck by its original decision. The case involved a television lighting designer who claimed he used his pleasure boat on business. The court reiterated that the man's guest book, which each guest signed his first time out, wasn't nearly sufficient. It also said that a list of alleged business guests was "merely another form" of the man's oral testimony.

The court gave no credence to vague testimony by the designer's secretary, and it said that testimony by two business associates established that they had been on board, but no more.

(Fiorentino v. Commissioner, T.C. Memo. 1970-344.)
12/30/70

❦

It was worth it for a fisherman to take the IRS to court.

Richard Haman fished for crab, tuna and shrimp off the California coast. He and his crew spent part of their time at sea and the rest in various ports, painting the boat and equipping it for the next fishing excursion. Haman frequently took the crew members to lunch and dinner while in port. And during the Christmas season he threw parties for them. Haman deducted these outlays as business expenses. Their main purpose, he reasoned, was to induce his men to continue to work for him.

Haman kept detailed records of the expenses as required by tax regulations. Each time he bought a meal or gave a party, he entered in a diary the amount spent, the date and place and the individuals participating. The IRS flatly rejected all the deductions for "lack of substantiation." But the Tax Court allowed them. Haman hadn't noted the business purpose of each meal in his diary, but the court said the purpose was evident because those entertained were the man's crew members.

(Haman v. Commissioner, T.C. Memo. 1972-118)
5/31/72

Tale of two boats: One was deductible, the other wasn't.

A New York lawyer had a 46-foot sailing sloop on which he frequently entertained guests. He kept informal diaries and telephone records indicating many of the guests were either law clients or prospective clients. The IRS said the records weren't adequate to support a business expense deduction for the boat. But the Tax Court has ruled the lawyer can deduct 60% of his costs, even though his records weren't formal.

A Nashville automobile dealer sold $180,988 of cars to people he entertained on his boat at a cost of $11,000. But his mistake in tax terms was using the soft-sell. He didn't initiate business discussions on the boat, but waited for his guests to get the idea that's why they were there. A circuit appeals court ruled he would have had to solicit business overtly for the boat costs to be deductible.

(Handelman v. Commissioner, T.C. Memo. 1973-27, and Hippodrome
Oldsmobile v. U.S.A., U.S. Ct. of Appeals, 6th Cir., 1973)
3/21/73

Country club set: The Tax Court denies a deduction for food and drinks and dues.

An Alabama C.P.A. lost on a tax issue that comes

up again and again even though the taxpayers hardly ever get to first base. Like many professionals, the C.P.A. tried to deduct his country club dues and part of his club expenses as business outlays to promote his practice. He argued that because his profession forbids advertising, it was necessary to use social contacts to drum up business. Most of the expenses came when he took his turn buying lunch or drinks after playing golf.

The Tax Court ruled he didn't prove the expenses were primarily for business, rather than personal. Beyond that, he didn't come close to substantiating the outlays as the law requires. He often played golf with clients, but that didn't prove the ties were more than friendships among professionals. Typically, foursomes were formed on the links, not set up in advance. This suggested that "friendship and camaraderie" were primary.

The C.P.A. contended that most of his outlays qualified as business meals. But the court didn't consider "the '19th hole' and the 'gin rummy table' . . . generally conducive to business discussion."

(Randall v. Commissioner, 56 T.C. No. 67.)
8/4/71

Business and pleasure don't mix, at least not to the Tax Court's satisfaction.

The court ruled twice on the "oft-encountered combination of personal and claimed business elements," and it denied deductions both times. In one case, a North Carolina doctor, an avid golfer, earnestly regarded the links as a good spot to meet prospective patients or gather referrals. He had no records, but from a list of his 1966 golf rounds, he inferred that 60% of his club dues usually went for business purposes. But the court said that estimate fell far short of the strict record-keeping required for business entertainment.

(Ross v. Commissioner, T.C. Memo. 1970-110.)

In another case, a New York architect wanted to deduct landscaping expenses for a site he owned at Martha's Vineyard, where he had a summer place. He said he was building a showplace house to display his design abilities. There was a connection, the court conceded, but not enough to "transform the essentially personal character" of the project.

The house might be "commercially or professionally advantageous," but it was basically the same as a manufacturer showing off some of his products in his home.

(Page v. Commissioner, T.C. Memo. 1970-112.)
5/20/70

><

Bah, humbug! The Tax Court disallows the deduction of Christmas tips.

A New York City salesman of television time for ABC spread Christmas cheer in the form of $10 tips to office helpers, delivery boys, elevator starters, doormen and maitres d'. He sought to deduct the $160 total as a business expense. When challenged, he rebutted that the payments sped his deliveries, kept elevator doors open as he rushed up, and yielded better tables and quicker taxis.

The Tax Court flatly rejected the deduction for tips to office hands, delivery boys and elevator starters. The salesman had failed to show how these were even proximately related to his business, it said. The court conceded, however, that tips "on occasions too often to be mere coincidence" do secure a better table location or a taxicab more promptly. Such tips could reasonably be deducted, it said.

But it nevertheless turned down these deductions, too, because the salesman didn't give the documentation required for business entertainment expenses.

7/9/69

No bonus: A lawyer gave his secretary $200 at Christmas, but the IRS refused to let him deduct more than $25 of it. The Tax Court agreed: Reasonable bonuses made in good faith are deductible, it said, but the lawyer didn't say the payment was anything more than a gift. Not until late—too late—in the trial did he raise the claim that the money was additional pay for services rendered.

(Steel v. Commissioner, T.C. Memo. 1969-254.)
12/10/69

Deductions for Employment Fees?

An employment fee paid to find a better job is deductible, the Tax Court says.

Deductions have been permitted for "fees paid . . . for securing employment," but the IRS has tended to split hairs over which "fees" actually qualify. Now, over six dissents, the Tax Court has ruled that the $3,000 a financial executive paid an executive placement agency was deductible as a business expense even though he already had a job and the fee was nonrefundable.

According to the court, the man was in the business of "being a corporate executive," and in an economy where executives hop from job to job, the expense was "ordinary and necessary from every realistic point of view." The outlay wasn't personal in nature, the court said, because it was directly related to producing income. The IRS had argued that only contingent employment fees warranted a deduction, but the court disagreed.

In concurring opinions, five judges indicated they would go even further. They scored a 1969 decision which had denied a deduction because the taxpayer had merely sought employment but failed to secure it.

(Primuth v. Commissioner, 54 T.C. No. 36.)
3/11/70

◗◁▷◖

The tax court gives short shrift to further IRS nit-picking on employment fees.

Court rulings have nearly eliminated a long-standing IRS position on deductibility of employment agency fees. The Service had allowed deduction of a fee if it resulted in a new job. If the seeker didn't get a job, the fee wasn't deductible. Courts generally have decided that's a "distinction without a difference." But the IRS hasn't given up.

In one case, an electrical engineer hired an employment agency to help him search for a new job. Eventually he became dissatisfied with the service he was getting and withdrew from the deal. He still had to pay the fee, though, and deducted it. The IRS balked because the man voluntarily stopped using the service before getting a job. But the Tax Court upheld the taxpayer and said the IRS's distinction "surely" was of "minor significance."

(Blewitt v. Commissioner, T.C. Memo. 1972-247.)
1/3/73

Last gasp? The IRS's position on employment fees is dealt another blow.

Tax Court rulings have undermined much of the IRS's notion that a fee paid to an employment agency isn't deductible unless it actually results in a new job. But the IRS is clinging to its view, so if a fee you paid doesn't bear fruit, you still have to go to court in order to deduct it. That's not only because of the IRS's refusal to yield, but also because employment fees are an issue the IRS prefers to litigate, rather than compromise, thereby encouraging a final judicial determination.

A new Tax Court ruling is the court's most unequivocal yet on the employment fee question. The court allowed a comptroller for a New Jersey company to deduct an $1,875 fee he paid to Frederick Chusid & Co., even though the fee didn't directly get him a new job. The court said: "It is settled . . law in this court that expenses incurred in either seeking or securing new employment within the taxpayer's established field are deductible."

(Black v. Commissioner, 60 T.C. No. 13.)
5/2/73

◦⟨⟩◦

Employment fees: The Tax Court rules on a long-standing dispute.

The question is whether a fee paid to an employment agency is deductible as a business expense. The IRS historically has held that a fee is deductible if it leads to a new job, but isn't deductible if it doesn't. In 1970, three Tax Court decisions broadened the circumstances where fees are deductible. And the court now has nearly eliminated the IRS's distinction.

Leonard Cremona, an "administrator" for a small company, tried to deduct a $1,500 fee he paid an agency to help him find a similar position elsewhere. The IRS said no; he didn't get another job or even an offer. But the court ruled Cremona was "in the business of being an administrator" and the fee was "no less" a legitimate expense of that business "merely because" he didn't land a job. A Tax Court judge originally handed down the Cremona ruling, but it was recalled for a look by the full court.

There weren't any dissents, but in concurring opinions a few judges indicated the broader policy isn't limitless. Without being specific, they made clear that only fees legitimately related to searching for a new job would be deductible.

(Cremona v. Commissioner, 58 T.C. No. 20.)
5/17/72

◦⟨⟩◦

Employment fees: A higher court takes a traditional stance on deductibility.

In the tax standing of employment fees, nothing succeeds like success. The IRS has traditionally drawn a sharp line between fees paid in seeking employment and those paid in actually securing it. Only the latter have been deductible as a business expense. The Tax Court appeared to be moving away from this position, but an appeals court has upheld the IRS stand.

The case involved an executive who paid $2,170 in nonrefundable fees and expenses to Frederick Chusid & Co. to help him find a job. He eventually found a new job on his own hook. Because he didn't obtain employment through Chusid, the IRS denied the deduction, and a circuit court agreed. "Under no theory" could the sum be deducted, it said. The firm didn't get him a job, and its fees weren't contingent on finding him one.

In one case, a man found a job through Chusid, and the Tax Court allowed the deduction. But it based its decision on broader reasoning than the distinction between seeking and securing. Five judges went even further in concurring opinions and said the distinction wasn't helpful.

(Morris v. Commissioner, U.S. Ct. of Appeals, 9th Cir., 1970.)
4/8/70

∘⟷∘

Forcing the issue: A design engineer for General Electric in Cincinnati deducted a $1,781.75 fee he paid an employment consulting firm for getting him a job offer from another company. The offer, including a higher salary, induced GE to promote the engineer and meet the competing pay offer. The employe decided to stay with GE. The IRS disallowed the deduction, but the Tax Court ruled for the taxpayer, calling the fee deductible as an "ordinary and necessary (business) expense."

(Kenfield v. Commissioner, 54 T.C. No. 113.)
6/10/70

Life Is Very Taxing
These Days (II)

April 15 sends some people to a psychiatrist rather than to an accountant.

Reactions to the annual ritual are "as specific to each person as his fingerprints," says Dr. Henry Krystal, a psychiatrist with Wayne State University. But "to the extent we harbor guilt, and we all do," he believes, "the income tax return mobilizes feelings of anxiety and vague self-accusation." Amassing wealth builds up guilt, Dr. Krystal declares, and some people assuage that guilt by paying more taxes than they actually owe.

Tax-paying can become a form of atonement through suffering, Dr. Robert Beavers, a Dallas psychiatrist, says. Psychoanalysts also report that emotional hang-ups can keep a person from filing. In one instance, a wealthy young woman had always relied on her "distant and frightening" father to handle money affairs. When the time came to handle her own, the trauma was too much. Her problem wasn't licked until she took her records to her analyst and "we spent an afternoon sorting them all out on the floor."

One "manic-depressive" Dallas businessman evaded all taxes. His business brought in up to $40,000 a year, which let him feel prosperous despite pressing financial concerns. "Filing a return would have destroyed the fantasy," his analyst explains. But severe depression overtook him when the IRS got him for tax evasion.

4/15/70

The Private Tax People

Why do taxpayers flock to private tax services when the IRS gives advice for free?

The IRS in 1970 had almost 1,300 full-time staffers, plus numerous temporary clerks, fielding taxpayers' questions. Yet private services boom. One Boston tax lawyer believes there's often scant difference in the quality of advice. A wage-earner with routine deductions "could go to the most expensive tax service or the Government man and wind up with almost the same tax," he says.

Other tax advisers and taxpayers are considerably more dubious. Some complain of long waits, sketchily trained clerks, cut-and-dried treatment, and occasional surliness at the IRS. "They wouldn't take time to go over my proof," says Mrs. Dorothea Stibbs of Chicago. She says the IRS advised her against claiming a dependent that she subsequently claimed without challenge. But beyond such complaints, "people confronted with their tax return simply become flustered," says Henry Rush of Chicago Tax Service. "They come to us to take it off their hands."

The IRS helped almost 29 million taxpayers in 1969. "The (private) tax preparer is going to sit down and prepare the return," an IRS spokesman says. "We more or less help you prepare your own."

2/18/70

➤◁

Fear and mistrust channel many taxpayers to private tax return services.

"Do you honestly think I'd level with the IRS—or they'd level with me?" asks a 27-year-old music teacher in Evanston, Ill. Other taxpayers feel the IRS is unlikely to show them all the angles, and a private tax service will. Still, Business Control Service, a San Francisco firm, says it discourages many claims for deductions. "We don't want the client to get his finger caught in the ringer."

Does this mean many taxpayers are out to cheat? "No," replies Mrs. Elaine Mason, a tax adviser in Chicago. "People fear the IRS, and many even tend to be reluctant about (legitimate) deductions." One Chicago man turned down deductions that could have saved him $125. "I just don't want the tax people to investigate me," he declared.

2/18/70

The IRS shows its sensitivity over professional tax-return preparers.

"Filling out your tax return may be easier than you think. . . . You can do it yourself!" That's what the new IRS instruction packet for 1971 returns assured taxpayers in big black type. Last season, confused taxpayers turned in droves to tax-preparation services. Many proved not entirely expert, and some exploited clients' tax data for sales prospects and credit checks. Complaints spawned demands for federal licensing of tax preparers.

There are no signs that such proposals are getting anywhere, but the IRS is taking pains to allay taxpayers' anxieties. It doesn't look good for the IRS when the annual filing chore is considered fearsomely complicated. A "special message" from the Commissioner asserts there's "no reason" for almost 30 million taxpayers with simple returns to resort to outside help. The message stresses free IRS assistance.

If you do turn to a professional, the Commissioner urges, "Satisfy yourself that you employ someone who is competent and trustworthy and will not misuse the confidential data."

11/10/71

Dealing With the IRS

The IRS report gives the nitty-gritty on separating taxpayers from their money.

The IRS collected $209,855,737,000 in fiscal 1972, according to the Commissioner's annual report. That's up 36% since 1968, five years earlier. In fiscal 1972, receipts from alcohol taxes alone ($5.11 billion) almost equalled total federal tax collections for 1940 ($5.34 billion).

It cost the Revenue Service 44 cents to collect each $100, it says. (The figure has been under 50 cents every year but one since 1950.) Of total collections, individual income taxes accounted for $108.88 billion, or 52%. About 55 million taxpayers, or two out of three who filed the 1040 Form, were due refunds, averaging $251 each. The IRS says that $31.1 billion in taxes was collected in New York State alone. California was a distant second with $18.96 billion.

5/12/71, revised 9/73

○━━▷◦

Here's a rundown on how things go when the IRS and a taxpayer disagree.

The IRS audited 1.7 million returns in fiscal 1972, 49,920 more than the year before, for the first year-to-year increase in nine years. About 1.3 million were audits of individual or fiduciary income tax returns, which works out to about one in 58. The IRS auditors recommended additional taxes and penalties totaling $3.4 billion.

More than 98% of tax disputes are settled without

going to court, the IRS says. Its internal appeals procedure disposed of 52,189 cases in fiscal 1972, compared with 1,556 decided by the lower federal courts. Of cases decided by the federal Courts of Appeal, the IRS won 237, lost 95, and had 23 split decisions.

5/12/71, revised 9/73

It takes a college grad to fathom itemized deductions, a study shows.

IRS Commissioner Johnnie Walters says Form 1040 is so simple a fifth-grader can fill it out, if the standard deduction is used. But a study released by Rep. Aspin (D., Wis.), indicates Walters is exaggerating. The HEW-funded study examined tax materials in terms of reading difficulty and concluded a taxpayer must read at the college graduate level to "comprehend without assistance the entire content of the tax instructions."

Giving some credence to Walters' view, the study showed a taxpayer with a fourth-grade education can "understand 1971 tax rate schedules and their instructions." But "it takes a college graduate" to handle itemized deduction of medical expenses and contributions and "some college education" is needed to figure interest expense deduction, the study says.

Another key point: An eighth-grade ability is needed to "understand" Walters' introduction to the Form 1040 instruction book, the analysts assert.

4/12/72

Thirty million taxpayers may have the IRS compute their taxes due for 1970.

Under the rules, eligible taxpayers may fill in the rest of their returns, but have the IRS figure the tax. The IRS then dispatches a bill or a refund. The provision has been expanded to include taxpayers with incomes up to $20,000 who take the standard deduction and whose income comes from salaries and wages, dividends, interest, and—a newly eligible category—pensions and annuities. The IRS also will compute the retirement income credit for the elderly.

The Treasury has found that more people make mistakes in computing the tax than in any other part of the return. Assistant Secretary Cohen also has cited findings that 75% of those who receive pension or annuity income report it wrong. Most pay too much tax. And one-third of those eligible for the retirement income credit don't claim it because it's too complicated.

"I worry about the simplicity," Cohen has said, "not for the thousands who can afford expert (tax) advice, but for the millions who cannot and shouldn't be required to."

12/2/70

◦⟨⟩◦

Here are the latest average deductions taken by people who itemize.

Some tax men say if your deductions are close to these averages, your chances of being audited are slim. That's because IRS computers are presumed to be set to select for audit only returns that depart from the norm. The IRS claims its system is much more sophisticated than that and strongly discourages taxpayers from taking any deductions they aren't entitled to. If you are audited, you have to be able to substantiate your deductions, average or not.

The figures are for 1970, the latest year available:

Adj Gr Income	*Contribs*	*Interest*	*Taxes*	*Med*
$10,000-15,000	$313	$783	$858	$325
20,000-25,000	557	1,181	1,548	358

30,000-50,000	1,077	1,900	2,615	490
50,000-100,000	2,186	3,376	4,581	681
100,000 or more	13,553	11,832	13,068	1,146

1/23/73

The odds you'll be audited vary among regions of the nation.

In the fiscal year ended June 30, 1971 (the latest year available), people who lived in the IRS's North Atlantic Region (New England including New York) stood a 50% greater chance of having their returns audited than residents of the Midwest Region (Illinois, Wisconsin and the upper plains states). Here are the percentages of the individual and corporate returns audited.

| Region | Individual | | Corporation | |
	Fis. Year 1971	Fis. Year 1970	Fis. Year 1971	Fis. Year 1970
North Atlantic	2.1	2.5	6.5	8.2
Mid Atlantic	1.7	2.1	8.7	13.3
Southeast	1.7	2.2	7.9	11.0
Central	1.8	2.0	10.0	12.4
Midwest	1.4	2.0	10.5	12.2
Southwest	1.3	2.1	7.4	9.7
West	1.9	2.3	10.2	12.3
U.S. returns filed abroad	5.0	5.9	12.5	10.5

The IRS says the 1971 percentages were lower than 1970 because of increases in the number and complexity of returns filed.

The regional breakdown comes from a secret IRS statistical study the agency refuses to release. It was obtained from reliable sources. The study doesn't explain the regional variations.

2/7/73

How efficiently does the IRS use its tax return auditors?

The agency audits a far greater portion of rich taxpayers' returns than poor peoples', and averages more hours on each big return than on small ones. But those aren't the only differences. Internal IRS statistics show that for every hour of audit time, the agency finds considerably more additional tax to be due from wealthy individuals and big companies than from less affluent taxpayers. Because each hour on big returns is so much more productive, some critics are suggesting the IRS should be devoting even more attention to big taxpayers than it currently does. The following table shows alleged additional tax due per audit manhour in each financial category of taxpayer. The statistics are for fiscal 1971, the latest period available.

Individuals

Income	—*Extra tax alleged*—	
	IRS office audits	*Field audits*
Under $10,000	$ 81	$108
$10,000-50,000	90	126
$50,000 and over	159	351

Corporations

Assets	*Extra tax alleged*	*Assets*	*Extra tax alleged*
Under		$ 1 mil-	
$ 50,000 ....$ 66		5 mil $217	
$ 50,000-		$ 5 mil-	
100,000 72		10 mil 358	
$100,000-		$ 10 mil-	
250,000 88		50 mil 376	
$250,000-		$ 50 mil-	
500,000 120		100 mil 498	
$500,000-		$100 mil-	
1 mil 146		and over 859	

The statistics are from a secret IRS report the agency refuses to release. It was obtained from reliable sources.

2/28/73

What recourse exists for a taxpayer hit with a jeopardy assessment?

If the IRS thinks a taxpayer intends to skip the country, hide his assets, or otherwise render "ineffectual" the routine tax collection procedures, it can step in and make an immediate assessment of taxes. The process, known as a "jeopardy assessment," starts with notice to the taxpayer that his "taxable period" is terminated and certain taxes immediately payable. The IRS gave such notice to two men because of their alleged gambling activities and assessed $68,000 in taxes.

The two men sought to resist in Tax Court, but that court said it lacked jurisdiction until the IRS issued a "notice of deficiency." The termination notice didn't amount to that. Some federal courts have required the IRS to follow a jeopardy assessment with a deficiency notice within 60 days to give the taxpayer "a ticket to Tax Court." The Tax Court didn't agree.

An audit of the men's 1972 returns was still going on. The Tax Court found it "unfortunate" that IRS delay caused "some inequity," but that wasn't enough to give it jurisdiction.

(Riley v. Commissioner, T.C. Memo. 1973-180)
9/5/73

◦⟷◦

State computers playback Federal tapes, confiding who tells the taxmen what.

Since 1935, Congress has authorized the IRS to tell state tax authorities what you put down on your Federal return. The states may pass on the data to localities. Now some 34 states get the information on magnetic tape. Plugging the tapes into state computers can pinpoint which Federal taxpayers neglect to file state or local returns. It can also check the consistency of certain income figures. The IRS says it can't estimate what this information is worth to states, but state tax officials are enthusiastic.

"Our program would be crippled without this material," says Martin Huff, a California tax official. "It's worth millions of dollars"—in fiscal 1969, some $10.3 million in additional tax collections, he says. The Federal data are especially useful to California because the state doesn't require withholding of state income taxes. In Michigan, where an income tax was adopted in 1967, the Federal list of names and addresses was used to mail out tax returns. Currently, the state is gearing up to use the Federal tax data to make comparisons.

The IRS stresses that state and local officials who receive the information are bound by Federal restrictions on disclosure.

7/23/69

◖━◗

Trading tapes may be modern, but old-fashioned audits pay off, taxmen say.

Tax authorities always single out some returns for close audits, and 44 states have agreed to exchange this audit information with the IRS. Generally, the audit sharing is "more productive" for states than uses made of the computer tapes, an official of the Federation of Tax Administrators says. "The first time around, matching lists of filers can be productive, but then the word gets out," he explains.

The audit information is worth $10 million a year to California, Mr. Huff estimates. New York State nets $10 million to $13 million annually by having its taxmen review audit changes ordered by Federal taxmen. (Taxpayers sometimes fail to tell state authorities when the IRS finds they owe more taxes than they originally declared.) In addition, New York says it has realized "tremendous savings" in manpower by splitting up audits with Federal taxmen and sharing the results.

7/23/69

Failure to file: "An unsigned return is no return at all," the Tax Court rules.

The IRS assessed a Pennsylvania man with additional taxes of $17,500 and then socked him with a 25% penalty tax (5% a month, up to 25%) for failure to file. The taxpayer protested that he had turned in his return, together with a signed check for the $1,169 he thought due, but had "overlooked" signing the return.

The Tax Court agreed with the IRS that even with a signed check, an unsigned return wouldn't do. For one thing, signing a return normally makes a taxpayer subject to perjury proceedings if the information is false. The signature on a check wouldn't bring a person under this possible penalty, which the court considered "one of the principal sanctions available to assure that honest returns are filed." It didn't find willful failure to file but the oversight still meant a penalty.

(Vaira v. Commissioner, 52 T.C. No. 106.)
10/15/69

◦───◦

The IRS padlocked a premises and was ordered to pay rent as the occupant.

A U.S. district court came to the rescue of a party caught in the middle when the IRS moved against a delinquent taxpayer. The IRS seized the assets of a Chicago restaurant and locked up the premises until the assets were sold or released. (It took about a month.) That was all well and good, except the restaurant was also in arrears on its rent. A court had already awarded its landlord repossession, though the order had been stayed for 30 days.

The Revenue Service refused to pay the landlord rent, so he sued, and the court sided with him. It decided that by its actions, the IRS had "implicitly agreed and contracted" to pay the reasonable value for use and occupancy of the place. The court awarded the landlord a month's rent ($1,300), plus interest and legal costs.

When the IRS padlocked the place, that amounted to a "condemnation of (the landlord's) rights and property without just compensation," the court said.

(Weber v. U.S.A., U.S. Dist. Ct., No. Dist. Illinois, 1970.)
6/2/71

◦◁▷◦

A great many taxpayers are legally obliged to file a declaration of estimated taxes, but many boast they've never filed and believe the IRS doesn't care. The IRS contends that isn't so. There's no penalty simply for failure to file, it says, but the penalty of 0.5% a month for underpaying an installment is automatic, it insists. Exceptions to the provision are liberal, however, and many nonfilers aren't subject to penalty.

By law, a taxpayer must file if his tax for 1971 is estimated to exceed his withholding by $40 or more, and (a) his income not subject to withholding exceeds $200, or (b) his income exceeds a certain figure ($5,000 for single taxpayers). If a taxpayer's tax will come to $9,000 and his withholding to $7,000, he should pay the other $2,000 in quarterly installments. But if at each installment date, he has paid 80% of the amount due by that date, there's no penalty. And the law provides four different ways to estimate the tax and avoid the penalty.

During fiscal 1970, only 7.4 million taxpayers filed declarations, the IRS says. It has no count of how many were penalized for underpayment.

6/16/71

◦◁▷◦

Invisible tax boosts continued as incomes edge upward into higher tax brackets.

As incomes rise, Uncle Sam not only has more income to tax but a bigger chunk of it comes under higher rates. According to newly released figures, the proportion of total returns with $10,000-or-more in adjusted gross income jumped better than 50% between 1965 and 1968. That's true even though three out of four returns still report less than $10,000. The proportion falling between $15,000 and $20,000 leaped 92% to one in 20.

To some extent Uncle Sam is benefiting from nominally higher incomes due to inflation. It's hard to say how much, but as a rough indication, Government figures show that per capita disposable income advanced 21% between 1965 and 1968. In 1958 dollars, however, the gain came to only 11%. Treasury people say the Tax Reform Act took some account of inflation when it liberalized personal exemptions and standard deductions.

But Treasury officials also contend the Government doesn't reap that much extra from the movement into higher brackets, whatever its cause. "The progressiveness of the tax system doesn't have that much bite," one official says.

3/20/70

❦

IRS gobbledygook must be explained in plain English when proposed tax regulations are published in the Federal Register. A new Register rule requires the IRS (and other rulemaking agencies) to include a preamble clear enough to tell a non-expert what a proposed regulation is all about. When final regulations are published, a similar summary must explain how they differ from earlier proposals.

(Announcement, Federal Reigster, 37 F.R. 23602)
2/21/73

❦

Quit quibbling and pay up, a court tells Uncle Sam in a case of two men who had been fined for violating a tax law that later was declared unconstitutional. The men felt their fines should be refunded immediately, but the Feds told them they would have to sue the U.S.

to get their money back. The Fifth Circuit appeals court said the government's reasoning "characterizes the worst features of impersonal and unresponsive bureaucracy."

(U.S.A. v. Lewis and Willoz, U.S. Ct. of Appeals, 5th Cir., 1973)
8/15/73

o⊂⊃o

How diligently does the IRS search for taxpayers who have refunds coming to them? When the Albuquerque, N.M., IRS office gave an "unable to locate" list to the local newspapers for publication, an editor spotted the name of Robert W. McCoy. He's the U.S. magistrate who holds court across the street from the IRS office.

12/8/71

o⊂⊃o

Errata: Back in 1967, a Texas man tried to deduct the $4,726 loss he took in the sale of his home. When the IRS objected, he pointed to the Form 1040 instructions for that year, which clearly, and wrongly, provided for the deduction. The Tax Court recently ruled for the IRS. "It has long been settled," the court said, that the IRS isn't blocked from correcting "a mistake of law."

(Elliott v. Commissioner, T.C. Memo. 1971-239)
9/29/71

o⊂⊃o

Helping hand? A Massachusetts woman got some free assistance from the IRS in preparing her 1967 return. Later, when the IRS challenged her deductions, she expressed "surprise and annoyance." The Tax Court found her chagrin understandable, but it ruled against her on every count. According to the court, the IRS "informally" helps millions of taxpayers a year, and its employes "cannot be expected to be correct as to every question asked or held to a standard of infallibility," especially when they may not know all the facts.

(Stokes v. Commissioner, T.C. Memo. 1970-200.)
8/5/70

Most tax disputes are settled by officials within the taxpayer's IRS district, the IRS says. When the IRS calls taxpayers in for an audit, and they disagree with its results, the first step in a chain of appeals is a conference with the district director's representative. (A handful of cases start at a higher IRS level or go directly to the courts.) Of the disputes that go to a district conference, better than seven out of 10 are resolved there without further ado, the IRS says.

12/23/70

◦⊂⟩◦

Turnabout: A taxpayer reached a compromise with the IRS, paid the tax, then sued for a refund. The IRS then decided to take another look at his return and said it had additional taxes in mind. The taxpayer sought an injunction to bar the IRS from reopening the case after an agreement had been reached. But a U.S. district court ruled the taxpayer had rejected the agreement by going to court, and the IRS was entitled to as much. "Otherwise, the matter would be a one-way street," the court declared.

(Crocker v. U.S.A., U.S. Dist. Ct., No. Dist. Miss., 1971.)
6/23/71

◦⊂⟩◦

Filing a tax return containing a new address isn't sufficient notice to the IRS that you've moved, the Tax Court says. To be safe, you should send the new address separately. The court recently rejected a complaint from a taxpayer who had received a tax deficiency notice late because the IRS sent it to his old address. He had told the IRS his new location only via his tax return.

(Budlong v. Commissioner, 58 T.C. No. 81)
9/13/72

◦⊂⟩◦

Nit-picker: An IRS notice of deficiency (meaning, it wants more money) is valid if mailed to a taxpayer's last-known address. Recently a taxpayer sought to quash a notice as invalid because he had never notified the IRS that he had moved. Thus, he claimed, his "last-known" address was his old one, not the new address to which the IRS sent its notice. (It had obtained his new address from his lawyer.) The Tax Court, however, found it far-fetched that the rule would block the IRS from using an address from a reliable source.

(Clodfelter v. Commissioner, 57 T.C. No. 9)
10/27/71

◦⊂⟩◦

When the GNP goes up 1%, federal revenues go up a comfortable 1.5%. That's a key point in the Nixon version of revenue-sharing. By contrast, Rep. John B. Anderson, speaking for the administration, claims only 27% of state revenues come from high-growth levies. He says general sales tax yields barely keep pace with GNP growth, and property taxes go up only 0.7% for each 1% rise in GNP. Tobacco taxes (0.35%) and motor-fuel taxes (0.35%) are even more laggard.

2/17/71

◦⊂⟩◦

Farm and household workers may ask to have income taxes withheld from their pay, under regulations recently made final by the IRS. An employe can make the request by filing Form W-4 with his employer, the IRS says, but the voluntary withholding can't proceed unless the employer agrees.

(IRS News Release IR-1118, 1971.)
3/24/71

◦⊂⟩◦

By the book: IRS Commissioner Thrower suggests that the Revenue Service take a tip from Robert Townsend's bestseller, "Up the Oganization." Townsend said no executive should approve a new form without first filling it out himself. A great idea, the IRS staff replied

—so good it had been suggested a number of times in the past. So why hasn't it already been applied to working out new tax forms? Well, Thrower was the first commissioner to suggest it, he was told.

7/1/70

Valediction: Retiring IRS Commissioner Thrower says he will leave office with "a special and deep affection" for Form 1040. "The trials of little Eva on the ice wouldn't compare with those of Form 1040," he declares. According to Thrower, the IRS considered its new 1040 a first-rate achievement. "We sat back and waited for the applause," he says, but the acclaim was hardly overwhelming. Thrower discovers a lesson in this for his successor, whoever he may be: "Keep trying, but you can't win."

5/5/71

Ah, progress: Edwin S. Cohen, Assistant Treasury Secretary for tax policy, marvels over IRS prowess in using computers. Still, he was disturbed to find that the computers sent him two sets of 1040 forms, one to his current address and the other to his Charlottesville, Va., home. Cohen wasn't eager to pay his taxes twice, so he asked the IRS computer people to fix things up. Sorry, Cohen says he was told, there was no way to correct the error because it was impossible for it to have happened.

5/5/71

Appraising art has always been a bane for the IRS, which at times finds more creativity in the donor's tax return than in the art work he gives away. In 1968 the IRS set up a panel of experts to appraise works involved in tax disputes. Since then, the panel has looked at 300 works, for which donors claimed deductions totaling

$35 million. The panel chopped that figure by $10 million. In estate tax cases, where higher values mean higher taxes, it boosted values to $7 million from $2 million.

11/4/70

◦⬦◦

Baring one's soul? In Amsterdam, an aggrieved taxpayer entered a tax office, stripped to the buff, put his clothes on the counter and shouted, "Take it all then!" He stalked out, but was later persuaded to return for the clothes and a mental examination.

2/25/70

◦⬦◦

How wordy is the tax law? Edwin S. Cohen, Assistant Secretary of the Treasury, gave an indication in discussing a pending piece of legislation. The proposal would substitute the word "Secretary" wherever the phrase the (Treasury) "Secretary or his delegate" appears in the law. Then in one place "Secretary" would be defined as including his delegate, too. That change, Cohen says, would shorten the Revenue Code by about 5,000 words.

2/3/71

◦⬦◦

Anyone who tells the tax men about someone else's tax evasion can claim a reward of up to 10% of the extra money collected. But in fiscal 1969, the IRS paid out $299,000 in rewards to 426 informants. That's off sharply from $403,000 collected by 462 informers the previous year and off even more from the year before that. In fiscal 1969, seven out of eight claims were turned down as unsubstantiated.

4/15/70

◦⬦◦

Washington tax lawyers note that a major revamping of the tax law apparently comes along every 15 years, for example in 1939, 1954 and 1969. They're already bracing for the next round—in 1984.

5/5/71

Your Day in Tax Court

The Tax Court says it will defer to individual circuit court views.

Though it can be reversed by any one of 11 appeals courts, the Tax Court has considered itself a national court and sought to apply its thinking uniformly in all areas of the country. Reversal by an appeals court hasn't been binding on the Tax Court as a precedent in future cases. As a result, when the Tax Court and a circuit court disagreed, a litigant could expect to go through a losing bout in the Tax Court before winning on appeal.

In two cases, however, the Tax Court said it intends to respect a circuit court's rulings in cases arising in its circuit. "Better judicial administration requires us to follow (such a) decision which is squarely in point where appeal from our decision lies to that court and that court alone," the lower court said. This opens the way for it to rule one way in one circuit and another way in a second circuit.

The Tax Court noted it can still follow its own bent when the circuit court hasn't spoken. Even when it has, the Tax Court can indicate its own disagreement, it says.

(Golsen v. Commissioner, 54 T.C. No. 70.)
4/29/70

⚬⊂⟩⚬

The Tax Court gears up for its new Small Tax Case Division.

The division was authorized by the Tax Reform Act and is limited to tax disputes involving up to $1,000 for any one taxable year or in estate taxes. Taxpayers may hire lawyers to represent them, but, in most cases, the stakes would be too small. The small-case procedures are geared to taxpayers representing themselves. Recently the court put out a simplified five-question form that will serve as a petition to the court. The forms will be available about Dec. 15 from the U.S. Tax Court, Box 70, Washington, D.C. 20044.

Four commissioners have already been appointed to handle the small cases, supervised by a Tax Court judge. The new division won't take full effect until Dec. 30, but the commissioners have already been assigned cases under interim rules. The court has scheduled small-case calendars in 11 cities next January to March and in 17 next April through June. The idea, Chief Judge Drennen says, is "to give the small taxpayer a fair, fast, informal, and inexpensive hearing close to home."

According to the court's new rules, "any evidence deemed by the court to have probative value" will be admissible in small cases, which are to be conducted "as informally as possible."

10/29/70

Small claims channels at the U.S. Tax Court are busy but not flooded.

Since last fall, commissioners, rather than judges, have handled small tax cases under simplified procedures. These permit taxpayers to argue their own causes in tax disputes involving $1,000, or less. The commissioners' decisions can't be appealed. Thus far the five commissioners have held sessions in 31 cities and were assigned 1,337 cases. Of those, 965 were settled before trial. Forty-one were dismissed when the taxpayers didn't press them. Two hundred have been continued, and only 131 actually have gone to trial.

At trial, many more taxpayers lose than win. The small cases include "a fair number of hopeless causes," says Chief Judge William M. Drennen of the parent Tax Court. Many taxpayers don't grasp what they must do to prove their point, even under relaxed rules of evidence. Others push "a concept of what the law should be, rather than what it is," says Judge Howard A. Dawson Jr., who supervises the Small Tax Case Division.

At 2,400 a year, the small cases are no more numerous than before the special rules were set up. But Judge Dawson says the new channel has prodded the IRS into settling more disputes out of court.

7/21/71

߷

Too many taxpayers miss the Tax Court's deadlines, the court says with distress.

If a taxpayer intends to contest a tax bill in the Tax Court, the law requires that he file a petition with the court within 90 days from when the notice of deficiency was mailed to him by the IRS. According to the court, it's had to toss out an increasing number of petitions because they weren't filed in time. Some petitioners misread the 90 days as three months, or as beginning on receipt of the notice.

The blunder is made most often by taxpayers representing themselves, Chief Judge William M. Drennen says. He has no exact count of how many cases have been rejected. "Whether there's an increase or a decrease, there are too many of them," he declares, "and I'd like to get the word out." The court must get the petition within the 90 days, or the petition must be correctly addressed, mailed and postmarked before the period runs out.

12/10/69

An Indian gets his day in court, but still no answer to his troubled "Why?"

Gordon Wallace Dymond Jr., an American Indian, went to Tax Court after the IRS assessed him for filing no returns for five years. He claimed the IRS erred in trying to force him "to voluntarily pay Federal taxes into a governmental structure whose overall objective he finds incomprehensible." Dymond asked for "conscientious objector" status, "so that I could maintain my convictions officially even while being forced to part with my material acquisitions."

"I find the thought of financially supporting something which I do not understand to be less than wise," Dymond said. He felt "these IRS Caucasians" were trying to impose their values on him by force. If the IRS tried reason, chances are he would pay up, Dymond said. Unfortunately, "the average citizen cannot understand me or my values until such time as this citizen understands his own." And in Dymond's view, most white Americans don't.

According to Dymond, the IRS told him he could put his views in a letter, but it would probably be disposed of because it "interfered" with the computer records. The Tax Court heard Dymond out, then ruled for the IRS. "He has selected the wrong forum," the court said.

(Dymond v. Commissioner, T.C. Memo. 1970-277.)
10/14/70

◖━━▷◗

If you deal with the IRS, better keep it posted on your latest address.

If the IRS notifies you it thinks you owe it more taxes, an appeal to the Tax Court must be filed (or postmarked) within 90 days of when the IRS mailed its notice of deficiency. If a taxpayer misses that deadline, the court has no choice but to dismiss his appeal for want of jurisdiction. In two cases, taxpayers missed the 90-day mark, but blamed it on the IRS for sending its notice to the wrong address.

Neither taxpayer got very far. Both had indeed moved, but neither, the Tax Court ruled, had officially let the IRS know. In one case, a California woman's lawyer mentioned to an IRS man that she had moved, but the court didn't think that was enough. In the other case, the taxpayer wrote one IRS agent he was moving, but the agent was looking into his 1967 return. The man said nothing about all other tax mail, so the notice didn't count for a separate proceeding involving his 1966 return.

Anyone who claims the IRS notice went to the wrong address must show he filed "a clear and concise notification concerning a definite change of address," the court reiterated.

(Stewart v. Commissioner, 55 T.C. No. 22,
and McCormick v. Commissioner, 55 T.C. No. 17.)
11/18/70

Canceled: If a taxpayer appeals an IRS "notice of deficiency" to the Tax Court, his petition must be received, or postmarked, within 90 days. In one recent case a New Yorker swore he mailed his petition on time, but the envelope showed up with no postmark at all. Dismissing the petition, the court declined to accept other evidence that the petition was mailed on time. "The risk of postmarking is on the taxpayer," it declared.

(Rappaport v. Commissioner, 55 T.C. No. 71.)
2/10/71

Dead letter: A Massachusetts couple mailed off a petition to the Tax Court within the 90-day period set by law, but unfortunately they mailed it to the IRS. By the time the letter was returned, the couple had missed the deadline for the Tax Court. The court ruled it couldn't accept the petition because the law clearly says it had to be filed "with the Tax Court" within the allotted period.

(Garland v. Commissioner, T.C. Memo. 1971-79.)
4/28/71

◄═══►

Time flies: Every calendar day counts, the Tax Court ruled, in figuring the deadline for a taxpayer's appeal of an IRS assessment to the court (150 days for petitioners abroad, 90 days for others). A taxpayer argued the law meant business days, by which count her petition arrived on time. But the law merely says the appeal period can't end on a Saturday, Sunday or holiday, the court concluded.

(McGuire v. Commissioner, 52 T.C. No. 50)
6/25/69

◄═══►

Faraway places: A taxpayer assessed with a deficiency normally has 90 days to appeal to the Tax Court but 150 are allowed if he's outside the U.S. A California taxpayer claimed the extra time because, coincidentally, the day the notice was mailed to him, he spent about 10 hours across the border in Tijuana. The court conceded the law made no distinction between residence abroad and a temporary stay, but it still found his claim far-fetched.

(Cowan v. Commissioner, 54 T.C. No. 60.)
4/8/70

◄═══►

Time will tell if privately-metered mail meets Tax Court deadlines. Normally, the court accepts petitions by mail if postmarked before the period for appeal expires. But as private-meter postmarks aren't authoritative, such letters must also take no longer than usual in transit. Recently, the IRS acquiesced in the court's acceptance of a South Carolina petition mailed late on a

Thursday (the deadline) and received in Washington the following Monday. But the court rejected a New York petition that took six days. The petitioner couldn't prove mail delays were to blame.

(Fishman v. Commissioner, 51 T.C. No. 86.)
4/2/69

Our "Voluntary" Tax System?

The IRS frets that voluntary compliance in paying taxes may be slipping.

A certain amount of hand-wringing is to be expected because it's time to ask Congress for money, but top IRS officials are expressing unusual concern. Commissioner Randolph W. Thrower has told Congress that signs point to "serious noncompliance in every tax area." According to Donald Bacon, assistant commissioner for compliance, the 1968 curbs on federal employment may well have left a lasting dent in voluntary compliance. "Audit coverage has declined to low levels," former Treasury Secretary John Connally told Congress.

An IRS survey of 400 taxi drivers found that every last one had either underreported his income or failed to file, Bacon says. In one city, the IRS turned up "industry-wide collusion" in the hairdressing business to underreport employes' earnings. The IRS is also discovering problems with large, publicly owned corporations, Bacon says. There will always be "honest differences" over interpreting the tax law, he says, but the IRS is turning up underpayments that "go well beyond professional judgment or prudent tax planning."

Bacon also chafes mildly at having to divert so many IRS agents to work on organized crime. Such investigations require six times as much time as investigating "our 'legitimate' tax evaders," he quips.

5/5/71

Ever wonder why you read about so many tax fraud cases in March and early April?

One reason is that the statute of limitations for prosecuting most offenders runs out at the April return filing deadline. More important, though, is an IRS practice of planting tax evasion articles in your local newspaper as April approaches. Papers print a lot of information the government hands them, of course. But the IRS's motive in promoting stories of tax fraud investigations isn't a general desire to keep the public well-informed. Rather, the articles are the IRS's way of instilling fear in potential tax cheats that they might live to regret any misdeeds. An internal IRS policy manual that recently became available to The Wall Street Journal spells out detailed procedures for seeking "optimum news coverage of (IRS) enforcement activities." The IRS calls this coverage "deterrent publicity."

Three and a half weeks ago, for example, The New York Times ran a story headlined "Dogged IRS Inquiry on Dellacroce's Spending Habits Led to His Conviction." The article detailed a "painstaking" investigation culminating in the tax evasion conviction of Aniello Dellacroce, a reputed mobster. On March 27 last year, exactly three weeks before the filing deadline, the Times published a story headlined "IRS, For Income Tax Cheats, Has Many Unhappy Returns." It told how agents had trapped a cheating New York accountant.

IRS sources acknowledged in answer to a question that the agency offered both stories to the Times. The Times says it regarded the articles as legitimate news stories and their timing was coincidental.

3/7/73

◆━◆

The IRS revives its dismay over gross disparities in penalties for tax fraud.

According to the IRS, it's something like Monopoly: Land on the wrong square and you go to jail. Last week, Chief Counsel Worthy noted that in the Western District of Tennessee, 22 of 24 persons convicted of criminal tax offenses drew prison sentences. In the Western District of Virginia, one in 36 was jailed.

Such contrasts have persisted for years and seem no better now, Commissioner Thrower said. In the First Circuit, prison sentences run 65%, but in the Third, only 18%. In the Fifth Circuit, the three Florida districts average about 50%; the three Georgia districts, less than 6%. The Federal district courts in New Jersey impose prison terms in about 2% of tax convictions.

No one can explain very well why some districts fall one way and some the other. In fact, Thrower contends such disparities continue in the face of a consensus among authorities that incarceration is essential to deter potential offenders. The IRS views tax fraud as a singularly rational, calculated crime—and singularly corrosive in a tax system based on trust.

"But for the ultimate threat of imprisonment, the odds for cheats could look very good," Thrower said.

12/9/70

◦⟨⟩◦

Jail terms for tax offenders often prove easier in theory than in practice.

There he stands, a reputable citizen, with solid family, community and business ties—and a convicted tax cheat. "No other duty causes more sleepless nights" than sentencing such a man, a Federal judge once said. Tax offenders rarely repeat, and their records are otherwise clean. They have suffered through uncertainty and been shamed by exposure.

About 75% of the Federal judges polled for the Practising Law Institute said they believe prison terms deter potential tax violators. But many judges are obviously loath to send such a man to jail.

Perplexities exist on both sides. One judge asks whether tax compliance is actually better in districts where tax evaders go to jail than in those where they don't. But in the view of one judge, short sentences (or none) for tax offenders "supply ammunition for those who would claim our law discriminates against the poor."

12/9/70

❮❯

To err is all too human, the IRS discovers. In fiscal 1970, one taxpayer in 12 had a math error on his return, but as in past years, the mistakes weren't distributed randomly. About 2.8 million taxpayers made errors that cost them money, a total of $212 million. But fully 4.2 million made mistakes in their own favor. Had their errors gone undetected, they would have cost the government $507 million.

5/12/71

❮❯

Small businesses that cheat on taxes will get a closer IRS look.

Informed sources say possibly less than two-thirds of the nation's eight million small firms (generally those with assets of $1 million or less) are conscientiously paying the taxes they owe under the law. That compares with a 97% compliance rate for all corporate and individual taxpayers. IRS officials say small business compliance has slipped substantially over the past four years.

To combat the problem, the IRS plans to begin next January screening all small business returns by computer. That move alone is expected to hike tax revenues by as much as $42 million next year, says John Hanlon, an assistant IRS commissioner. In addition, it's anticipated the small business area will get a large hunk of a planned increase in IRS manpower.

Congress has been asked to appropriate funds for 1,342 additional audit personnel in the fiscal year beginning July 1. And it has been learned the IRS is seeking another "substantial" increase beyond that in auditors and revenue agents.

6/14/72

◦━━◦

Bar behind bars? The IRS says the legal profession tops its "most wanting" list.

"As a lawyer," IRS chief counsel Worthy said recently, "I am ashamed to say that in recent years more lawyers have been convicted of tax fraud than members of any other profession." During 1966-70, 224 lawyers were indicted for tax fraud and 203 convicted. Next worse among professionals were doctors and dentists (170 indicted and 154 convicted), followed by certified public accountants (42 indicted and 36 convicted). Total convictions ran 2,533, but the IRS says it has no breakdown for nonprofessional occupations.

Another trouble spot is small, closely held corporations, the IRS says. One IRS district recently ran intensive audits on 42 such firms. None had been audited in five years, and all consistently reported operating losses. The results: Twenty-seven of the firms (and 21 of their officers) had underpaid taxes by significant amounts. "Most shocking," according to Worthy, was that the audits turned up 11 probable instances of outright tax fraud.

The IRS says that sample was too small to merit any general conclusions, but it contends that small, closely held firms are a perennial tax problem. "There's more room for finagling," the IRS says.

12/16/70

◦━━◦

The IRS finds widespread underreporting in certain doctors' and dentists' returns.

Goaded by a flap some months ago before the Senate Finance Committee, the IRS has checked the returns of about 8,400 individuals, mainly doctors and dentists, who received $25,000 or more in Medicare or Medicaid fees in 1968. The IRS assessed additional tax in more than half the cases, it says, and in such cases, the underpayments averaged $2,800. There were 47 cases of possible tax fraud.

The 8,400 taxpayers averaged $107,300 in total receipts, and they paid an average of $23,100 in taxes, the IRS says. About 15% of the taxpayers underreported their gross receipts, but such underreporting came to only 1% of total gross receipts for the group. Similarly, the IRS says, about four taxpayers in 10 underreported their net profits, but this involved only 3% of total net profits for the group.

The IRS notes pointedly that its findings don't necessarily hold true for "the entire health care profession."

5/19/71

◗◗◖◖

How much money is stashed away in Swiss banks to evade U.S. income taxes?

A whopping $5 billion in the last four years is the estimate pieced together by Arie Kopelman, a New York tax lawyer and UN consultant. Kopelman says his estimates are "admittedly incomplete," but he offers them as "very well supported hypotheses." They are based on something called the "errors and omissions" account in balance-of-payments figures.

That account covers money that shows up in one country without being recorded as leaving another. Tourist spending and cash sent to relatives abroad are entries, but studies suggest that short-term capital flows (which include bank deposits) are most important. Kopelman finds that over the last 10 years, the

U.S. has had an enormous $12.86 billion deficit in errors-and-omissions with Switzerland. Much of this was normal commercial deals handled through Swiss banks, he says, but allowing for this still leaves billions in an unexplained flow of funds in 1966-69.

"The great bulk" of these billions is quite likely tax-evasion money, Kopelman contends. A U.S. Treasury aide says it has made no estimate, but adds that Kopelman's is "certainly not unthinkable."

11/11/70

o⊂⊃o

Our tax system relies on "voluntary compliance," the IRS says, but it clearly works best when the IRS knows how much a taxpayer has earned, and he knows it knows. Compliance is much lower when the IRS lacks such independent verification, the IRS finds. It points out that back in 1963, the first year it got information returns on payments of interest, returns with interest income leaped 45% and the amounts reported jumped 28%.

2/24/71

o⊂⊃o

Frank George: During confirmation hearings for budget chief George Shultz as Treasury Secretary, Sen. Harry Byrd (Ind.-Va.) approvingly mouthed the traditional Treasury line that "98% of taxes are paid voluntarily." Instead of agreeing with the observation (which overlooks the fact that withholding is mandatory), Shultz chided: "Speak for yourself, Senator."

5/31/72

How Much Did He Really Earn?

An attorney offers some tips on countering an IRS reconstruction of income.

If the IRS suspects tax evasion, it may try to reconstruct a taxpayer's income by the "net worth" method. That simply assumes that an increase in net worth, plus nondeductible outlays but minus nontaxable income, equals taxable income. Obviously, attorney Jeffrey W. Loubet says in Taxes magazine, the IRS must have a sound figure for initial net worth. Thus the first defense step is to judge whether the IRS can come up with such a figure on its own.

After that, Loubet says, it's a common ploy to try to explain away a net-worth increase by claiming the IRS initially overlooked a large cash hoard. But the taxpayer's standard of living or his previous income might belie that. Loubet says it's essential for the taxpayer to avail himself of the "inherent uncertainties" in the circumstantial net-worth method. Often if he catches the IRS in "one or two flagrant errors," that's enough to discredit its entire computation, Loubet says. The taxpayer should also search for unclaimed deductions to offset any unreported income the IRS turns up.

According to Loubet, the courts have held that if the IRS substitutes its figures for a taxpayer's return, it assumes a heavy burden of proof. Thus, he says he feels the taxpayer will always win "the borderline case in criminal fraud" where the net worth method is used.

12/30/70

171

Shave and a haircut, four towels—by the Tax Court's count of a barber's income.

The IRS will devise practical means of checking a taxpayer's income, and the courts will be no less practical in reviewing them. A St. Louis man ran a small barber shop but apparently learned all his bookkeeping in barber college. His ledgers were poor, so the IRS counted the towels he used, figured how many haircuts and shaves he gave, and estimated his income.

The Tax Court took the IRS figure, trimmed it all around and took a little off the top. "This method is not unreasonable," it said, but "it must be used intelligently." The IRS had overlooked that a shave took three towels to a haircut's one. It also forgot the barber didn't charge for some trims. Finally, the court discounted IRS testimony that at times the barber used the same towel twice. "Any barber who stuffed a towel full of hair" down a customer's neck wouldn't last very long, it said.

(Newton v. Commissioner, T. C. Memo. 1970-103.)
5/20/70

ο⊂⊃ο

A "friendly favor" raises IRS suspicions of squirreling away untaxed cash.

The IRS socked a Chicago woman with a $3,700 tax deficiency, based largely on a report from her bank that she had changed $10,000 in small bills. The bank's records also showed she had entered her safe deposit box the same day. The woman owned a restaurant, and the IRS concluded she was stashing away part of her profits.

The woman was in a pickle, but the Tax Court accepted her explanation: She had encountered an acquaintance who wanted to change the money but lacked a bank account. She had helped him, but had never seen him again. Her financial records and living standard were consistent with this, the court said, and it was impressed with her accountant's testimony on her behalf.

(Collins v. Commissioner, T.C. Memo. 1970-91.)
5/6/70

o⊂⊃o

Wouldn't you know the IRS could find a use for the rising cost of living?

If a taxpayer isn't reporting income, the IRS has an arsenal of ways to construct its own figure. These range from counting towels in a bordello to checking published trade data on the average mark-up of a jewelry store. Still another method has passed muster at the Tax Court. The IRS estimated a convicted bookie's income by using Labor Department cost-of-living figures, plus a percentage increase each year to allow for inflation.

The bookmaker challenged the method as "arbitrary and excessive," but the Tax Court disagreed. The IRS had reason to believe the man was earning money from bookmaking, yet he filed no returns and also refused to cooperate with the revenue agent. The court noted that Congress laid down no guidelines on determining tax liability, and that suggested it meant the IRS to have "great latitude."

Thus it was reasonable to use the Bureau of Labor Statistics figures, especially since the man couldn't explain what he lived on.

(Giddio v. Commissioner, 54 T.C. No. 145.)
8/5/70

o⊂⊃o

Bank deposits that a couple can't explain lead to tax troubles.

If a taxpayer's bank account opened the year with $1,412, chalked up $239,283 in deposits, and contained $7.49 at year-end, how much did the taxpayer earn that year? About $224,590 more than he declared on his tax return, the IRS answered. Wrong, the Tax Court ruled. Actually, the man and his wife were kiting checks, it said. At least $184,078 in deposits merely reflected one check written to cover another falling due.

In this case, the IRS had questioned the couple's income and applied a method known as "bank deposits and cash expenditures" to make its own estimate. The taxpayer, a blind attorney, protested that in fact they were badly in debt and making payments to 10 lenders. In a desperate effort to keep up, they "availed themselves" of the time lag between when a check is cashed and when it is presented for payment. They devised at least eight ways to cash a check somewhere and make a quick deposit before previous checks bounced.

The Tax Court drastically chopped the IRS estimate, but it still found $34,889 in deposits and cash outlays unexplained. It was forced to conclude the sum was unreported income, the court said. On appeal, however, the Second Circuit found no unreported income at all.

(Teicher v. Commissioner, U.S. Ct. of Appeals, 2nd Cir., 1972.)
11/25/70

◦⊂◻▷◦

A swindler in the great salad oil scandal bests the IRS in Tax Court.

Before the bubble burst for Allied Crude Vegetable Oil Refining Corp., Ben Rotello had the chore of spreading bribes to keep the Anthony DeAngeles operation afloat. He drew checks against "petty cash" to pay bank clerks and New York dockworkers to give Allied Crude special treatment. Later he bribed a clerk at Bunge & Co., a creditor, to delay depositing Allied's remittances. Still later, he paid the clerk thousands of dollars to substitute Allied's ordinary checks for certified checks it had sent Bunge.

A Federal court sentenced Rotello to three years for his part in the swindle. When the IRS sifted the financial wreckage, it charged that Rotello had failed to report $139,000 in taxable income. The IRS claimed he had cashed or endorsed that sum in petty cash checks, with no evidence that the money was in fact used for business purposes. Rotello denied taking a cut, but the IRS said he couldn't be believed.

But the court believed him anyway. It found the pattern of under-the-table payments entirely plausible, and it saw no evidence that Rotello had lived beyond his means.

(Rotello v. Commissioner, T.C. Memo. 1970-213.)
8/5/70

◦⟨⟩◦

Bridge expert Oswald Jacoby didn't report $203,000 from gambling, a court finds.

The IRS claimed that Jacoby and his wife had more than $268,000 in unreported income during 1960-64, mainly from betting on cards, dice and sports (but not tournament bridge). Twice the couple filed no return at all. The IRS used their bank deposits and cash expenditures to reconstruct their income. But the Jacobys protested that his losses at least equaled his winnings. "Mr. Jacoby is a compulsive gambler," his wife testified. "If he would only follow what he writes in his books, he would be as winning a player in anything . . . as he is in bridge tournaments."

The Tax Court trimmed the IRS figure, but it basically upheld the Revenue Service. It did find, however, that Jacoby indeed had substantial gambling losses. "We are convinced (Jacoby) gambled frequently, compulsively, and unwisely," the court said. But it recognized only $139,000 in deductible losses because Jacoby had no records other than hundreds of cancelled checks.

Jacoby's "modest" scale of living indicated heavy losses. He enjoyed few of the luxuries that "would normally flow from (his) writings, his individual genius, and his gross gambling receipts," the court said.

(Jacoby v. Commissioner, T.C. Memo. 1970-244.)
9/9/70

Is It Fraud?

Failure to file isn't tantamount to tax fraud, the Tax Court decides.

An Oregon lawyer, a former assistant U.S. Attorney who once prosecuted tax cases, found himself on the other side of the fence. He pleaded guilty in 1967 to willful failure to file returns for 1961 through 1964. He claimed he failed to file for 1961 because he lacked the money to pay his taxes. Then he became afraid that filing later returns would give away his omission and possibly cause him to be disbarred. When the IRS caught up with him, he had all four returns in various stages of completion.

The Tax Court was asked whether the 50% penalty for civil tax fraud should apply. It noted that willful failure to file isn't necessarily fraud, but merely one fact to consider along with "other relevant facts." "Admittedly, this is a close case," the court said, but it concluded the lawyer intended ultimately to pay his taxes. He cooperated fully with the IRS and made no effort to hide what he owed.

The lawyer was "caught in a web of his own making," the court declared. But "a failing in judgment and character cannot be equated with intent to defraud," it said.

(Morrell v. Commissioner, T.C. Memo. 1971-99.)
5/12/71

◦⊂⊃◦

A run of cases finds the Tax Court refusing to find fraud in failure to file.

The Tax Court has ruled against the IRS after it

imposed the 50% penalty for fraud on a taxpayer who repeatedly failed to file. The Tax Court recited in each instance that the burden of proof is on the IRS to show fraud by "clear and convincing" evidence. The latest decision involved a New York attorney who didn't file for four years.

The lawyer was "an intelligent, well-educated man" who met the tax obligations of his law practice (such as paying withholding taxes on time), but whose personal tax affairs were a mess. In eight earlier years he had filed returns late, though entirely voluntarily. His only excuse for failing to file was that he lacked the money, and his law practice kept him too busy. He meant to file and pay up eventually, he claimed.

The court decided that his intent to file late returns, as he had done before, "belies any fraudulent motive." It wasn't impressed by his excuses, but a "merely inadequate" explanation doesn't amount to fraud, it said.

(De Pumpo v. Commissioner, T.C. Memo. 1971-115.)
5/26/71

◁▷

Proving fraud can be easier if the defendant is a Phi Beta Kappa.

To stick an underpayer of taxes with the 50% fraud penalty, the IRS must show "clear and convincing" evidence of fraud. This often isn't easy, and courts frequently reject IRS fraud allegations. The IRS's charges are measured against several criteria. One factor that influences judges is the sophistication of the taxpayer.

The Tax Court threw out fraud charges against a Springfield, Ohio, turkey farmer. Among other things, the court noted the man "received only a sixth grade education, worked long hours" and, like many farmers, "maintained only the most meager formal records." But in the case of a North Carolina accountant with a college degree and a Phi Beta Kappa key, the court upheld the IRS. One deciding factor: The accountant's "intelligence, business experience and formal education are such that he certainly was . . . cognizant . . . that he wasn't keeping accurate records. . . ."

The cases differed in another way. The accountant represented himself at trial. The farmer had a lawyer.

(Bevan v. Commissioner, T.C. Memo. 1971-312, and Hendrix v. Commissioner, T.C. Memo. 1972-29.)

2/16/72

◦⟵⟶ı

A "morally deficient" alcoholic with a guilty conscience beats a fraud penalty.

An ex-securities salesman, he ran out on his wife and children and moved to another city. He continued drinking, hopped from job to job and got involved with another woman. But after a year or so in his new surroundings, the man settled into a real estate sales job and eventually made a success of it.

He didn't file an income tax return the first few years away from his ex-wife. The IRS finally caught up with him and charged him with civil tax fraud, which carries a penalty of 50% of the back tax due, in addition to the tax itself. The Tax Court threw out the fraud charge. It found the man had failed to file a return for the first year on his own because he drank a lot and didn't earn much money. And in subsequent years he was afraid to file returns because doing so would have tipped off his failure to file for the first year. At one point his conscience bothered him so much he went to the nearby city where the IRS office was situated and checked into a hotel across the street from the office with the intention of confessing. But he lost his nerve at the last minute.

The court said he definitely was unstable and lacked a "well-defined sense of responsibility." But that isn't enough to prove he consciously tried to defraud the government, it ruled.

(Lord v. Commissioner, 60 T.C. No. 24.)
5/23/73

◁▷

"The largest bootlegger in Harlan County" fares pretty well in the Tax Court.

Maggie Bailey, born in 1904, has been in the moonshine business since 1921, the court said. She neglected to pay income taxes until 1955 when a Federal agent called her attention to the oversight. In 1965 she was in tax trouble again when the Kentucky State Police found $207,000 in cash in her footlocker. That hoard contrasted with her style of life, which was partial to denim dresses or cast-off National Distillers Co. work clothes and tennis shoes.

The court counted the cash as unreported income over the years since 1941, but it refused to penalize her 50% for fraud. She kept no records, it conceded, but she did her business in cash and had no use for banks. The court had "more difficulty" comprehending the failure to file, but even that wasn't necessarily fraudulent.

The IRS never proved a specific sum was due in a specific year and fraudulently withheld, the court decided. But it held Miss Bailey liable for back taxes and late-filing penalties.

(Bailey v. Commissioner, T.C. Memo. 1970-64.)
4/1/70

◁▷

A loophole for tax evaders is closed by a circuit appeals court.

The IRS accused a taxpayer of understating his income and assessed him $2,307 in additional taxes, which he paid. The man wasn't accused of fraud at that point. But after further investigation, the IRS found the man actually owed $12,339 in addition to what he had already paid and socked him with a fraud penalty on the total amount (50% of the tax deficiency).

The taxpayer contended the fraud penalty shouldn't apply to the initial $2,307 deficiency because he had paid it before the question of fraud arose. The Tax Court agreed. But the Second U.S. Court of Appeals said that interpretation would "make sport of the . . . fraud penalty." If you follow the Tax Court's reasoning, the higher court held, a taxpayer could file a fraudulent return on the chance the fraud wouldn't be detected; if he was investigated, he could simply pay the tax owed before fraud was formally alleged, and thus nullify the fraud penalty.

"It's highly unlikely" Congress intended to create a situation so favorable to tax evaders, the court added.

(Papa v. Commissioner, U.S. Ct. of Appeals,
2nd Cir., 1972.)
6/21/72

◦⟨⟩•

Former Governor William G. Stratton of Illinois was upheld in tax-fraud litigation.

The IRS claimed that Stratton's income for 1953-60, the years he was in office, came to $366,000, or $194,000 more than the $172,000 Stratton reported. The IRS used bank accounts and other records to reconstruct how much Stratton's net worth had increased while he was governor. It also levied penalties for under-payment of taxes due to fraud. Stratton had been acquitted of criminal tax fraud.

The Tax Court upheld Stratton, however, and the main point was the treatment of political contributions. A campaign contribution diverted to personal use becomes taxable income, but an outright gift isn't taxable. In Stratton's case, the court ruled that $43,600 of "unreported income" had been in fact "outright, unrestricted gifts." By the court's reckoning, Stratton had understated his income by only $82,000. But for most of this sum, the statute of limitations had expired because no fraud was proved, the court said.

The bulk of the unreported income came from contributions used for personal ends. But Stratton could have "reasonably believed" these contested sums were gifts.

(Stratton v. Commissioner, 54 T.C. No. 23.)
2/18/70

◦⟨⟩◦

An appeals court upholds a broker's conviction for willful failure to file.

Earl G. Baird conceded he hadn't filed returns for 1959 to 1963, when he made as much as $121,000 a year as a floor broker for Baird & Co., a firm headed by his brother, David G. Baird. But Earl Baird contended he wasn't criminally responsible because of mental disability. Two psychiatrists testified as to his incompetence. They were allowed to relate what Baird had told them in interviews, though normally this would have been excluded as hearsay. It was admitted solely to show what they had based their opinions on, even though it included Baird's saying he thought the returns were "taken care of" by a tax adviser.

The Government had Baird examined by its expert, who found him competent. That expert was also allowed to relate his out-of-court interview with Baird—but no admission about the willfulness of not filing. Baird's counsel said the examination was self-incrimination because Baird had to submit and answer all questions. But the court ruled that having raised the plea and introduced his own experts, Baird couldn't object to the Government's.

The court also noted that, through the psychiatrists, Baird had got a favorable explanation on the record without submitting to cross-examination.

(Baird v. U.S.A., U.S. Ct. of Appeals, 2nd. Cir., 1969.)
9/10/69

A fraud penalty was overturned despite a taxpayer's questionable actions.

A Pennsylvanian didn't report his capital gain on a $160,000 stock sale in 1963. As part of the deal he had insisted on being paid with thirty-two $5,000 bills and given a receipt for only $120,000. He said he didn't want his estranged wife to know how much money he had. Later he deposited the bulk of the $5,000 bills in his checking account.

The man died in 1964. After the IRS discovered the stock sale, the taxpayer's estate paid the tax on the profit but balked at an added assessment for fraud. The Tax Court sided with the estate. Among other things, it noted that while the use of currency rather than a check in such a large deal might suggest fraud, the taxpayer's demand for $5,000 bills (there were only 555 in circulation) and his putting the money in his checking account were easily traceable actions that weren't consistent with the typical fraudulent intent to conceal.

The court said the taxpayer's conduct was suspicious and wasn't easily explained by his desire to deceive his wife. But it also held that suspicious behavior doesn't necessarily indicate fraud.

(Estate of Kauffman v. Commissioner, T. C. Memo. 1969-20.)
2/19/69

⟡

The odds you'll be indicted for tax fraud are rising. Some 1,186 people were indicted for tax evasion and related crimes in fiscal 1973 ended June 30. That continues a steady rise from 1,085 in 1972, 956 in 1971 and 924 in 1970. The IRS credits improved administration in its criminal division, formation of additional investigative teams and computerization of some procedures for the increase.

8/22/73

Shade of difference: The IRS and the Justice Department sometimes use different standards when deciding whether to press a tax fraud case, says Bruce Hochman, a Los Angeles tax lawyer. In an article in Tax Adviser magazine, Hochman says the IRS asks itself whether a crime has been committed. But at the Justice Department, which decides whether to prosecute, the question, according to Hochman, becomes: Can this case be won?

4/26/72

◦⟷◦

In tax fraud, the burden of proof is on the IRS, and the Tax Court normally demands a clear showing that the IRS has met that test. The court recently declined to find fraud against a New Mexico man who ran a crap game and expanded into bookmaking. He falsified wagering tax returns, destroyed records and reported no bookmaking income. The IRS said that added up to fraudulent tax evasion, but he claimed he was just hiding from the police. The court had its doubts, but ruled the IRS didn't prove he was hiding income too.

(George v. Commissioner, T.C. Memo. 1970-231.)
8/19/70

◦⟷◦

The IRS had a bad day at the track. It brought charges of attempted tax evasion against a "ten-percenter": someone who, for a fee, will cash winning pari-mutuel tickets so that the true winner need not come to the attention of the IRS. The Third Circuit appeals court recently overturned the conviction. The government didn't prove the true winner actually underpaid taxes that year.

(U.S.A. v. Petti U.S. Ct. of Appeals, 3rd Cir., 1971.)
10/13/71

What Are a Taxpayer's Rights?

Fifth Amendment rights apply in a civil case, an appeals court rules.

The Seventh Circuit decision apparently breaks new ground in extending traditional constitutional guarantees to civil proceedings. The case involved an IRS raid on a Chicago liquor store and bar, where bets were believed to be taken. The owner, who later said he was scared and nervous, talked freely with IRS agents. At no time was he warned of his rights to remain silent and get a lawyer.

The IRS conceded that failure to give the warnings barred use of the owner's statements in a criminal prosecution. But it used what he said as evidence in dunning him for underpayment of taxes and the 50% penalty for civil fraud. The Tax Court upheld that. The circuit court, however, found it "unwholesome and an abuse of power" to let the government base its civil case on an infringement of the man's constitutional protections. It ordered a new trial, with his statements excluded.

Barring the statements from the civil proceedings was a good way to deter the government from relying on improper procedures, the appeals court said.

(Romanelli v. Commissioner, U.S. Ct. of Appeals, 7th Cir., 1972)
9/6/72

◄═►

A court rules out the use of tax return information in a non-tax case.

There's long been confusion over the extent to which the government can use information in an individual's tax return if it prosecutes him for a non-tax crime. There aren't any clear-cut precedents to go by. The Supreme Court in 1927 said a taxpayer is required to file a return but can, under the Fifth Amendment, refuse to answer certain questions on the return if he feels he would be incriminated. Several years ago, the Ninth Circuit Court of Appeals ruled that for those questions a person does answer, he's in effect waiving his Fifth Amendment protection if the answers incriminate him. But subsequent Supreme Court decisions have cast doubt on that line of reasoning.

Now, the Ninth Circuit has ruled on the issue again. A man was prosecuted for gambling law violations. He had listed gambling as his major source of income on his tax return. The U.S. used the return in its case, contending the man gave his occupation voluntarily. The court reversed his conviction. It said answering the occupation question was compulsory; the IRS couldn't verify his income unless it knew the source. And because the disclosure was compulsory, the court ruled, it shouldn't have been used against the man without his okay, which he hadn't given.

(Garner v. U.S.A., Ct. of Appeals, 9th Cir., 1972)
7/26/72

The Justice Department breaks a promise, but a court puts it back together.

Government attorneys questioned a man connected with a company they were investigating for tax fraud. The man claimed the lawyers promised him "informally" he would be immune from prosecution and his records wouldn't be turned over to the IRS if he cooperated—in effect waiving his Fifth Amendment right not to incriminate himself. The man gave the government his records and testified before a grand jury. Later, however, his records were given to the IRS and he was indicted. The U.S. attorneys denied there had been any agreement and said they never grant "informal" immunity.

A district court accepted the man's story and ridiculed the government's contention. It said Justice Department attorneys routinely grant immunity informally. If they didn't, they'd be constantly awash in the paperwork of formal immunity agreements, the court asserted. It ruled the man's grand jury testimony couldn't be used against him.

But the court said the records he had given up could be used because they were corporate records, to which personal immunity agreements don't apply.

(U.S.A. v. Robbins, U.S. Dist. Ct., No. Dist. Ohio, 1972)
6/28/72

Two partners in a New York resort hotel take the Fifth with a court's approval.

Ben and Julius Slutsky, brothers who run the large Nevele resort in Upstate New York, were accused of tax fraud. The IRS subpoenaed their partnership records. The Fifth Amendment allows individuals to refuse to turn over their records, but it doesn't protect corporations. The law covering partnerships is less clear. Generally, partnership records are protected because they are assumed to constitute the individual records of the partners instead of the records of a business separate from the individuals. But in some cases courts have denied Fifth Amendment protection to partnerships that are large and impersonal enough to resemble corporations.

The IRS contends the Slutskys' Nevele operation is too much like a corporation for them to use the Fifth Amendment. It pointed out the place takes in roughly $4 million a year and employes a full-time accountant.

A federal district court, however, upheld the brothers. Despite its size, the Nevele resort remains essentially a personal family business, the court said.

(U.S.A. v. Slutsky, U.S. Dist. Ct., So. Dist. of New York, 1972)
2/14/73

◑⫸◐

A tax fraud case shows some of the limits on a taxpayer's rights.

The matter involved an investigation of a woman for possible criminal tax fraud. An IRS revenue agent had looked over her records (which were at her accountant's) and called in a special agent, a routine step when likely criminal violations crop up. The special agent subpoenaed the records from the accountant, over the woman's objection.

The Fourth Circuit appeals court recently upheld the subpoena. The woman had protested the subpoena was out of place in a potentially criminal investigation, but the court ruled the subpoena proper as long as the IRS investigation retained "a legitimate civil purpose." The woman also invoked her Fifth Amendment protections against self-incrimination. But those protections didn't help her, the court decided, because she had voluntarily given her records to the accountant.

When she did that, the records "passed from the sphere of privilege surrounding her," the court said. No privilege protected dealings between accountant and client.

10/27/71

◑⫸◐

A lawyer can't take the Fifth on behalf of a client, a split appeals court says.

The constitutional privilege against self-incrimination normally is considered purely personal. That is, it can be used only by an individual to turn back a request for information made directly to him. But some courts have said a lawyer can invoke the privilege for a client in a tax matter when it isn't convenient for the client to appear at every stage of an inquiry.

The IRS asked a Texas lawyer to turn over work papers bearing on the tax liability of one of his clients. The lawyer took the Fifth for the man and pointed out the client would have been protected if the documents had been in his possession rather than the lawyer's. But a circuit appeals court in a two-to-one ruling ordered the lawyer to give the IRS the papers. The court cited a Supreme Court decision that the Fifth Amendment doesn't protect a taxpayer's documents when they are held by an accountant.

The dissenting judge said a lawyer has much more leeway to act for his client than an accountant does and asserted the majority's ruling "seriously weakens" the attorney-client relationship.

(U.S.A. v. White, U.S. Ct. of Appeals, 5th Cir., 1973.)
5/2/73

Fourth Amendment protection extends to civil tax cases, the Tax Court rules.

"Unreasonable searches and seizures" are barred by the Fourth Amendment, and courts long have held that evidence thus obtained can't be used in a criminal prosecution. But whether such "tainted" evidence can be used in a civil tax case is another question—one which the Supreme Court has never answered explicitly and which the Tax Court hadn't confronted until recently. The tax case involved a Miami man who was charged with conspiracy to perform an abortion. Police raided his offices and seized various evidence including his financial records.

A jury convicted the man, but a higher court threw out the verdict. It found the police raid violated the Fourth Amendment; the officers didn't announce the purpose of the raid when it began and didn't have warrants. The IRS, meanwhile, used the seized financial records in a civil action against the man for underpayment of taxes.

The Tax Court ruled the IRS couldn't use the records because they were obtained illegally. The court noted the Fourth Amendment doesn't distinguish between criminal and civil cases. There were two dissents to the ruling.

(Suarez v. Commissioner, 58 T.C. No. 78)
8/23/72

◦⟨⟩◦

Seizing records from a taxpayer violates the Fifth Amendment, a court says.

According to his employes, an Illinois doctor kept two sets of books—one of which was to be burned if the taxman ever came to the door. With affidavits to this effect, an IRS special agent obtained a search warrant and seized 35 cartons of records from the doctor's office and home. The doctor protested that the seizure violated constitutional guarantees against self-incrimination, and the Seventh Circuit appeals court readily agreed.

Even the IRS conceded that had it obtained a summons, it couldn't force the doctor to hand over his records. It contended, however, that its search warrant was valid, and thus the seizure didn't infringe on Fifth Amendment rights. That struck the court as "constitutional question begging." The IRS also argued that the doctor wasn't compelled to testify against himself. Other witnesses would have to establish that the records were authentic.

The court found "more shadow than substance" in that distinction. A taxpayer's records "speak against him as clearly as his own voice," the court declared.

(Hill v. Philpott, U.S. Ct. of Appeals, 7th Cir., 1971.)
6/9/71

Were the agents going too far when they emptied the guest's purse?

Armed with search warrants, nine IRS agents in two groups descended simultaneously on a dentist's office and home. They searched the home for six hours, the office for four. They took not only financial records but also personal letters and appointment books. They even forced the dentist's wife and a guest to empty their purses.

The dentist claimed the searches violated the Fifth Amendment's protection against self-incrimination. But the IRS said the Fifth applies only to situations were an individual is directly compelled to furnish information. It reasoned that under a search warrant, a person isn't actually forced to give information personally; the agents merely help themselves.

The Ninth Circuit appeals court rejected that argument and barred use of the records against the dentist. "One need only ask," the court said, "what would happen if the (object) of a warrant refused to allow the search . . . to appreciate the magnitude of compulsion produced by a search warrant. Without the slightest hesitation his doors would be broken down, he would be placed under arrest and the desired material would be seized. How the imminence of such force can be considered anything other than compulsion escapes us."

The ruling agrees with a similar one in the Seventh Circuit, but conflicts with one in the Sixth, thus suggesting possible high court review.

(Vanderahe v. Howland, U.S. Ct. of Appeals, 9th Cir., 1973)
4/18/73

◦⟨⟩◦

Ever wonder how you'd react if the Feds dropped in to check your finances?

Here's how it went for one Illinois dentist. Two IRS agents met him in the parking lot as he arrived at his office one morning. They hadn't called for an appointment and the dentist told them he had a golf date. But he agreed to spend an hour with them after treating two patients. (He'd read in a dental journal how to handle IRS interviews without a lawyer present.) The dentist's records revealed he hadn't recorded some payments from patients in his cash receipts book. He didn't have a ready explanation.

The questioning stretched beyond the first hour. The doctor got very nervous and began to sweat profusely. He asked if he could lie down, saying "I can't take it at this time." Occasionally the tension broke. The doctor talked about his academic achievements. He advised one of the agents what to do for emphysema. Twice, the agents asked if the dentist wanted to leave for his golf game. He didn't go and, after several hours, confessed he'd failed to record more than $40,000 in receipts.

The man was sentenced to three years in prison and fined $5,000 for tax fraud.

(U.S.A. v. Lehman, U.S. Ct. of Appeals, 7th Cir., 1972)
7/18/72

◘◁▷◙

Note to bankrupts: A circuit court says your tax refunds can't be seized.

A bankrupt person generally must give up his property to a trustee. But he's allowed to keep his wages; they aren't considered part of property. The purpose is to insure that as many debts as possible are paid but still let the man get a new start. Simple as that formula seems, it can get complicated. For example, bankruptcy courts commonly have seized tax refund checks, and the Supreme Court in the past ruled that some kinds of tax refunds are seizable property.

But an appeals court now says refunds of taxes that were withheld from wages two men were paid before they went bankrupt are part of their earnings and can't be seized. There's one qualification, though. If the

refund simply is the difference between actual tax liability and the minimum amount IRS formulas automatically withhold from a taxpayer in a particular category, the bankrupt taxpayer can keep 100%. But if he
chose to have more than the minimum withheld, he can
retain only 75% of the refund; the trustee gets the rest.

The court indicated the limitation was intended to
discourage a man who intended to go bankrupt from
drastically raising his withholding in anticipation of
keeping all the refund.

(In re James and Cedor, U.S. Ct. of Appeals, 9th Cir., 1927)
1/10/73

◊⊂◯◗

A masked fox dressed like Boss Tweed breaks into
a chicken coop with a torch.

That's the composite image a prosecutor apparently wanted to convey of a man on trial for tax evasion.
In his opening remarks to the jury, the prosecutor
stressed that much of the income the defendant hadn't
reported appeared to have been obtained illegally from
his company. The man "couldn't have done a more effective job of getting money out of the (company) if he
had gone out and bought a mask, got an acetylene
torch, gone in there one night and blown the vault door
open," the prosecutor said.

He also cast the man in the fabled role of the fox
who robs the chicken coop after being trusted to guard
it. And the government attorney further embellished
his attack on the defendant by showing the jury an enlarged cartoon drawing of Boss Tweed, the corrupt
Tammany Hall leader. The jury convicted the man, but
a U.S. appeals court threw out the verdict.

The court stressed he was on trial for tax evasion,
not for stealing from his company. It ruled the prosecutor's comments had prejudiced the case.

(U.S.A. v. Singer, U.S. Ct. of Appeals, 6th Cir., 1973)
8/8/73

A strict view of the IRS's criminal warnings policy is eased by a court.

The IRS policy, announced in 1967 after the Supreme Court's Miranda decision, provides that when an IRS special agent enters a case, the taxpayer must be warned that the agent's job is to investigate criminal matters. The agent also must tell the potential defendant of his right to remain silent. Courts since have thrown out evidence in some cases where agents didn't follow the announced policy. But a circuit court recently reversed what it considered a too-strict interpretation of the policy by a district court.

The special agent told the taxpayer that "one of my functions is to investigate the possibility of criminal violations of" the tax laws. The defendant contended, and the district court agreed, that this wording didn't go far enough in "describing the function" of a special agent. A previous IRS release on the subject had referred specifically to "criminal fraud" rather than simply "criminal violations."

But the higher court said it "failed to see" how the "violations" warning was less candid than the "fraud" statement. The higher court admitted the evidence.

(U.S.A. v. Bembridge, U.S. Ct. of Appeals, 1st Cir., 1972)
6/7/72

The IRS' warnings policy in criminal cases can be flexible, a court says.

The IRS is supposed to warn a potential defendant of his right to remain silent when an investigation turns up evidence of criminal tax fraud. The tipoff usually is when an IRS "special" agent (they work only on criminal matters) takes over from a "revenue" agent. But one recent case showed there isn't a set way of deciding when the warning has to be given.

Having decided to start a criminal inquiry, a spe-

cial agent accompanied a revenue agent to see the taxpayer. The revenue agent introduced the special agent
only as "another man with the government." The
agents asked for the man's records and he released
them. Only later did the special agent identify himself
and tell the man his rights. After he was indicted, the
taxpayer claimed the special agent had tricked him into
cooperating and tried to bar the evidence the agent obtained. But a circuit court admitted the evidence, ruling
the special agent's reticence wasn't a "material misrepresentation" under the circumstances.

The taxpayer previously had loaned his records to
the revenue agent for copying, and anything one gives
the IRS voluntarily at the outset of a civil inquiry can
be used later in a criminal action without his permission. Also, the man had disregarded his accountant's
advice to stay silent.

(U.S.A. v. Bland, U.S. Ct. of Appeals, 5th Cir., 1972)
11/19/72

◂━▸

An Exxon unit, with a federal court's help, stops an
IRS fishing expedition.

The Revenue Service tried to subpoena certain
lease records from Humble Oil, a part of what used to be
Standard Oil of New Jersey and is now Exxon. The IRS
said it was doing "research" to see whether people who
had one kind of leasing relationship with Humble were
paying all their taxes. It stressed it wasn't at that time
auditing any specific company or person in connection
with the leasing matter.

Humble protested the subpoena was an "unreasonable search" and an "unwarranted invasion" of confidential records. The company said responding to it
would be a "substantial economic burden." In a recently
reported ruling, a federal district court in Houston generally agreed with Humble.

Broad as the IRS's powers are, the court said, they don't encompass extracting information from a third party when the tax agency isn't investigating a specific taxpayer.

(U.S.A. v. Humble Oil & Refining Co., U.S. Dist Ct., So. Dist. Texas, 1972)
3/14/73

A related type of IRS "fishing expedition" also is causing court controversy.

The Revenue Service asked a Jackson, Miss., milling company for records of the company's dealings with soybean farmers in the state. The IRS said it was making a survey to determine whether the farmers were paying all their taxes. The company refused to give up the records. It argued that such a request could be proper only as part of an IRS investigation of a specific person. But a federal district court in Mississippi ruled that the Service has the authority to subpoena such information on broad groups of taxpayers.

The Mississippi ruling clashes with another in Texas. There, the IRS asked Exxon Corp. for records of its leasing relationships with unnamed outsiders the government wanted to check on. Exxon claimed the request was unreasonable and an "unwarranted invasion" of confidential files. A U.S. district court in Houston upheld Exxon on somewhat the same grounds cited by the Fourth Circuit: The IRS can't extract information from a third party when the tax agency isn't investigating a specific taxpayer.

The Texas and Mississippi rulings would be appealable to the Fifth Circuit.

(U.S. v. Anderson Clayton & Co., U.S. Dist. Ct., So. Dist. of Miss., 1973)
6/6/73

IRS access to a credit bureau's files is upheld over the firm's objections.

A circuit court case spotlighted a longstanding IRS practice of quietly tapping credit-bureau data banks for financial information about taxpayers. TRW Credit Data, whose files hold information on 20 million New Yorkers and Californians, contested the IRS right to compel it to give data on a taxpayer. The company demanded fair compensation, and it also asked a hearing on whether the IRS summons was burdensome or injurious.

"We question their right to such information in the first place," declares Gerald Davey, head of Credit Data. The circuit court disagreed. It ordered another hearing to set fair compensation (a lower court had said 75 cents a report), but it brushed aside Davey's substantive objections. "The Government has the right to require the production of information wherever it may be lodged . . . so long as it pays," the court said.

Industry sources say most credit companies cooperate with the IRS, sometimes under a summons issued on the spot. But in some instances, companies have refused and heard no more about it.

(U.S.A. v. Davey, U.S. Ct. of Appeals, 2nd Cir., 1970.)
6/3/70

The Swiss bank decision comes up with an important grant of authority.

The Swiss Federal Supreme Court upheld the right of Swiss authorities to give U.S. tax officials data from the "secret" bank account of a U.S. citizen under investigation for tax fraud. When the full text of the decision, X v. The Federal Tax Administration, became available, U.S. Treasury officials expressed delight with it. The decision interprets the U.S.-Swiss tax treaty, which authorizes the exchange of information necessary "for the prevention of fraud or the like."

The court brushed aside Swiss bank secrecy laws as inapplicable. In several cantons, it said, tax law pro-

vides that tax fraud be prosecuted under ordinary criminal procedure, and such procedure doesn't permit
banks to withhold evidence in criminal investigations.
The tax treaty extended this doctrine to all cantons, the
court said. Otherwise, offenders could defeat the "spirit
and purpose" of the treaty by switching their "fraudulent machinations" to cantons with laxer laws.

The Swiss insist their law has always provided for
such disclosure, though they certainly haven't advertised it. They also note that under Swiss law, "simple
tax evasion" isn't fraud.

(X v. The Federal Tax Administration,
Swiss Federal Supreme Court, 1970.)
6/9/71

The IRS moves one more small step toward crack-
ing Swiss bank secrecy.

The Treasury's efforts to get more information on
U.S. citizens' dealings with Swiss banks got a big boost
in late 1970. Then, the highest Swiss court ruled that
Swiss tax authorities had to give the IRS information
about an American tax fraud suspect's dealings with a
Swiss bank. For such information to be useful in court,
however, the IRS must lay its hands on Swiss bank records from which the information is gleaned. And the
U.S. Tax Court has authorized the IRS to take the first
step toward obtaining records.

The step amounts simply to the U.S. government's
asking Swiss officials for permission to take depositions
from officials of a Swiss bank, Commercial Credit Bank
Ltd., Zurich. The taxpayer involved contested the IRS's
right to proceed. But the Tax Court said his objections
were "more technical than legal."

The Tax Court cautioned it wasn't ruling on
whether evidence the IRS might obtain would be admis-

sible in court. That will be up to the trial judge if there's a trial, the court said.

(Ryan v. Commissioner, 58 T.C. No. 10.)
5/3/72

◦⊂⊃◦

A five-year gap between indictments and trial isn't necessarily undue delay.

That's what the U.S. District Court for the Southern District of New York decided in ruling against a man indicted in 1965 on charges of helping to prepare a fraudulent tax return. The case had been adjourned a dozen times and then, in May 1966, removed from the court calendar at the government's request. Not until last February did the government indicate it was ready for trial.

The defendant claimed that was undue delay and asked to have the indictment dismissed. The district court reluctantly refused. Clearly the delay required an explanation, the court said, and the only explanation the government offered was inadvertence. But the defendant failed to show the delay had hurt his ability to rebut the government's case. (He had been at liberty the entire time.) Nor had he ever asked that the case be taken up.

Precedents in the Second Circuit left no ground to dismiss the indictment, the district court said. Failure to demand a speedy trial amounts to a waiver of the claim, the court recited.

(U.S.A. v. Schwartz, U.S. Dist. Ct., So. Dist. New York, 1971.)
5/26/71

◦⊂⊃◦

Jersey Standard (now Exxon) loses a legal test to close its board minutes to the IRS.

Auditing Standard Oil of New Jersey's consolidated tax return is a mammoth task, requiring the full-time work of four IRS agents. Since 1957, the IRS auditors have requested the minutes of meetings of directors and executive committees of Jersey Standard and many of its affiliates, including Humble Oil & Refining Co. Jersey complied for a decade, but in 1967 a new general counsel decided the IRS was asking more than the law allows. Instead, he offered to inform the IRS of top-level actions affecting the company's tax return.

A U.S. district court ruled, however, that Jersey must produce the minutes in full. The law allows the IRS to demand books and records that "may be relevant or material" to its purpose. The IRS can't be expected to take Jersey's word for what is relevant, the court said. Indeed, it noted, Jersey's accounting firm routinely requires full access to Jersey's files for its auditing.

Similarly, "IRS agents must inevitably look at things that are irrelevant and immaterial to avoid overlooking some that are relevant and material," the court said.

(U.S.A. v, Acker, U.S. Dist. Ct., So. Dist. New York, 1971.)
3/31/71

The IRS was barred from the records of an ongoing grand jury investigation because agents were looking for civil tax liability. Grand juries are limited to criminal matters, and a federal district judge ruled such access would amount to widening the jury's scope. The judge didn't foreclose the possibility that evidence unearthed by a grand jury's criminal inquiry might later be used for civil purposes. But widening the investigation in advance or while in progress would "expand the already awesome powers of the grand jury beyond tolerable limits," the judge said.

(U.S.A. v. John Doe, U.S. Dist. Ct., So. Dist. of N.Y., 1972.)
3/15/72

Stretching the Fifth: A taxpayer contended that requiring him to file a return one year violated his protection against self-incrimination. He had illegally failed to file returns in the previous three years, and the return for the year at issue included a question whether he had filed for the prior year. Filing a return with a truthful answer to that question would have amounted to admitting a crime, he reasoned. The court indicated the Fifth Amendment might have permitted him to leave the question blank. But it said he still was required to file the return.

(U.S.A. v. Egan, U.S. Ct. of Appeals, 2nd Cir., 1972)
5/24/72

◁▷

Start the clock? A Colorado man, convicted in 1971 for tax evasion in 1963 and 1964, claimed the long span violated his Sixth Amendment right to a speedy trial. A U.S. circuit court recently disagreed. The right didn't apply, the court said, until the man somehow became an "accused." And that didn't happen until 1969, when a complaint was filed and an indictment returned. It didn't matter that he had been under IRS investigation since 1963.

(U.S.A. v. Merrick, U.S. Ct. of Appeals, 10th Cir., 1972)
8/2/72

◁▷

Logical: A man filed a tax return containing only his name, address and signature. He claimed if he completed the return truthfully he would be incriminating himself and the Fifth Amendment protects him from doing that. If he completed it untruthfully he would be perjuring himself. If he didn't send in a return at all he would be guilty of failure to file, also a crime. An appeals court upheld his conviction on the last point: Filing a return that omits the taxpayer's income is the same as not filing at all.

(U.S.A. v. Daly, U.S. Ct. of Appeals, 8th Cir., 1973)

The lady took the Fifth, so the IRS asked a court to compel her to answer questions about her taxes. The IRS said its investigation was civil; thus she wasn't protected by the Fifth Amendment's self-incrimination provisions as she would have been in a criminal case. But the court found the case had "dominant criminal overtones," despite what the IRS said. The woman allegedly had been involved in illegal gambling and hadn't filed tax returns for six years. So she was within her rights in refusing to answer questions, the court held.

(U.S.A. v. Dean, U.S. Dist. Ct., So. Dist. Fla., 1972)
7/5/72

◦⸺◦

The source of your income is nearly as important to the IRS as how much you earn. And you can be indicted for lying about where your money comes from, even if you give the correct amount on your return. So ruled an Illinois district court. Two men had claimed the only "material" misrepresentation for which one can be indicted is falsifying the amount of his income. The court pointed out the IRS can't verify the amount if it doesn't know the source.

(U.S.A. v. DiVarco and Arnold, U.S. Dist. Ct., No. Dist. Ill., 1972)
6/21/72

◦⸺◦

What happens if your accountant discovers that, through error, you materially underpaid your taxes in a previous year? According to the American Institute of Certified Public Accountants, a CPA must promptly notify a client if he turns up a material understatement. The CPA isn't ethically bound to tell the IRS, however, or even allowed to do so without his client's permission. If the client doesn't correct a material error, the institute says "the CPA will want to satisfy himself that (keeping the account) is compatible with . . . service to other taxpayers who assess themselves fairly."

10/14/70

Cough up: An accountant did a couple's tax returns for 11 years and routinely kept a copy for his files. There the copies rested until an IRS special agent called for an interview. The accountant put him off four days, then told him that regrettably, all copies and working papers had been returned to the couple two days earlier. A district court recently decided the papers remained the accountant's property, and the couple couldn't refuse to produce them.

(U.S.A. v. Widelski, U.S. Dist. Ct., East. Dist. Mich., 1970.)
11/11/70

o⟨⟩o

No Fifth: A U.S. district court in California ordered an accountant to comply with a summons and produce working papers related to a corporate client's return. It wasn't impressed by a claim of Fifth Amendment protections against self-incrimination. It is "well settled law" that neither a corporation nor its officers or employes can invoke Fifth Amendment privilege with respect to corporate records.

(U.S.A. v. Machtinger, U.S. Dist. Ct., Central Dist. Calif., 1971)
6/30/71

o⟨⟩o

A routine audit led the IRS to believe a banker had probably violated Federal law. The IRS wrote the Justice Department and told it so. At trial, the defendant claimed that initial letter was an unlawful disclosure of his tax return. But a U.S. district court in Connecticut said no. The letter gave nothing more specific than the man's name and address. (The IRS turned over its files later under authorized procedures.)

(U.S.A. v. Tucker, U.S. Dist. Ct., Dist. Conn., 1970.)
9/9/70

o⟨⟩o

Sacred trust: The IRS called in an attorney to ask about $12,000 in interest he allegedly paid a client who owed the Government taxes. The attorney replied that the client was in litigation, and any questions about the man were barred by the privilege covering dealings between lawyer and client. But a U.S. court of appeals was unimpressed. The IRS was merely looking for assets to get its tax money, it said. For the attorney to make a blanket claim of privilege "borders on the cavalier," the court declared.

(U.S.A. v. Finley, U.S. Ct. of Appeals, 5th Cir., 1970.)
11/25/70

An Illinois man charged the IRS with violating his civil rights by picking his return for audit, thus requiring more supporting data from him than from the millions who went unaudited. The Tax Court was baffled but unmoved.

5/13/70

There are few exceptions to the law requiring that income tax returns be kept confidential. So when the receiver of a defunct savings and loan association wanted to examine the tax returns of the association's employes, they resisted. A court backed them. It noted that if the employes themselves had made an issue of their income, they would have had to open their returns. But this didn't happen, and the receiver failed to sway the court on other grounds.

(Federal Savings & Loan Insurance Corp.
v. Krueger, U.S. Dist. Ct., No. Dist. Ill., 1972)
9/13/72

Breaking Down IRS Secrecy

The end of secrecy should mean fairer tax rulings with less hanky-panky.

That at least is the hope of Tax Analysts and Advocates, the public interest tax law firm whose suit prompted a U.S. district judge in Washington to rule that private IRS rulings must be made public. Citing the Freedom of Information Act, the judge's order covers both the roughly 30,000 secret rulings issued annually and secret guidance from IRS headquarters to field offices on how to handle particular taxpayers, records of related letters and phone calls, and indexes to rulings and guidelines. The IRS must get court permission to keep any part of such material secret. The judge implied that won't be easy.

The decision should, among other things, force an increase in the quality and uniformity of tax rulings, says Thomas F. Field, executive director of Tax Analysts and Advocates. "The prospect of disclosure means you can assume those handling the rulings will be more thorough; there should be less slipshod work," Field asserts. He adds that "unknown corporations who get large windfall concessions won't be unknown any longer, and Congress can correct abuses more promptly." Tax Analysts plans to put rulings on microfiche and assemble a computer index of them.

The Treasury has appealed the court's ruling. As this book goes to press, the outcome isn't known.

6/13/73

Two secret IRS documents must be made public, a federal judge decides.

Internal guidelines the IRS follows in negotiating conflicts with taxpayers and a report showing how the IRS allocates audit manpower between small and large taxpayers were ordered turned over to a Bellevue, Wash., taxpayer who had sued to get them. A U.S. District Court judge, after reading the IRS materials privately, said "prejudice to the government from disclosure of the documents is outweighed by the public's right to know" their contents.

After his own returns were audited, the taxpayer, Philip Long, accused the IRS of following audit and negotiation guidelines that are kept secret from the public, thereby placing taxpayers at a disadvantage. Long also charged the IRS audits small taxpayers more vigorously than large ones. His suit followed a number of unsuccessful attempts to get the IRS to let him see the documents.

The IRS has given Long the negotiation guidelines, but hasn't yet decided whether to appeal the judge's ruling on the audit manpower report.

(Long v. IRS, U.S. Dist. Ct., West. Dist. Wash., 1972.)
9/13/72

◦⟨⟩◦

More access to a secret IRS manual is likely from a Sixth Circuit decision.

Increasingly, taxpayers are using the Freedom of Information Act to force disclosure of the IRS Manual, which governs agents in examining returns and questioning taxpayers. A U.S. district judge in Seattle decided the manual should be turned over to a taxpayer who sued to get it. And the Sixth Circuit appeals court, whose area is Michigan, Ohio, Tennessee and Kentucky, has expressed much the same opinion.

The Sixth Circuit interpreted exceptions to the Information Act narrowly. The law requires disclosure of "administrative" manuals, except those pertaining to law enforcement. The court said the exemption applies only when disclosure would significantly impede enforcement—such as by detailing FBI stake-out procedures. If a manual merely describes "an agency's understanding of the law," disclosure isn't harmful, the court said. It thought "several sections at least" of the IRS Manual should be released.

The Information Act also exempts from disclosure matters related "solely to internal personnel rules and practices." The court said this only applies to things like employe lunch hours, not to matters the manual deals with.

(Hawkes v. IRS U.S. Ct. of Appeals, 6th Cir., 1972.)
10/11/72

IRS secrecy can make it hard to know when to appeal an audit ruling.

One obvious reason for appealing is knowing you have a good chance of having an agent's determination overturned at a higher level. But unless you have a savvy lawyer, it's often difficult to tell what your chances would be. If you knew there was disagreement within the IRS over the merits of your case, that would be a tip-off that appealing might be worthwhile. It's general IRS policy, however, to refrain from telling you of such disagreement.

In the St. Louis IRS district, for instance, an internal document strongly warns agents against telling taxpayers "of any disagreement between (agents) and reviewers (people who check agents' work). Conveyance of such an idea can result in taxpayer relation problems and lead to the belief that one branch of the Service is at odds with another."

Some critics of IRS procedures feel agents should

be allowed to give taxpayers a candid idea of the strength of the IRS's case against them.

4/25/73

◦◁▷◦

"Secret" tax rulings by the IRS draw new criticism.

The Treasury publishes only about 600 of the 35,000 decisions it makes annually on how to treat specific taxpayer circumstances. The IRS considers most rulings too narrow to be of interest generally. But since millions of dollars ride on many private decisions, "there's a likelihood of improper pressure" from taxpayers seeking favorable rulings, asserts Thomas F. Field, executive director of Taxation With Representation, a nonprofit Arlington, Va., group.

Columbia University law professor George Cooper contends the "backroom" rulings erode public confidence. Publication of more rulings would increase the uniformity of tax law application, many critics say. Sen. Proxmire favors advance public hearings on any IRS decision that could cost the Treasury $5 million or more in revenue. But some lawyers say such hearings would overburden the IRS and wouldn't be worth the time they'd consume.

2/16/72

◦◁▷◦

The Treasury agrees to make public most of its correspondence on tax matters with Congressmen and other outsiders. The action was sought in a Freedom of Information suit filed by a group of public interest tax lawyers. The Treasury has agreed to ease access to the documents by maintaining an updated public list of correspondents and subjects.

6/6/73

◦◁▷◦

Turnabout: A California man filed suit in Federal court under the Freedom of Information Act on behalf

of something called "Taxpayers Anonymous." He asked
to do to the IRS what the law permits it to do to an individual taxpayer—"to examine (its) books and records."
All he wanted was "a spot check," he said, "which
shouldn't prove unduly burdensome." But the district
court gave him the short shrift. He hadn't exhausted
his administrative remedies—gotten a definite "no"
from the IRS—and he didn't specify the records he
wanted.

(Abel v. I.R.S., U.S. Dist. Ct., Central Dist. Calif., 1970.)
9/23/70

Tactics for the Taxpayer

"Silence is golden" in criminal tax fraud cases, a defense attorney says.

In The Tax Adviser, Paul P. Lipton, a Milwaukee lawyer, argues "the advantages of non-cooperation." It's vital, he says, that rights be protected "from the earliest possible moment." The entry of an IRS special agent means the IRS has criminal charges in mind, but Constitutional rights may be claimed even earlier. The taxpayer should deal with the IRS only through his lawyer, he says.

The taxpayer can't be compelled to talk with IRS agents, Lipton advises, and "such interrogations seldom should be permitted (because they) invariably produce damaging admissions." Personal papers are also privileged, and "in most instances . . . it isn't advisable" to give them to the IRS. (On "rare occasions . . . full cooperation is proper.") The taxpayer should get his records back from his accountant, and it's "preferable" that the accountant (or others) talk to the IRS only under summons, with the taxpayer's lawyer present. Waiving the statute of limitations could mean giving away a good bargaining tool.

"Ironically, the cooperative taxpayer fares much worse," Lipton contends. "Tax prosecutions almost invariably are based in whole or large part on evidence furnished by cooperative taxpayers."

8/26/70

If you're audited, be sure to ask the IRS whether your case is a "prime issue."

Even though the Service's prime issue list was made public recently, it is still official IRS policy to refrain from telling a taxpayer whether his case involves a prime issue until well into the audit process. Prime issues are unresolved tax questions that the IRS prefers to litigate rather than compromise.

"While a case is under the jurisdiction of the District (IRS) Director (where it remains during the audit and until it is appealed to the IRS appellate division or the courts), the taxpayer won't be advised" that the case involves a prime issue, says the IRS's internal procedures manual. The manual alerts IRS agents in prime issue cases to "obtain data necessary to assist the government's attorneys to litigate." But by letting the taxpayer believe the matter will be settled out of court as most tax cases are, the IRS leaves open the possibility the taxpayer will give more information than he would if he knew the case might go to court.

A spokesman for the IRS says the agency "is considering" changing the disclosure policy in view of its recent release of the prime issue list to people who asked for it under the Freedom of Information Act. But he says the current policy will remain in effect for the time being.

4/11/73

Some tips for the taxpayer threading his way through the audit process:

In an audit, the taxpayer must make a series of tactical decisions with no pat answers to guide him, an article in The Tax Adviser magazine warns. Its authors, Richard S. Helstein and Alan R. Bialeck of J. K. Lasser & Co., stress that pro's and con's must be weighed at every step. They urge the taxpayer to turn to expert advice, bringing in his attorney and his accountant. (Almost never, they say, should the accountant voluntarily turn over informal work papers to the IRS auditor. That could embarrass the client.)

If the revenue agent claims more tax is due, sometimes it's best to pay up and sue for refund. But it's "generally wise," the article says, to follow the IRS appeals route of a district conference and, if needed, an appellate conference. The authors urge that the taxpayer himself stay away from such conferences. Some taxpayers clash with IRS conferees. Others, surprised to find "a sympathetic ear" at IRS, talk too much, the authors say.

If the IRS conferee is flatly unresponsive, that may mean the Revenue Service is bent on a court fight. Care should be taken not to tip the taxpayer's legal hand. And "unfavorable factual information should never be volunteered," the two CPAs write.

If the appellate conference fails to produce a good settlement, the authors encourage the taxpayer to press on into court. That step, with little added expense, often results in a better settlement in pretrial stages.

2/21/73

◦⟨⟩◦

The Cohan rule helps a taxpayer who couldn't document his donation deductions.

Taxpayers who aren't as diligent about keeping records as they might be have long found some shelter in a precedent involving George M. Cohan, the composer. A tax tribunal had refused to allow Cohan any deduction at all for substantial business expenses because, it said, it was impossible to establish exactly how much he spent. Judge Learned Hand overruled that decision, however.

Complete certainty in such matters is usually impossible, Judge Hand said. If a court was satisfied that "something" was spent, it could make an estimate of what the minimum must have been. The court could of course "bear heavily" on a taxpayer whose "inexactitude is of his own making." In one recent Tax Court case, however, the taxpayer did pretty well under the Cohan rule. He had claimed $715 in charitable contributions, of which the IRS allowed only $15 for Christmas seals. The Tax Court restored an additional $625.

The Cohan rule doesn't apply to business deductions for travel, entertainment or gifts. Since 1962, the tax law has required detailed records of such outlays.

(Cohan v. Commissioner, U.S. Ct. of Appeals, 2nd Cir., 39F. 2d 540.)
4/28/71

Here's a good example of how the Cohan rule is applied.

Many years ago, the U.S. refused to allow George M. Cohan a tax deduction for some sizable business expenses because he couldn't document exactly how much he had spent. But a federal appeals court ruled that if a court is satisfied the taxpayer spent some amount in such a case, it can make an estimate and allow him to deduct that much. The ruling became known as the Cohan rule, and has helped many a taxpayer persuade a court to okay part of a contested deduction.

In a recently decided case, the IRS seized the inventory and fixtures of a bookstore and auctioned them off to pay the store owner's back taxes. The IRS set the man's deductible business loss resulting from the seizure at $1,400. But the owner asserted it was $48,388. The IRS said he had 3,500 books in his inventory. The owner said it was closer to 18,000. The Tax Court settled on 6,000 books and left it to the IRS to revise the deductible loss.

Among other things, the court noted the IRS man

who counted the books was testifying from memory several years after the seizure.

(Chandler v. Commissioner, 58 T.C. No. 86)
9/27/72

◖━━◗

In many cases, if a taxpayer can show he filed a return late because of a lawyer's advice, the IRS won't assess a penalty. But in one instance, a late-filing company's lawyer, in addition to giving it legal advice, also was a director and prepared its tax returns. Thus, the IRS said, his advice wasn't sufficiently objective to qualify as a legitimate excuse for filing late. But a district court has ruled otherwise. It found the lawyer thoroughly analyzed the point of law behind the late-filing. Besides, a ruling for the IRS would put at a disadvantage the thousands of small companies that can't afford to hire lawyers just for legal work, the court said.

(Burruss Land & Lumber Co. v.
U.S.A., U.S. Dist. Ct., West. Dist. Va., 1972)
9/27/72

◖━━◗

If you file late, there may still be a way to avoid a penalty.

There's no penalty if a taxpayer can show the lateness was due to "a reasonable cause." Sometimes he can do that by showing he relied on a professional's advice in a tax situation beyond a layman's ken. But this excuse has its limits: The tax adviser must be competent, and he must be sufficiently informed about the taxpayer's financial affairs.

Two closely held Oklahoma corporations pleaded that their accountant had advised them they needn't file for 1967 because they had no income that year. But they hadn't bothered to tell him that in 1967 they had settled back taxes for less than they owed. The concerns' failure to disclose "this critical fact" nullified their reliance on the accountant's advice, the Tax Court ruled. (The settlement was a "discharge from indebtedness" and thus taxable income.)

The court also questioned the accountant's advice. It noted he didn't know that even a corporation without taxable income may still be required to file a return.

(Yale Avenue Corp. v. Commissioner, 58 T.C. No. 103)
10/11/72

◖━▷◗

Attention embezzlers: Here's a way to avoid taxes if you're caught.

Get your employer to treat the missing money as a loan. Sign a pledge to repay him. And start payments immediately. If you do this the same year you steal the money, you apparently can exclude the haul from taxable income for that year under a Tax Court decision. Seven judges dissented; one called the ruling "simple hokey." The IRS hasn't decided yet whether to appeal. So, for now at least, the decision stands.

The case concerned a man who embezzled $22,740 through the first five months of the year. When caught, he admitted the crime and signed an affidavit commiting him to repay the money. He borrowed $1,000 from a bank as an initial installment and paid his employer $25 a week. The IRS tried to tax the amount taken, citing a Supreme Court decision that embezzled funds generally are taxable income. But the Tax Court ruled that even though the man took the money, it could be considered a loan in this case because the embezzler and his employer formally agreed to treat it as such and repayment was begun.

One dissenting judge said the ruling "rewards the thief with an unintended tax benefit." Another said the decision would cause "doubts, confusion and uncertainty."

(Buff v. Commissioner, 58 T.C. No. 21)
5/17/72

The IRS loses a tax dispute because it switched its ground in mid-argument.

If the IRS socks you for more taxes, it has to say why. That sounds simple enough, but in complicated tax litigation there's sometimes a temptation to slip from one issue to another. In one recent case, a Mississippi steel company bought a development company, but immediately sold off two chicken farms the subsidiary owned. It incurred a $227,257 loss. The IRS disputed the steel company's right to the deduction on the ground that it hadn't shown it acquired the subsidiary for a valid business purpose, rather than to take advantage of the loss.

At trial, lawyers for both sides agreed that was the only issue. But as things went along, the IRS abandoned that line of attack and seized on another possibility the taxpayer's lawyer alluded to. The steel concern couldn't take the deduction, the IRS then said, because the loss grew out of events before the merger.

The Tax Court refused to consider that argument, however. The IRS doesn't have to be consistent in what it argues, the court said, but it can't spring an issue it hasn't raised in its notice to the taxpayer or in its written pleadings.

(Mississippi Steel Corp. v. Commissioner, T.C. Memo. 1971-18.)
1/27/71

◦⟨⟩◦

IRS access to a taxpayer's books is subject to a mild restriction.

The restriction isn't onerous, but sometimes it will do. By law, the IRS is limited to one inspection a year of a taxpayer's account books unless it notifies the taxpayer in writing that additional inspection is necessary. The IRS must also be able to show it doesn't already have the information it seeks.

In one case, a U.S. district court decided the IRS

hadn't given notice. The IRS tried to get around it by contending that another look was part of a continuing investigation, but the court was unimpressed. IRS agents had spent at least 60 days working over the taxpayer's records. "The government has had its 'one inspection,' " the court declared.

(U.S.A. v. Schwartz, U.S. Dist. Ct., No. Dist. Ga., 1971)
11/17/71

It sounds strange but a taxpayer can't use the figures the IRS uses against him.

A taxpayer was in a dispute with the IRS over how much support he had provided for his child, but he was willing to accept the IRS estimate of what his former wife contributed. The taxpayer had to prove he had put up more than she had. Apparently, he found it easier to take the IRS figures than to document his own version of the former wife's share.

The Tax Court, however, wouldn't accept the IRS agent's report as "competent evidence" of the former wife's share. The IRS based its conclusions on the report, but the taxpayer couldn't rely on it. For one thing, the court said, the IRS never claimed its estimate was complete. Once it decided her share topped his, it might well have stopped counting, the court surmised.

(Blanco v. Commissioner, 56 T.C. No. 39.)
6/23/71

A lawyer's word counts, even if it's wrong, the IRS says.

If a taxpayer realizes a gain from "involuntary conversion" of property—say a building that cost him $100,000 burns and he gets a $120,000 insurance settlement—he doesn't have to pay taxes on the $20,000 gain if he invests the settlement in similar property within two years. If he wants to put off deciding whether to replace the building beyond the two years, he must apply to the IRS for an extension before the two years are up.

In one case, a taxpayer's attorney and accountant advised him there hadn't been any gain on an involuntary conversion. But some time after the two-year replacement period, the man discovered he had a taxable gain after all and applied for an extension of the authorized period. The IRS ruled that "good faith" advice from a reputable lawyer and accountant is "reasonable cause" for a late application if they are experienced in tax work and were given full details on the property conversion. The IRS uses the same reasoning in deciding whether to assess penalties for filing regular tax returns late.

1/26/72

◠

No peeking: When the IRS threw out almost all of the $16,000 in deductions a Chicago attorney claimed for business entertainment and gifts, he tried to subpoena the tax returns of 11 other law firms. The idea apparently was to show that such deductions were common, and his weren't out of line. But the Tax Court considered the other returns irrelevant. They wouldn't show that the lawyer kept the expense records required by law. Nor could the court assume that the deductions the others claimed were legitimate.

(Bane v. Commissioner, T.C. Memo. 1971-31.)
2/24/71

◠

Mixed motives are evident in the IRS's latest blast at tax-return preparers.

Commissioner Johnnie M. Walters promises the Revenue Service next year won't slow its attack on crooked return preparation firms. The current boxscore: 103 convictions, nine acquittals, 56 pending indictments, and 315 cases under investigation or "in prosecution." (Of course, that's relatively few of the thousands of return preparers around the country.)

But rooting out fraud isn't the IRS's only aim. By making broad threats about auditing professionally prepared returns, the IRS hopes to encourage more people to do their own returns instead of hiring a tax service—reputable or otherwise. Return preparation fees are deductible, and Walters frets that nearly 40 million individual returns, more than half the total, were prepared by tax services this year at an average fee of $16 per return, or a total of about $640 million.

The government "cannot afford" that kind of revenue drain, Walters says.

12/13/72

◦◁▷◦

A major IRS enforcement tactic is ruled illegal by a circuit appeals court.

As part of a continuing assault on fraudulent tax return preparers, IRS undercover agents pose as customers of "questionable" preparation firms. An agent takes "assumed" personal financial information to a preparer and asks that a return be filled out. If the return is handled improperly, the IRS immediately asks the firm to turn over all its clients' records, which then are examined for evidence of further wrongdoing. In one case, the IRS issued a summons to a South Carolina accounting firm for records, work papers, correspondence and other documents relating to all its customers for a three-year period. The firm claimed the action was an "unreasonable search and seizure," barred by the Fourth Amendment. A U.S. district court upheld the IRS.

The Fourth Circuit appeals court, however, reversed the district court. Calling the summons "unprecedented in breadth," the court said the "IRS isn't to be given unrestricted license to rummage through the office files of an accountant in hopes of perchance discovering information (establishing) increased tax liability for some as yet unidentified client." The law only allows the IRS to demand information on a particular taxpayer, the court held. It added, however, that the IRS is entitled to a list of the firm's clients.

The IRS hadn't any immediate comment on the ruling.

(U.S. v. Theodore, U.S. Ct. of Appeals, 4th Cir., 1973.)
6/6/73

0<>0

A tax return preparer is ordered to give a list of his clients to the IRS. The federal circuit appeals court in Chicago said an IRS request for the names didn't violate the preparer's Fourth Amendment protection against unreasonable search and seizure or his Fifth Amendment protection against self-incrimination.

6/27/73

0<>0

A quiet Senate move makes it a crime for tax preparers to misuse tax data.

Sen. Mathias (R., Md.) slipped through a little-noticed amendment to the tax bill. His measure makes it a misdemeanor for a tax-return preparer to disclose a client's tax data to someone else or use the data for any purpose other than filing his return. Doing so without the client's consent could mean a fine of up to $1,000 or a year in prison.

The amendment sailed through by voice vote. The Treasury registered no objection, and Sen. Long, Finance Committee chairman, backed the measure as "a forward step." Last tax season, reports cropped up of some tax preparers exploiting clients' confidential tax data for sales prospects or credit checks. There were calls for federal licensing of tax preparers, but the Treasury clearly wasn't eager to take on that task.

The Mathias amendment was approved by the House-Senate conference committee and signed into law.

11/17/71

Life Is Very Taxing
These Days (III)

Who could oppose mother, God, and country? You'd be surprised.

In California, William T. Bagley, chairman of the state assembly's revenue committee, became irked by incessant pleas for special tax consideration. He offered his own measure, which asked an exemption from sales tax for "white canes for the blind, Bibles, the United States flag and Mother's Day cards."

The bill was meant as a wry attempt at "legislative enlightment," Bagley says, but it isn't clear how much light is being shed. One legislator suggested a $10 tax credit for anyone who bought a flag. (It would be cheaper to give every Californian a flag, Bagley retorted.) Then a minister objected to favoritism for religion and asked equal treatment for Darwin. Even the blind complained that they don't need special treatment.

Nothing's been said about the Mother's Day cards. "Everybody's in favor of motherhood," says a Bagley aide. But no one's heard from the population people.

5/27/70

A Few Shelters and Loopholes

Tax shelters come into season, with a new hard look at investment merits.

Interest always quickens toward year-end as taxpayers get a firmer fix on what their income will be. But the stereotyped high-bracket fellow in desperate "need" of a loss is badly out of date. "A tax shelter is primarily an investment and secondarily a way to reduce taxes," says Medical Monetary Management Inc., New York. One reason for the new stress is a new top rate of 60% on "earned income" (50% next year). But also there's more recognition that good deals and bad deals come under the same tax law.

Tax-oriented investment ventures have proliferated, mainly in real estate, oil and gas and cattle. At least nine out of 10 aren't good investments, some analysts say. The arrangements are sometimes rife with conflicts of interest. For example, Bruce Trainor of Tax Shelter Advisory Service Inc. considers the cattle business basically sound but badly discredited by "a lot of horrendous deals."

Cattle-feeding is relatively simple, for instance. The investor has someone buy him steers, truck them to a feedlot and fatten them up. But extra markups on the cattle, steep trucking charges and inflated feed costs can put more fat on the price than on the animals.

9/1/71

o⟷o

If many shelters have pitfalls or snares, how do you find a decent one?

According to the man who screens such investments for a major bank's clients, the first test is the basic economics. In an apartment project, for example, will projected rents materialize? And how good is the management company?

Secondly, the banker says, how are the proceeds shared? He demands that an investment "program" come to the investor "at its basic price." The "packager" shouldn't get a fat markup just for putting it together. The promoter deserves to profit, the banker adds, but along with investors, not before them. No "big slice of the action" for the promoter until investors have recouped their original stake.

9/1/71

◦⟨⟩◦

Who should seek a tax shelter? Tax advisers almost always say an investor should be in at least the 50% federal tax bracket, but there's no hard-and-fast rule. One banker considers a client's "sophistication and temperament" a key factor. Investment adviser William E. Aaron looks to a client's "sleep test": No matter what the economic and tax benefits, an investor must be able to sleep nights without fretting over his money.

9/1/71

◦⟨⟩◦

Tax loopholes? Here's a tax reform provision that comes personally engraved.

One part of the Tax Reform Act was widely known as tailored to benefit Station WWL, the CBS affiliate in New Orleans. The station belongs to Loyola University, a Jesuit institution. Senate Finance Committee Chairman Long pushed through an exemption for WWL from a tax on what religious groups earn from businesses unrelated to their religious functions.

The exemption is subject to three qualifications,

which apparently only WWL can meet. A recent discovery makes that intent all too clear: In writing the law, the draftsman began each of the qualifying phrases so that together they spell out the station's call letters. Here's how it goes:

"Except . . . in the case of a trade or business . . .
"(A) Which consists of . . .
"(B) Which is carried on by . . .
"(C) Less than 10% of the net income . . ."

Capitol sources swear there was no coincidence.

5/27/70

0⟨⟩0

California is seen as "the great mother lode" for tax-shelter deals.

"People out here won't look at an investment unless it has a tax angle," one former New Yorker declares in amazement. A Los Angeles attorney finds currently "probably as great a demand for tax shelters as at any time." One reason, he says, is that California has "a lot of no-capital, high-income people"—for example, entertainers with high salaries and short working lives.

Currently, Californians find federally assisted housing a popular tax shelter. But there's growing interest in investment partnerships in agricultural commodities, in particular to develop vineyards. Such ventures offer an immediate deduction of much of an investor's costs. California agricultural interests are increasingly turning to public offerings for capital. One Los Angeles attorney is working on an offering to raise $16.5 million.

Many agricultural deals aren't registered with the SEC and thus can be sold only to California residents.

1/5/72

0⟨⟩0

Watch out for "conflicts of interest," drilling investors are warned.

People who invest in oil and gas drilling for tax benefits and income should be wary of "retained leases" and "functional allocation," says David Gracer, a New York oil investment counselor. When an oil company invites tax-shelter investors into a partnership in certain leases, but retains adjoining leases for itself, "shenanigans" may result, Gracer contends. He cautions that the company may use the investors' money to determine whether oil is in the area, then put most of its efforts into drilling on its own leases.

Under functional allocation, outside investors pay all currently tax-deductible costs (essentially drilling expenses) and the company pays capitalized costs (mainly for completing the well). This gives the outsider the maximum tax advantage. But it also gives him most of the risk, as many capitalized expenditures aren't made until it's determined whether the well will produce. The company can wait for sure producers and pass up moderately promising wells already drilled with the outside investors' money, Gracer says.

Gracer recommends investing in companies that agree to a "substantial, fixed investment," obliging them to pay part of the drilling costs if capital costs don't consume all their committed investment.

3/29/72

A tax shelter shelters less after a look by a circuit appeals court.

Most oil drilling ventures try to funnel as much investor money as possible into so-called "intangible" drilling expenses, which comprise most of the costs of drilling a well. That's because these expenses are deductible immediately, and thus can be readily used as a tax shelter. In a case decided recently by the Second Circuit appeals court, a group of investors was accused of inflating their deductions beyond legal limits by claiming higher intangible drilling expenses than had been incurred.

The group invested in a package deal covering interests in a lease and shares of the drilling expenses. They claimed the deductible expenses amounted to $205,000. But the IRS was unable to verify that from their records. So it made its own estimate of what an "ordinary prudent operator" would have paid, came up with $117,000, and rejected the remaining deductions.

Taking note of the "obvious incentive for padding the drilling costs," the court upheld the IRS.

(Bernuth v. Commissioner, U.S. Ct. of Appeals, 2nd Cir., 1972)
1/23/73

◦⊂⊃◦

A new twist in oil and gas drilling ventures is stirring controversy.

The twist is having an investor put up part of his investment in cash and borrow the rest. In other fields, such leverage is routine, but banks don't consider speculative oil leases the best collateral. One way the leveraged ventures try to get over the hurdle is by having the drilling company or a related concern hold the investor's note. This is done on a "non-recourse" basis, which limits the investor's liability to the cash he put up.

Supposedly these ventures yield a tax deduction two or three times an investor's actual cash stake. Many tax experts consider that too good to be true. If it were, a high-bracket investor would automatically make money—his tax savings would exceed his investment. "No matter how the government has to do it, they are going to get rid of these things. They are going to fight like hell," predicts David A. Gracer, a specialist in oil and gas investments. The law isn't clearcut, but many doubt the IRS will recognize the "loan" as a valid debt. If it doesn't stand up, neither do the deductions.

The leveraged ventures have blossomed in the last

year as private deals. The SEC says it's considering "problems" they would pose in public offerings.

9/1/71

⚬━⚬

The IRS drops another shoe on leveraged oil and gas drilling funds.

It's the second IRS attack this year on an asserted tax shelter feature of the funds. Presumably, a person had been allowed to put up part of his investment in cash, borrow the rest, and deduct two or three times his cash stake. Such arrangements are common in fields where collateral is secure. But in drilling, the only collateral often is a speculative oil lease and the loans are "non-recourse," limiting the investor's liability to his cash contribution.

Last March, the IRS ruled that non-recourse loans a drilling fund's general partner makes to the limited partners as part of their investment won't be considered loans at all but merely contributions to the fund's capital by the general partner. This wiped out part of the limited partner's tax advantage because it meant he couldn't deduct the "loan," only his cash outlay.

Now, the IRS has applied much the same reasoning to non-recourse loans to the limited partners from the contractor who drills the partnership's wells, or from other sources outside the partnership, if the "loans" are convertible into an equity interest in the drilling venture.

(Rev. Rul. 72-350)
7/19/72

⚬━⚬

The tax court hits a widely used tax shelter technique.

Many wealthy people put off tax planning until late in the year when they know how much income they want to shield from taxation. Thus, a number of tax shelter plans are designed to allow investments in sheltered industries like oil drilling or cattle-feeding shortly before year-end, and deduction of much of the investment from that year's taxable income. But the IRS over the past several months has shown increasing resistance to such deductions if the activity the money is invested in doesn't begin until the following year. Many year-end investments don't serve any business purpose other than manipulating tax liability, the IRS feels.

The Tax Court bolstered this tough line. It rejected an Iowa farmer's deduction for 1966 of a $20,731 payment he made for feed on Dec. 31 of that year. The farmer didn't actually possess or use the feed until 1967. Furthermore, the prepayment didn't benefit his business and thus couldn't be considered a business expense, the court said. Paying in advance didn't get him preferential treatment and wasn't necessary to assure the feed would be available when needed.

The payment was deductible for 1967, of course. But the Tax Court's stance makes the type of year-end planning that lends to such prepayments more difficult.

(Mann v. Commissioner, T.C. Memo. 1972-162.)
8/9/72

Timing that counts: A farmer figures a way to avoid income until he wants it.

Controlling when you receive income sometimes can save taxes. Postponing income from one year to the next, for instance, means a smaller tax bite if you know your total income, and thus your tax bill, will be smaller in the second year than in the first. But the IRS sometimes tries to thwart such timing if it feels it misrepresents when income was effectively received.

A Mississippi farmer agreed to rent part of his land to three planters for a year for $14,500. He asked that they put off paying him until the following year. But they harvested their crops by October of the first year and wanted to pay him then. He insisted on the delay, however, so they paid the money to a bank and instructed it to hold the cash for the farmer until January. It did so, and he reported the rent on his income tax return for the second year. The IRS said the arrangement was a sham and claimed the farmer in effect had taken control of the money when it was paid to the bank toward the end of the first year.

But the Tax Court okayed the deal. It said the farmer hadn't any legal control over the money until the bank released it to him.

(Millsaps v. Commissioner, T.C. Memo. 1973-146.)
7/18/73

◦━━◦

Year-end tax planning could be more difficult under a Tax Court ruling. An Idaho potato farmer had the option of receiving an $18,000 payment on Dec. 31 one year or Jan. 5 the next. He took it in January and reported it as income for that year. But the court said that, as he could have taken the money in December, he effectively received it then and had to pay taxes on it for the earlier year.

(Patterson v. Commissioner, T.C. Memo. 1973-39.)
3/28/73

◦━━◦

Two cheers for the DISC, Nixon's shot in the arm for export sales.

That's what businessmen are saying about the controversial new tax break for U.S. companies that sell overseas. The DISC, or Domestic International Sales Corporation, is intended as a selling arm for export sales of U.S. manufacturers. (A DISC can't make anything itself.) An indefinite deferral of U.S. taxes is granted on 50% of a DISC's income, provided that 95%

of its receipts and assets are export-related. The provisions take effect next year.

Business reaction ranges from wait-and-see (often from big concerns with extensive overseas operations) to open enthusiasm (smaller companies). "We're definitely going to take a very close look," says Koehring Co., a Milwaukee-based maker of construction equipment. A Detroit source considers the DISC mainly "for the small or medium company that doesn't have a full-blown export program now." Central National Bank, Cleveland, finds some belief that Congress watered down the DISC too much.

Not all big companies are dubious. "We're setting up a DISC just as speedily as we can," says Dow Chemical Co., the $2 billion, world-wide chemical concern.

12/22/71

◦◁▷◦

Slipped DISC: An expected penalty cuts the lustre of a key DISC provision.

Something called "producers loans" are central to the DISC idea. The law permits DISCs to use their tax-deferred profits to make such loans to U.S. manufacturers, presumably their parent companies. This is the vehicle by which U.S. concerns may put the DISC tax savings to work. (The money needn't be used exclusively for export purposes.)

The Senate, however, added a provision to insure that U.S. concerns didn't pour their tax savings into building plants abroad. If the parent company or related companies have a net increase in foreign assets beyond their 1971 holdings, the loans made from deferred DISC profits can be penalized: the profits may lose their tax deferral. The upshot of the complex provisions is that a DISC could be completely useless to a company with both exports and extensive manufacturing operations abroad.

The National Foreign Trade Council hopes the Treasury will be "as liberal as possible" in interpreting the penalty provisions. "Otherwise, it's going to be terrible," an official says.

12/22/71

ο⊂⟩οι

Will tomorrow ever come? The law provides a "deferral" from taxes for 50% of a DISC's income, but Prof. Stanely Surrey of Harvard contends the tax break is more generous than it seems. "In these days of high interest rates," he says, "a postponement of tax—a borrowing interest-free from the government—is the equivalent of exemption." For a profitable company, putting off a tax for 15 years is about the same as not paying it, he declares.

12/22/71

ο⊂⟩οι

Eureka? There's a hot new multipurpose tax shelter, a CPA firm advises.

It's called a tax-exempt bond. According to a Coopers & Lybrand study, the combination of high interest rates and "tax reform" curbs on other devices has resurrected municipals and "moved (them) to the fore as investment vehicles." The Lybrand firm is advising its clients to consider tax-exempts in many cases where trusts are now used. These include supporting elderly parents, providing for a child's future needs, paying alimony and giving to charity.

For a 70% bracket investor, it would take $250,000 in 8% corporate bonds or $400,000 in stock paying 5% to match the $6,000 after-tax net of $100,000 in 6% taxexempts. That's the nub of the matter, but Lybrand says tax-exempts may be worthwhile regardless of the bracket. And using tax-exempt income to support a relative, for example, avoids the legal costs of a trust, retains the relative as a dependent, and keeps control of the income-producing assets.

Inflation has favored equities over tax-exempts and other debt, but according to Lybrand's Jack Crestol, investors have found the stock market "is a two-way street."

5/13/70

◦◁▷◦

The maximum tax on earned income "isn't the bonanza we expected," a lawyer says.

It was intended to wean executives and professionals away from complicated tax gimmicks by providing a lower top rate on earned income—60% in 1971 and 50% scheduled for 1972 and after. But V. Henry Rothschild II, speaking at a New York State bar association session, said his clients have found the tax saving isn't that great unless the taxpayer earns $100,000 or more. The ordinary marginal rate doesn't exceed 50% until the taxpayer makes about $60,000 (assuming a joint return and some deductions).

Other provisions may curb the advantage of the new ceiling, Rothschild said. The ceiling doesn't apply to deferred compensation, but if an executive takes all his pay currently, that may push whatever "non-earned" income he has into a higher bracket. Through another provision, the taxpayer with both earned and non-earned income loses part of his deductions. And more than $30,000 in "tax preference" income cuts use of the new ceiling rate.

2/3/71

◦◁▷◦

The IRS gets a shearing when it tries to trim a Christmas-tree shelter.

Raising certain crops is a popular tax shelter because many costs are fully deductible as current business expenses while proceeds from the eventual sale of the crop are usually taxed at lower rates as a capital gain. But the Tax Court rebuffed an IRS effort to tighten the loophole. A taxpayer owned a stand of Scotch pine trees, which he raised for sale as Christmas trees. The IRS refused his sizable deduction for fees he paid to have the trees sheared.

If Scotch pines aren't sheared annually, they lose their neat conical shape and their sales appeal. The tax-men contended that shearing converted the pines to a new and more valuable use as Christmas trees and was therefore a nondeductible capital expenditure. But the Tax Court ruled that, in practice, Scotch pines have only one use, and their marketability is the outcome of natural growth. The shearing was maintenance.

(Kinley v. Commissioner, 51 T.C. No. 102.)
4/2/69

◁▷

The Treasury won't try to plug the new loophole in the minimum-tax provision.

"We have too many other higher priority items to make an issue over this," says one official. The change, passed in the closing days of the last Congress, modified the 10% minimum tax on certain "tax preference" income, and it will cost the Government about $100 million annually in revenues. The Treasury knew what was afoot, registered its opposition, but didn't—or couldn't —block the measure. It won't seek repeal this session.

Under the 1969 tax act, a 10% minimum tax has to be paid on "tax preference" income above $30,000, although that's offset by any Federal tax liabilities already paid. This was passed following publicity that 154 persons with gross incomes of $200,000 or more paid no Federal taxes in 1966. But the newly passed amendment allows a taxpayer to carry forward for seven years any Federal tax payment and thus offset the minimum tax on future tax-sheltered income.

1/13/71

One yacht owner went aground in the Tax Court when he claimed business losses.

In this case, the court refused to recognize a wealthy Californian's "losses" because he failed to show a bona fide intent to make money. The man owned two boats in turn, including a luxurious 70-footer originally built for a Spanish nobleman. He set up a business to produce coastal surveys and to charter his craft for pleasure or oceanographic work.

The Californian opened an office and bought some letterheads. He also spread the word that his boats were available for charter. He actually obtained some business—but not much. Of the 1,523 days he owned the nobleman's old yacht, it was used on business only 20 days. The court was more impressed by his personal use, which included living aboard for a year.

(McCormick v. Commissioner, T.C. Memo. 1969-261.)
3/25/70

❦

A scheme for financing movies and skirting taxes takes a beating in court.

The IRS chose to make an example of writer Paddy Chayefsky, but his technique is used widely in the movie business. Chayefsky formed a company called Carnegie Productions to make a picture for distribution by Columbia Pictures. Columbia loaned Chayefsky the $735,-401 the picture cost. Even though it hadn't put up any money, Chayefsky's company depreciated the film for tax purposes as if it owned it. That might have been okay had the deal been financed with a normal loan. But Chayefsky hadn't any liability to repay this loan. Columbia expected to get its money back from distribution profits.

No-liability loans, often called "non-recouse," also have been used by some oil drilling tax shelters to increase tax deductions for investors. But the IRS has declared such loans invalid in some oil deals, and it did so again in the Chayefsky case. The IRS reasoning: As Columbia Pictures bankrolled the film without expectation of direct repayment, it, rather than Chayefsky's company, owned the movie in effect. So the Chayefsky concern hadn't anything to depreciate. The Tax Court has just agreed that Columbia owned the completed film.

The IRS is expected to press challenges of similar film deals. But the Chayefsky decision may be appealed.

(Carnegie Productions v. Commissioner, 59 T.C. No. 63.)
2/14/73

❧

The tax haven business is booming, says an Economist Intelligence Unit survey.

The research group, associated with The Economist, says developing countries are vying to give investors the most favorable tax deals. Most are tailored to the needs of the multinational company. According to the survey, the "artificial" holding company has probably become "a moribund tax avoidance device," thanks largely to loophole-plugging efforts by U.S. and British tax authorities. But havens abound for truly multinational firms.

"Every tax avoider is a special case and needs a particular kind of tax haven," says the survey, which profiles the dozen most prominent havens. The essentials are political stability, accessibility, and a low tax, or none, on at least one important income source. But while safe havens exist for firms or funds, "few people should flee to a tax haven purely to avoid tax," the survey advises. Higher living costs often wipe out any tax saving.

2/3/71

Tax reform should begin with a look at "tax subsidies," a professor says.

Harvard Law's Stanley Surrey figures the federal government "spends" from $55 billion to $60 billion a year through tax breaks. That is, its collections are lower by that amount than they'd be without the tax preferences given to millions of individuals, companies and institutions. Many such preferences actually constitute indirect subsidies that ostensibly are intended to encourage social goals, Surrey points out in The Tax Adviser magazine. But he asserts a number of tax breaks produce "upside-down" results.

Among Surrey's examples: Deductibility of mortgage interest benefits rich people a lot but middle-income people relatively little. An interest deduction of $100 is worth $70 to a 70%-bracket taxpayer, but only $14 to a 14% individual. Thus, if the government intends to encourage people to own homes, it is giving a disproportionate amount of aid to the relatively few wealthy people. The impact of such tax "expenditures" should be analyzed as if they were direct payments, Surrey contends.

He says the 1971 tax act was "dominated" by tax subsidies and weakened the "fairness and structure" of the income tax.

4/12/72

◦━━◦

Ireland offers a tax haven for artists to draw creative people to the Emerald Isle.

"It is a way to improve the quality of life in Ireland with little or no cost," a tax official says. "Tax-wise, we are losing next to nothing." Since April, the Irish Republic has offered a tax exemption for original, creative work in writing, musical composition, sculpture, painting and similar arts. Both Irishmen and foreigners may qualify as long as they live in Ireland.

If an artist isn't already recognized, he may submit a sample of his work to the Revenue Commission to determine its merit. The commission can consult an outside panel of experts, and the law is to be interpreted liberally, taxmen say. The exemption applies only to an artist's income from artistic pursuits.

Mervyn Wall, secretary of the Irish Arts Council, expects about 600 artists will benefit the first year. Tax officials say they have inquiries from about 20 foreign artists. "I don't think Picasso is going to move up here," says Mr. Wall, however. "An elderly man isn't going to move to a damp climate."

11/26/69

◦———◦

Businesses may save on taxes by using appreciated property to pay dividends.

If a company has stock it bought for $10 but is currently worth $100, the firm can avoid taxes on the $90 appreciation by distributing the shares to stockholders as their dividend. In its newsletter, Coopers & Lybrand, the CPA firm, says many of its business clients are doing this. Large, publicly held companies often use stock they acquired many years ago. Smaller, closely held firms often turn the trick with appreciated real estate.

For an individual shareholder, the fair market value of the property is his dividend. But if the shareholder is a corporation, it gets a real tax break, Lybrand says. Its taxable dividend is limited to the issuing company's cost basis—the $10 in this example—and the normal corporate 85% dividend credit would apply to that $10. This would leave a mere $1.50 taxable on the stock dividend worth $100, Lybrand says.

Previously, businesses often used appreciated property to re-acquire their own shares, Lybrand says. But a provision of the Tax Reform Act restricted that.

3/17/71

The IRS proves no dummy: It nails the owner of a wax museum for its taxes.

Back in 1962, a Canadian set up a wax-figure display at the Seattle World's Fair and dubbed it Tussaud's Wax Museums Inc., although records in the case don't show any connection with Madame Tussaud's in London. He leased wax dummies from their manufacturers for $20,000, and the display grossed better than $330,000 for its tax year 1963. But the Canadian tried to chop its tax bill through an intricate sale-and-leaseback plan. That called for setting up a Netherlands Antilles corporation to buy the dummies and lease them to Tussaud's for a hefty royalty. That corporation would be owned by a Bahamas corporation, wholly owned by the Canadian.

But the Tax Court ruled that he "played a shell game" with Tussaud's assets. It held him responsible for $70,000 in taxes Tussaud's owed. (The court had already set aside the sale-and-leaseback as nonexistent and disallowed a $118,000 deduction for purported royalties.) The court said Tussaud's had in effect transferred property (about $183,000) to the Canadian for no economic consideration. This rendered Tussaud's insolvent and hindered or defrauded its creditor (the IRS).

Under Washington State law, this made the Canadian, as transferee, responsible for Tussaud's debts, the court said.

(Hicks v. Commissioner, T.C. Memo, 1970-267.)
10/7/70

o⟨⟩o

Nest egg: According to Warren Shine of S. D. Leidesdorf & Co., some Midwesterners find a tax-sheltered investment by buying pullets and going into the egg business. Like cattle-feeding, the venture offers a tax deferral: Most of the deductible expenses come one year, and the income later. But the chickens have an extra tax wrinkle. In addition to outlays for feed, the full costs of the chickens are immediately deductible the first year.

9/1/71

One investment adviser offers a rule of thumb for sizing up intricate tax-sheltered investments: If I sold it tomorrow, what would I get for it?

9/1/71

In his dissent from the University Hill Foundation decision, Judge Schnacke dusted off a quotation from Judge Learned Hand that bears repeating every so often. To wit: "Any one may so arrange his affairs that his taxes shall be as low as possible; he is not bound to choose that pattern which will best pay the Treasury; there is not even a patriotic duty to increase one's taxes."

6/9/71

You Can't Take It With You

The unitrust, a Tax Reform Act creation, draws interest as an inflation hedge.

The Tax Reform Act of 1969 laid down tough new rules for "split interest" trusts—typically, where someone leaves property in trust with the income to his wife or children for their lifetime, then everything to charity. To get favorable tax treatment, such a trust must be one of two types: An "annuity trust," which guarantees the income beneficiary a fixed sum every year, or a "unitrust," which must pay a fixed percentage (at least 5%) annually of the market value of the trust assets.

That new unitrust, according to one major accounting firm, offers "the best hedge against the vagaries of the economy." It gives the income beneficiary protection against inflation: As the trust assets appreciate, the annual payment goes up. Some attorneys say this makes the trust a good vehicle for investments in growth stocks. Of course, if the investments go awry, the beneficiary's income suffers.

The assets held by a unitrust must be valued annually. This can pose a problem if that's hard to do—as with the stock of a closely held corporation.

12/29/71

〜

The foreign trust ranks high on the agenda at tax conferences these days.

Paradoxically, the Tax Reform Act of 1969 was largely responsible for the current interest in foreign trusts (sometimes called Bermuda trusts, after a favor-

242

ite site for such matters.) The reform act extended to all U.S. trusts certain severe rules that already applied to foreign trusts. (The rules are meant to block a high-bracket taxpayer from letting income pile up in a trust, which likely pays taxes in a lower bracket.)

According to Julian S. Bush, a New York attorney, the reform act "placed the foreign trust, for the first time, squarely within the tax mainstream." The advantage is that foreign trusts are considered nonresident aliens and pay no U.S. income tax on capital gains. When the trust earnings are distributed to the beneficiary, he must pay a tax. In the meantime, however, the entire proceeds from capital sales are free to build up untaxed. "Obviously, such a trust is primarily designed for a growth-oriented investment policy," Bush writes in The Tax Adviser magazine.

Indeed it is. Depending on where it's located, a foreign trust may have to pay up to 30% in withholding taxes on ordinary income like dividends.

12/29/71

◇

It gets harder to leave something to charity and postpone the gift.

When the wealthy make out their wills, they often set up what's known as a "charitable remainder" trust. This permits family or other beneficiaries to enjoy income from the estate during their lifetimes. After that, the remainder (the principal) goes to charity. This saves estate taxes because the estate gets an immediate deduction based on what the charity will eventually get. The Tax Reform Act set up stiff new rules for such trusts, but thousands of wills and estates remain under the old law.

These "old law" estates have been thrown into confusion. There's no deduction if the value of the eventual gift to charity can't be "readily ascertained." The Third

Circuit appeals court shook things up when it overruled the Tax Court and denied a deduction. The appeals court said the trustee's powers were so broad that he could shortchange the charity in favor of the immediate beneficiaries. Thus the remainder couldn't be ascertained.

The Tax Court had ruled that the trustee's obligations under New York law were an adequate check on him, but the circuit court disagreed. Its decision has been appealed to the Supreme Court.

(Estate of Stewart v. Commissioner, U.S.
Ct. of Appeals, 3rd Cir., 1971.)
8/11/71

◦⟷◦

IRS semantics over what's "necessary" in a trust don't impress the Tax Court.

You can give someone up to $3,000 a year without being subject to gift tax, provided the gift is genuine and immediate, and not simply a future interest in property. Normally a gift in trust to a minor isn't considered a "future interest" if the money can be spent for the minor's benefit and the trust funds are turned over to him when he becomes 21.

The IRS, however, has challenged more than a score of trusts a wealthy Florida family set up for its children and grandchildren. Each trust agreement authorized the expenditure of income and principal "as may be necessary" for the education, comfort and support of the minor beneficiary. The IRS argued that the "may be necessary" phrase restricted the trustee's discretion to spend the funds and made the transfer a future interest.

The Tax Court disagreed. It found the wording "a gratuitous directive" that told the trustee to do what he had to do anyway: to decide what was necessary for the child's education, comfort and support.

(Heidrich et al. v. Commissioner, 55 T.C. No. 77)
2/17/71

A doctor's trust wasn't part of his estate, the Tax Court rules.

An Albany, N.Y., physician was planning to serve two months one summer on the hospital ship Hope. Two weeks before he was to leave, his wife died suddenly. Despite his grief, the doctor decided against changing his plans. But he did hurriedly set about rearranging his financial affairs before departing. He made out a new will and a day later converted some insurance policies he'd held for his wife's benefit into a trust for his two sons. Less than two years later, the doctor himself died unexpectedly.

The law says one's taxable estate includes interest he transfers to others "in contemplation of death" within three years of dying. Thus, the IRS tried to collect taxes on the trust the doctor created for his sons. The use of life insurance policies to form the trusts and drafting a new will at almost the same time the trust was created indicated thoughts of his own death were the doctor's main motive, said the IRS.

The Tax Court disagreed. It's unlikely the doctor expected to die that soon; he was healthy and only 48 when his wife passed on, the court said. It reasoned he took care of the will and trust within a day of each other because he was in a hurry to leave for the ship.

(Estate of Barton, T.C. Memo. 1972-30)
2/16/72

◦⟷◦

A court bars estate taxes on a payment settling a car crash death suit.

The estates of three people killed in a car-truck collision sued the owner of the truck that hit their car. The suit was settled before trial for $320,000. The IRS tried to tax the money, contending it was part of the accident victims' property. Generally, all property a person owns when he dies is subject to the estate tax.

A district court agreed with the IRS that under the laws of Connecticut, where the victims had lived, proceeds of a "wrongful" death suit are considered property owned at death, and therefore are taxable. But the Second Circuit Court of Appeals has reversed that stance and held that payments stemming from such a suit are property produced after death, not owned at death.

Thus they aren't part of the estate and aren't subject to estate taxes, the court said.

(Connecticut Bank & Trust Co. v. U.S.A.,
U.S. Ct. of Appeals, 2nd Cir. 1972)
8/16/72

◦⟨⟩►

Deduction of a lawyer's fee sparks a spirited debate among Tax Court judges.

It's well known that a fee paid to a lawyer or accountant to figure your tax and prepare your return is deductible. But there's a good deal of controversy over whether other tax-related legal services should be deductible. A doctor's attempt to deduct what he paid a lawyer to get his estate in order prompted an unusual array of comment from the Tax Court last week.

The doctor reasoned the fee was deductible because all the legal work on his estate related to taxes in one way or another. His lawyer testified he spent "a great deal of time" on the tax aspects of the arrangement. But the IRS said at most only a part of the fee went for tax work and, as the bill wasn't itemized, it was impossible to say how much. But the Tax Court majority figured 20% of the fee was tax-related and allowed deduction of that much. More than half the majority judges, however, had reservations about the ruling. Some of them said it's questionable whether any estate expenses should be deductible.

Four dissenting judges said the only deductible portion of the fee should be that which went for preparation of gift tax returns associated with a transfer of property (7% of the fee). In general, the expense of planning future tax liability (as distinct from figuring existing liability) shouldn't be deductible, they said.

(Merians v. Commissioner, 60 T.C. No. 23)
5/8/73

◦⊂⊃◦

A tax break at death will live on despite recent congressional action.

Congress passed a law ending the long-standing provision under which certain Treasury bonds are redeemable at par for payment of estate taxes even though their current market value is well below their face value. The new law abolishes this tax break for bonds issued after March 3, but more than $40 billion of such issues are already outstanding and aren't affected. Their maturities range as late as 1998, so the tax device will take time to fade away.

Of course as dates of maturity draw nearer, the dollar difference between par and market value declines, and so does the tax saving. It will also be reduced if bond prices continue their recent rise. But attorney A. L. Suwalsky Jr. of the Washington tax firm Silverstein & Mullens estimates that roughly $15 billion of the outstanding issues are selling low enough to consider buying with the estate tax saving in mind.

According to the attorney, the tax feature should remain attractive, at least to certain taxpayers, for another ten years.

3/24/71

◦⊂⊃◦

Savings bonds can unexpectedly be held subject to estate taxes.

More than 500 million Series E U.S. savings bonds are outstanding, and three-fourths of them are registered in the name of two co-owners. The Tax Court has sifted conflicting precedents and ruled that when a co-owner of such bonds died, the bonds fell in her taxable estate. The case involved a Texas woman who stashed $95,000 in bonds in a safe deposit box. The bonds were in her name and that of her daughter or one of two grandchildren. Many times the woman assured the co-owners the bonds were theirs.

The Tax Court nevertheless included the bonds in the woman's estate. Savings bonds are clearly marked nontransferable, the court pointed out. A co-owner couldn't give up ownership and rights to the bonds simply by handing over the bonds to the other co-owner. The transfer could only be done, the court said, by having the Treasury reregister the bonds in the donee's name.

Five concurring judges would have decided the case more narrowly. It was enough that the transfer wasn't complete under Texas law, they said.

(Estate of Elliott v. Commissioner, 57 T.C. No. 14)
11/3/71

◦━━◦

End-game: Estate planning sometimes borders on the macabre.

Take, for instance, one new provision among several estate tax changes enacted in 1970. It provides that any capital asset included in someone's estate may qualify as a long-term gain or loss when sold, even though not held by the estate for the usual six months. (The new rule is meant to speed up settlement of estate taxes.)

Of the 1970 changes, this provision "opens up the broadest new avenue for effective after-death estate planning," writes Bernard Barnett, a certified public accountant, in The Tax Adviser magazine. "An individual who has just been told he has cancer and will not live more than another three weeks can buy stock which his investment adviser recommends for a short-term investment." Thus the terminally ill taxpayer sets the stage for his estate to turn a quick profit at bargain long-term tax rates.

12/29/71

◦◁▷◦

A longer wait for that inheritance seems to be the trend.

Some lawyers who work with wills and trusts report an interesting shift by people who put money in trust for their children: The age they set for when the children are to get the money is rising noticeably. Currently it isn't uncommon for the funds to be held back until age 35, 40, or even 45, attorneys say. In fact, two special tax provisions—the Uniform Gifts to Minors Act and something called Section 2503(C)3 Trusts—are often ignored because they require that the money be handed over at age 21.

Today, feelings are pronounced that "by giving money to children, you're going to destroy them," John J. McDermott, a Manhattan attorney, relates. He calls this concern "the biggest bugaboo" in estate planning. One of his wealthy clients passed up $13,000 or $14,000 in gift tax savings, rather than give money to his grandchildren before he considered them ready for it.

"It just wasn't worth it to him to do it at the expense of the kids," the attorney relates.

12/29/71

◦◁▷◦

Two more cases lay to rest a particularly strained piece of IRS reasoning.

In one instance, a U.S. appeals court granted a widow's estate a deduction for a $68,000 coin collection left to the State of Israel. In another, the U.S. Court of Claims upheld a similar deduction for $275,000 left to a Bavarian town to build an old people's home. The IRS had opposed both deductions on the ground that if the law expressly permits an action, it bars a similar act if not explicitly allowed.

The law gives a deduction for bequests to a U.S. or state governmental body for a public purpose. Foreign governments aren't mentioned, so the IRS contends it follows that bequests to them aren't deductible. The IRS has stuck to that logic, even though another part of the law allows a deduction for bequests to trustees for a charitable purpose, without mention of any geographic limit. But the courts decided the coin collection and the old people's home were charitable purposes, and Israel and the Bavarian town could qualify as trustees.

"At best, the (IRS) argument is a highly technical contention," the Court of Claims said.

(Kaplun v. U.S.A., U.S. Ct. of Appeals, 2nd Cir., 1971, and National Savings & Trust Co. v. U.S.A., U.S. Ct. of Claims, 1971.)
2/24/71

ᗢ

The family farm survives an onslaught by the Internal Revenue Service.

Any time an elderly taxpayer makes a substantial gift, the IRS may challenge it as a subterfuge to avoid estate taxes. In one recent case, an elderly couple deeded over their 372-acre Texas farm to their four children and then leased it back under a sharecropping arrangement. Not long thereafter, health and financial problems cropped up, and the rent wasn't paid for four years. When the father died, his estate made up the payments.

The IRS insisted the gift wasn't valid because the parents kept an interest in the property. It also regarded the alleged "rent" as mere gifts to the children. But the Tax Court found nothing to suggest the lease was a sham. The parents were obligated to pay "a fair, customary rental" to the children, the court said, and "he who receives the rent in fact enjoys the property."

True, the parents missed some payments, but that couldn't be foreseen, and it didn't mean they kept a right to the farm's income.

The father owed the back rent when he died, the court said, so the estate was clearly entitled to a deduction for paying it.

(Estate of Barlow v. Commissioner, 55 T.C. No. 67.)
2/3/71

◦⟨⟩◦

The Tax Court decided both an estate and the IRS were off base in valuing land.

Fixing a fair value on real estate for tax purposes has long been a thorny process, particularly when prices are rising rapidly. Usually the value is based on sales of comparable land in an area but even so, taxpayers and the IRS often wind up sharply at odds. In a recent estate case, an estate valued 170 acres of land in northern Delaware at $586 an acre, although property sales in the area around that time ranged from $1,000 to $2,600 an acre. The IRS said the estate land was worth $3,000 an acre. Subsequently, the estate raised its valuation to $1,000 an acre while the IRS came down to $2,000.

The Tax Court decided the value was $1,400 an acre after taking into account such things as the relation of sales of nearby land to the date of valuing the estate, whether such sales were for cash or on credit, the residential desirability of the land compared with nearby parcels and the topography of the various parcels.

The court rejected the IRS estimate because it was based on land that wasn't comparable and on mere offers to sell rather than actual prices. The estate's estimate wasn't accepted because it was based simply on the lowest sales price for land in the area.

(Estate of Mitchell v. Commissioner, T.C. Memo. 1968-297.)
1/15/69

A Dillon family trust is upheld in a complicated transaction.

In 1923, Mrs. Clarence Dillon set up a trust in which she kept a life interest in its income. Its corpus was to go to her husband if he survived her and to their children if he did not. In 1932, Mrs. Dillon created another trust to benefit their children, C. Douglas Dillon, later to become Secretary of the Treasury, and his sister.

In 1958, Clarence Dillon (acting through still another trust) turned over 72% of his interest in the 1923 trust to the 1932 trust. For this, the 1932 trust paid him $1.2 million.

Mrs. Dillon died in November 1961. In the same month, the 1932 trust began to write off what it had paid Clarence Dillon for his life interest in the earlier trust. In 1962, it sought to deduct $198,000 from taxable trust income. The IRS denied $22,000 of the deduction, however. Part of the acquired life interest consisted of tax-exempt bonds, it said, and the cost of acquiring tax-exempt income shouldn't be deductible, it claimed. But the Tax Court ruled that acquiring a life estate wasn't subject to such a limit.

7/8/69

◦━━▷◦

How much should you have before it becomes worthwhile to fiddle with trusts and other sophisticated estate-planning techniques? Lawyers sometimes cite $250,000 or thereabouts as a threshold figure. They also say, however, that many executives are worth more than they realize at first blush. With assets like group life insurance, stock options, and lump-sum payment of pension benefits, it isn't hard for an executive to be worth $400,000, they say.

12/29/71

A du Pont dies and Delaware balances its budget. Maybe that old saw was once true, but Delaware's Gov. Russell Peterson went out of his way to note that the state's share of the late Henry B. du Pont's estate won't alter its financial plight very much. (Insiders say the state will reap a mere $2 million or so when the estate is finally settled.) The governor has emergency tax measures pending.

8/25/71

Confused: The sheer complexity of the new rules on "split interest" trusts has caused some taxpayers to throw up their hands, according to Hewitt Conway, a New York attorney. "Where a guy might have said, all the income to my wife, remainder to Harvard," Conway explains, "today he's liable to say, oh, the hell with it. He leaves it all to his wife and gives Harvard $5,000, and Harvard never knows what it has missed."

12/29/71

Death and taxes: A person's taxable estate includes interests he transfers to others "in contemplation of death" within three years of dying, the law says. Thus, two $40,000 gifts an Oklahoma invalid gave her son and daughter two years before she died were taxed as part of her estate. But a district court disagrees. It held the daughter's gift—an interest in the parent's home—was mainly an inducement to move in and take care of her mother. The son got $40,000 because of a family tradition of giving the children equal gifts. Both gifts were motivated by "purposes associated with life rather than death," the court said.

(Stewart v. U.S., U.S. Dist. Ct., West. Dist. Okla., 1970.)
7/29/70

No place like home: An elderly Kansas City woman transferred title on her house to her three children seven years before she died. They began paying real estate taxes and insurance premiums on the place. But the mother continued living there until her death, paying no rent. The Tax Court ruled the house was part of her estate, even though she'd given it away, because there had been an "implied understanding" she would retain actual possession.

(Estate of Kerdloff, 57 T.C. No. 66)
3/1/72

Never say die: An "estate tax closing letter" from the IRS usually indicates it has set the estate's final tax liability. But not necessarily, says the Tax Court. It okayed reopening a recent case, after the "closing letter" was sent, when the IRS decided some stock in an estate was worth more than the taxpayer had claimed. For an estate tax return to be finally closed, the court said, the IRS and taxpayer must execute a formal agreement.

(Estate of Meyer v. Commissioner, 58 T.C. No. 5)
5/3/72

A mother gave her son some stock. He sold it and bought other stock. Two years later, she died, and her gift had to be valued as part of her estate. Question: is the value what the original stock would have been worth at the time of her death? Or is it the value of the replacement stock her son bought (a considerably higher figure in this case)? The IRS ruled the value is what the original shares would have been worth when the mother died.

(Rev. Rul. 72-282)
6/14/72

She bought a mink coat, played bridge, shopped for

groceries, went to the theater and did a lot of other things a person 89 years old usually doesn't do. So a U.S. district court has decided that $406,564 an Ohio woman gave her relatives a year before she died at 90 wasn't given "in contemplation of death" and thus wasn't taxable as part of her estate.

(Skall v. U.S.A., U.S. Dist. Ct., No. Dist. Ohio, 1972)
2/14/73

Planning for death is often cloaked in euphemisms. One frequent turn of phrase used by lawyers to their client is "when the will becomes effective"—rather than, bluntly, "when you die."

12/29/71

Sometimes people get in trouble when they sally forth with their own estate planning. For instance, it's not unheard of for someone to put all his property in the name of his wife. "And then he meets Sara Stewardess, and the trouble starts," attorney John J. McDermott chuckles.

12/27/71

Law in Flux on Life Insurance

They hardly expected to die in a hotel fire, so their insurance wasn't taxable.

That essentially is what a federal district court concluded in the case of a young Georgia couple, Jerry and Gail Kahn. They each joined an accidental death insurance plan available through Jerry's company. On the advice of an insurance broker, they took out the policies in each others' names; that is, Jerry owned Gail's policy; Gail owned Jerry's. Barely a year after the insurance took effect, the Kahns died in a hotel fire in Jacksonville, Fla.

The Justice Department contended Jerry and Gail had given their policies to each other "in contemplation of death." Under the law, if a person gives away an asset because he expects to die fairly soon, the asset is taxable as part of his estate. Barring proof to the contrary, the government applies that rule to anything given within three years of death. But the court refused to believe that expectation of early death motivated the Kahns to give the insurance to each other. Jerry and Gail both were under 30 and healthy.

The court didn't indicate how it would have ruled if the government had contended that because the Kahns owned each others' policies, Jerry's insurance was taxable as part of Gail's estate and vice versa.

(Kahn v. U.S.A., U.S. Dist. Ct., No. Dist. Ga., 1972.)
11/8/72

An Appeals Court excludes some life insurance proceeds from estate taxes.

The Fifth Circuit Court, the first appellate court to rule on the issue, has reversed a district court and ruled against the IRS. The case involved two daughters who in 1953 each took out a $10,000 policy on their father's life. He and their mother paid the premiums, however, until his death eight years later. The IRS then claimed that the portion of the insurance proceeds attributable to premiums he paid in the last three years of his life should be included in his taxable estate as a transfer in contemplation of death.

The circuit court disagreed. It was unmoved by the IRS argument that the father had given his daughters insurance benefits, "a bundle of rights." The daughters already owned these rights, the court said, because they had taken out the policies. They could have paid the premiums as well, and their father's gift was simply the cash amount of the premiums he paid. An IRS ruling otherwise is "without support," the court said.

Because of a technicality, the court didn't rule on whether the premiums paid in the last three years became part of the estate. But the plaintiffs conceded they would have been.

(First National Bank of Midland v. U.S.A., U.S. Ct. of Appeals,
5th Cir., 1970.)
11/8/70

◦⟨⟩◦

Taxing Insurance: The IRS wins an important skirmish in a long battle.

If you give away an asset within three years before you die, your estate generally has to pay taxes on the asset as if you still owned it at death. When insurance is involved, applying this rule can get complicated. A wealthy person commonly will try to keep proceeds of insurance policies out of his estate by having someone else, say his wife or child, buy the policy, so the insured

person himself doesn't own it. But often the insured
still will pay the premiums himself. When all this happens within three years of death, thus bringing estate
taxation of transferred assets into play, how much is
taxable? There isn't much dispute that the premiums
are. But courts have struggled to different conclusions
on whether the proceeds of the policy are, too.

The Sixth Circuit appeals court ruled in one case
that the full proceeds of a policy are taxable, even
though the insured never technically owned the policy.
A Michigan man had a trust buy a $100,000 policy on
his life; the proceeds were payable to his children. He
paid the initial premium, $9,600, and died six months
later. His estate contended the only asset he gave away
was the premium payment; the kids' trust owned the
policy all along.

A district court agreed, but the Sixth Circuit in a
two-to-one decision says the $100,000 also is part of the
estate. In effect, the court held, the man wasn't giving
away just the premiums but also the insurance protection the premiums bought.

(Detroit Bank & Trust Co. v. U.S.A., U.S. Ct. of Appeals,
6th Cir., 1972.)
9/20/72

◦⟨⟩◦

Another court rules insurance proceeds taxable in
the insured's estate.

If you give away something within the three years
before your death, that's presumed a transfer "in contemplation of death" and included in your taxable estate. A long-standing controversy has been waged over
insurance proceeds where the insured person pays the
premiums but has someone else, usually his wife or children, actually take out the policy. The Sixth Circuit appeals court ruled the entire proceeds taxable, but previously other courts had included only the premiums.

Now a U.S. district court in Oregon has also included the entire proceeds in the taxable estate. In this case, the insured paid the premiums but had his wife sign policy applications. In the court's view, a "transfer" isn't limited to a direct passing of property. It also covers anything that the deceased paid for with the idea that, upon his death, it would pass to someone else.

Actually the man died in an auto accident. But the court said that lawyers for his estate failed to show the transfer wasn't nevertheless in contemplation of death.

(First National Bank of Oregon v. U.S.A.,
U.S. Dist. Ct., Oregon Dist., 1972.)
10/11/72

◦⟨⟩◦

An estate bests the IRS in a complex tussle over insurance policies.

Hector Skifter gave his wife all his interests in nine insurance policies on his life. She died several months later, and her will directed that her estate be placed in trust. Hector was named trustee and given broad powers to control the trust as he saw fit. The estate, of course, included the nine insurance policies.

Hector eventually died, thus bringing his own estate into question. A person's estate generally includes insurance policies over which he exercises control. As Hector had broad power over his wife's estate, and it included insurance policies, the IRS contended those policies actually were part of his estate for tax purposes. But a federal appeals court has ruled otherwise.

It said Hector's control over his wife's trust didn't include power personally to benefit economically from the policies. That generally was what the framers of the law had in mind when they included insurance policies in estates, the court ruled.

(Estate of Skifter v. Commissioner, U.S. Ct. of Appeals,
2nd Cir., 1972.)
11/1/72

A tangled question involving life insurance and estates is settled by a court.

Life insurance proceeds are taxable as part of an estate if the deceased owned the policy or exercised any control over it when he died. Simple as that principle seems, it frequently is difficult to apply, because what constitutes control over a policy can mean different things to different people.

A Richmond, Va., lawyer owned several life insurance policies during his lifetime. But he attached formal statements to three of the policies that had the effect of transferring all control over them to the beneficiaries—his wife and son. However, he also, jointly with his wife and son, designated the policies as collateral security for any loans which he, his wife or son might take out from a particular Richmond bank. The IRS contended that as the lawyer himself could have used the policies as collateral, he hadn't relinquished total control over them; thus, the tax agency ruled, their proceeds should be included in his taxable estate.

But the Tax Court decided the lawyer's using the policies as collateral didn't amount to control over them. He had transferred ownership to his wife and son. So presumably he would have needed their permission to use the policies as collateral. Therefore the policies' proceeds don't have to be included in the estate, the court said.

(Estate of Goodwyn v. Commissioner, T.C. Memo. 1973-153)
8/29/73

◦━━◦

The IRS drops a restriction on giving away group life insurance.

It has got much easier in recent years for a person to give away his interest in a group life insurance policy, thus keeping the proceeds out of his taxable estate. But it's essential to give up all control over the policy, including the right to convert it from group to individual coverage. If this right isn't relinquished, the IRS has reasoned, the insured retains some control because he has the power to terminate his coverage by quitting his job at the company where the policy is in effect.

Until recently, the IRS has held that in states where conversion to individual coverage isn't explicitly allowed, the policy can't be given away for tax purposes because of this job-quitting power to cut off the policy that the insured automatically retains. But the Revenue Service has reversed itself and ruled that this power alone doesn't constitute control over the policy if all other controls (such as the right to name beneficiaries) are given up.

(Rev. Rul. 72-307)
6/28/72

◦⟨⟩⟩

A group life insurance policy can be given away, a U.S. court rules.

An insured man can often protect the proceeds of his life insurance from estate taxes by giving the policy to his wife or having her buy the insurance initially. This is frequent practice with policies individuals buy. Now the U.S. Court of Claims has upheld the transfer of a policy under a group life contract paid for by the insured's employer. The case involved the president and half-owner of a New York corporation who irrevocably assigned his $200,000 policy to his wife, also the beneficiary.

When the insured died, the IRS contested the transfer on the ground that he had kept "incidents of ownership," or control over the policy. For one thing, the IRS claimed, he could end his group coverage by quitting the company. But the court countered that the wife had acquired the usual right to convert group coverage into ordinary life. The tax men also argued the husband had control because by acting jointly with the other half-owner, he could cancel the company's group contract.

"A close question," the court said. But stock ownership wasn't enough. Proof was needed that an insured person held enough fellow holders in sway that he could end the contract at will. And this wasn't proved.

(Landorf v. U.S., U.S. Ct. of Claims, 1969.)
3/26/69

Another court decision upholds the assignment of group life insurance.

It's common for a person to exclude the proceeds of an individual life insurance policy from his taxable estate by assigning, or giving, the policy to someone else. The key is giving away "all the incidents of ownership." Now the practice is becoming more frequent with group life coverage, often paid for by an employer. The Tax Court recently upheld the transfer of two policies totaling $125,000 that a California man signed over to his wife.

One issue simply concerned the validity of policy endorsements permitting assignment. But the IRS also argued that California law bars giving away the right to convert the coverage to an individual policy. The Tax Court, however, found that right "just as much subject to assignment . . . as any other right."

The Revenue Service also objected that assignment could lead to a beneficiary who would suffer no financial loss if the insured died, and thus the policy would be void. Perhaps, the court said, but the possibility shouldn't prevent assignment.

(Estate of Gorby v. Commissioner, 53 T.C. No. 12.)
11/5/69

An oversight makes life insurance proceeds taxable as part of an estate.

Avoiding taxation when a policy pays off is tricky. The law says the proceeds are to be included in the taxable estate if the insured person had any control over the policy. Did he personally own it? Could he change the beneficiary or cancel the policy? Could he pledge it for a loan? If the answer to any such question is yes, the proceeds are taxable. So the idea is to transfer all such controls to someone else before you die.

When James H. Lumpkin Jr. died, he was participating in a group insurance plan at the company where he worked. Lumpkin had none of the normal controls over the policy. But he could vary the pace at which its proceeds would be paid out. The Tax Court earlier said that one control wasn't significant enough to make the proceeds part of the estate. But a U.S. appeals court disagrees. And it adds that Lumpkin could have avoided the problem if he had given the payout control to someone else.

(Estate of Lumpkin v. Commissioner, U.S. Ct. of Appeals,
5th Cir., 1973.)
3/28/73

∞

Interest grows in giving away group life insurance to avoid estate taxes.

This year some 15 states have passed laws authorizing the giving away, or assignment, of group life insurance policies. Others are considering such legislation. For years, insured persons have sheltered the proceeds of individual life policies from estate taxes by irrevocably assigning to someone else all the "incidents of ownership." These include the right to cancel the policy, borrow against it, or change the beneficiary.

Last year the IRS ruled that group coverage could also be assigned, where state laws and the group contract permit. Some insurance companies and business corporations report that the practice is growing. They note, however, that usually it's only worthwhile for those who have substantial coverage or more-than-moderate estates. (It's vital to give up the right to convert the policy to individual coverage. Otherwise, the insured could cancel his insurance by quitting his job.)

"It's a pretty serious step," one insurance official warns. "If you give your wife a $50,000 policy, and you happen to change wives, you're in trouble. The new wife gets nothing, you know."

7/9/69

○⊂⟩○

Two more states allow employes to "give away" their group life insurance.

Iowa and Missouri bring the total to 39 states authorizing the tax gambit, Commerce Clearing House Inc. reports. The idea is to allow an insured person to keep the proceeds of his policy out of his taxable estate by irrevocably assigning the policy to someone else. This means giving away all "incidents of ownership," such as the right to name the beneficiary, cancel the policy, or convert group coverage to an individual policy.

Three years ago, the IRS ruled that group policies could be assigned. But it has taken the position that state law (and the group contract) must explicitly permit the move. This set off a flurry of law-making that brought the number of states with such statutes from two or three to its current total. Typically, the new laws were framed to have retroactive effect.

Policyholders are assigning group policies "with some frequency," Prudential Insurance says, but "it isn't a land-office business." Not everyone's estate is large enough to justify the move.

7/14/71

Of Interest and Debts

A father, with his son's help, pulls off a maneuver to avoid taxes.

The father settled a huge back-tax claim with the IRS. A sizable portion of the amount he had to pay was interest that had accrued on the taxes owed. The interest, of course, was deductible the year he paid it. But he didn't have enough income then to take full advantage of the deduction. Solution: the father "sold" $122,820 in stock dividends he expected to receive over coming years to his son. The son paid $115,000 cash for the right to receive the anticipated dividends. That gave his father a big influx of income in the year when the large interest deduction was available and enabled him to utilize it fully.

But the IRS said the transaction wasn't valid. It said the son didn't assume any real risk in the deal. (Taking risk of ownership usually is considered an essential element of a valid sale.) The Tax Court agreed and called the payment to the father a "loan masquerading as a sale." But the Sixth Circuit appeals court has just okayed the deal by ruling that the sale of future dividends was legitimate.

The son paid a fair price and did risk the possibility that the stock wouldn't continue to pay dividends, the court said.

(Estate of Stranahan v. Commissioner,
U.S. Ct. of Appeals, 6th Cir., 1973)
2/14/73

265

The IRS rules on when bank credit card charges are deductible as interest.

Not only did the ruling clear the way for taxpayers to deduct the full "finance charges" on bank cards like Master Charge or BankAmericard. The IRS also said "this same general rule" would apply to charge or credit customers of department stores. If it can be shown that no part of the "finance charge" is a carrying charge or other fee, then the entire charge is for the use of money and thus fully deductible as interest. (Otherwise a taxpayer can assume only 6%.)

Strictly speaking, it may be tough for a taxpayer to prove such finance charges are solely interest, but it's unlikely that the IRS will challenge such a conclusion. One important factor, the ruling indicates, is that the bank charges participating merchants a percentage of their credit card sales, and these fees are meant to cover all costs of the credit plan except interest. Thus the cardholder's charges must be interest.

The IRS also cites precedent that if borrower and lender agree "at arm's length in the loan contract" as to what portion of a charge is interest, that agreement "ordinarily" will be accepted for tax purposes.

(Rev. Ruling 71-98.)
2/3/71

◦⟺◦

Here's a good example of how taxpayers get confused and tax lawyers get rich.

The U.S. Tax Court is supposed to interpret the tax laws uniformly nationwide. Usually the only exceptions to this policy are when the court is forced to take inconsistent positions in different regions of the country because of conflicts among appeals courts in various judicial circuits. But in one case, the Tax Court issued a ruling inconsistent with a previous decision, even though it wasn't forced by an appeals court to do so. The result:

It's anybody's guess how the Tax Court will rule the next time the issue arises.

The question concerns interest on money a brokerage firm borrows to finance its business in tax-exempt securities. Generally such interest isn't deductible. But in a case five years ago the Tax Court permitted Bache & Co. to deduct all interest on its total borrowings. The court found that though the firm did some business in tax-exempt bonds, it wasn't possible to tie any of its borrowing directly to those securities. The Second Circuit reversed the Tax Court and denied the firm a deduction for part of its interest.

Normally in such a case the Tax Court would stick with its own original view in circuits other than the Second. However, in a ruling involving facts identical to those in the Bache matter (but in a different circuit which hasn't ruled on the question), the Tax Court reversed its original position and disallowed part of a Nashville firm's interest deduction.

The court didn't give a specific reason for its action. Six judges dissented, saying the ruling can only confuse taxpayers and the IRS.

(Bradford v. Commissioner, 60 T.C. No. 30)
6/13/73

⊶⊷

Nice try: A rich doctor trips on a plan to get a little richer.

His taxable income rose from $3,156 his last year in the Air Force to $204,758 four years later. Naturally he wanted to make some investments. On his bank's advice, he put part of his money into tax-exempt municipal bonds. At about the same time he invested in the bonds, he took out a mortgage loan on his house. Most types of interest are deductible, so he deducted the interest he paid on the loan.

The IRS challenged the deduction after a close look at all the doctor's finances. One of the few types of in-

terest that isn't deductible is interest on money borrowed to finance the purchase of tax-exempt bonds. The
IRS claimed financing the bond purchases was the
main reason the doctor took out the mortgage loan. The
doctor, of course, tried to prove he had other reasons. He
contended he had borrowed the money to buy some
X-ray equipment and pay taxes. He paid for the bonds,
he said, out of his earnings.

But the Tax Court ruled the man hadn't adequately disproved the IRS's findings, which in a civil
tax case are presumed correct unless the taxpayer
shows otherwise. So the doctor couldn't deduct the interest on the mortgage loan, and as a result his tax bill
rose.

(Mariorenzi v. Commissioner, T.C. Memo. 1973-141)
7/18/73

⚬━━◗

An Irish Sweepstakes winner has a tax dodge
thrown out as a sham.

In 1962, when a California couple won $140,000 in
the sweeps, they looked around for shelter from the
huge tax bite. They decided to buy a $168,000 apart-
ment building, for which the owner asked $63,000 cash
and assumption of a mortgage. The couple's accountant
worked out a deal under which the seller kept the mortgage, but the couple paid him monthly instalments
pegged at $3 more than the mortgage payments. This
arrangement called for only $19,000 down—plus $44,000
as prepayment of five years' "interest" on the "debt."

The seller didn't care what the sum was called, as
long as he got his $63,000 in cash. But the IRS balked
when the couple deducted the $44,000 as interest. The
Tax Court recently agreed. "No genuine debt was created to support the so-called 'interest' prepayment," it
said. "The CPA merely juggled the figures."

But the court did permit the couple to deduct the

$4,511 to the accountant for his tax advice and services.

(Collins v. Commissioner, 54 T.C. No. 163.)
9/9/70

◦⊂⊃◦

Another winner in the Irish Sweepstakes goes through the Tax Court wringer.

The Court had set aside an apartment deal entered into by one sweeps winner. The court called it a "sham." Now the court has ruled on the business arrangements of another man who won $140,000 in the sweepstakes, and he lost on more points than he won. The man borrowed money to buy $210,000 in four-year Treasury notes, but the court disallowed deduction of $32,000 interest paid in advance. Interest isn't deductible on debts contracted solely to obtain a deduction, and the court found that was his sole intent.

The sweepstakes winner also bought 414 steers for fattening and resale. He claimed a $27,000 deduction for advance payments for feed, management services and interest on a mortgage. The court conceded that "the possibility of profit" was present, but it set aside $17,000 of the deduction. It said the sum wasn't clearly for a nonrefundable purchase of feed.

The court allowed him to deduct $15,000 paid New York State in income taxes, even though his actual tax bill came to $6,000. (The later refund was taxable income.) The $15,000 was what he would have owed, had none of his tax shelters held up.

(Estate of Cohen v. Commissioner, T.C. Memo. 1970-272.)
10/7/70

◦⊂⊃◦

The tuition burden may be eased slightly by a new IRS ruling. It concerned a student who borrowed money under a student loan program to pay tuition, fees and other expenses. His father was required to co-sign the note, and as interest payments fell due, it was in fact the old man who paid them. Under these circumstances, the father was entitled to deduct the interest because co-signing the note made him liable for the debt.

(Rev. Ruling 71-179.)
1/21/71

〜

A New Yorker claimed he made frequent gifts to family members by crediting accounts in their names carried by his firms as unsecured loans. He charged himself 10% interest on the unpaid sums, which was similarly credited. But the Tax Court denied his deductions of the interest "payments." Virtually no cash changed hands, it noted, and mere bookkeeping entries weren't actual gifts. Thus, no debts existed on which interest was due.

(Todd v. Commissioner, 51 T.C. No. 100.)
3/26/69

If You Live Abroad

An artist earns his pay, just as a con man or a tax lawyer does, a court says.

Mark Tobey is a U.S. citizen but does most of his world-renowned painting in Basel, Switzerland, where he lives most of the time. Americans who reside abroad generally don't have to pay U.S. taxes on the first $20,-000 they earn each year. But when Tobey tried to use that tax break, the IRS said he didn't really "earn" his income as the law defines "earning." The IRS claimed the only income that qualifies is compensation for "personal services." It reasoned that the people who buy Tobey's paintings don't receive any service from him; they merely buy a product.

The Tax Court saw things differently, however. It said Congress intended "personal services" to be interpreted broadly to mean pretty much any kind of labor. The court referred to a recent case where a man who earned money by "manipulating" slot machines in U.S. military service clubs overseas was permitted to take advantage of the $20,000 exclusion. An appeals court ruled that, questionable as the man's methods were, he "earned" his money.

In the Tobey matter, the Tax Court said it didn't see any reason for treating "income earned by the personal efforts, skill and creativity of a Tobey or a Picasso any differently from income earned by a confidence man, a brain surgeon, a movie star or, for that matter, a tax attorney."

(Tobey v. Commissioner, 60 T.C. No. 27)
5/30/73

Jackpot! An itinerant "teacher" beats the one-armed bandits and the IRS too.

An American civilian spent six years traveling the world from one American military club to another, hitting 500 in all. He made his way by "diagnosing and manipulating" slot machines, a skill he acquired while working for a firm that made slot machines. As he told it, he instructed GIs in his art, shared their jackpots and helped them "beat the game of gambling itself, hence breaking addiction to it."

He claimed his take was tax-exempt as earned income from sources outside the U.S. But the IRS said he had rendered no service to "earn" it and socked him for $46,600 in back taxes. His "joint ventures" with GIs were just to get him in the club, it said. At first, the Tax Court agreed, but after a legal fight, it took a second look. He didn't have to render a service, it decided, as long as his income wasn't passive, like rental income.

When the IRS protested that gambling income isn't "earned," the court didn't disagree. But whatever the man was doing, he wasn't gambling, it said. It was the "diligent application of an unusual skill."

(Robida v. Commissioner, T.C. Memo. 1970-86.)
4/22/70

∘⟨⟩•

A bank president, who went abroad to run a church mission, gets a tax break.

Americans who live overseas and don't work for the U.S. government generally don't have to pay taxes on their first $20,000 of annual income. Most people in this category are employes of foreign branches of U.S. companies. But the IRS ruled the tax advantage also applies to a bank president who took leave from his bank to manage his church's mission in a foreign country.

From the foreign post, the man continued to participate by mail and telephone in managing the bank, and the bank paid him a salary. The bank hadn't any foreign operations. But the IRS said this isn't necessary; the law requires only that a taxpayer work for] is employer and receive his salary while a foreign resident.

(Rev. Rul. 72-423)
9/13/72

◦━━◦

A husband and wife get a foreign residents' tax break over IRS objections.

Although their permanent home was South Bend, Ind., William and Carol Hagerty lived in France for well over a year while they tried to spur European sales of their company's products—silver polish and related items. The law generally entitles an American citizen who isn't a U.S. government employe but who lives and earns money in a foreign country for more than a year to exclude the first $20,000 of his income from taxation.

The IRS said the Hagertys weren't "bona fide" residents of France, but the Tax Court concluded they were. They rented a home in a town on the Riviera, took part in community activities there and enrolled their children in a French school, the court said. It also decided their company's business couldn't have been handled adequately on brief visits. And the Hagertys eventually returned to South Bend not because they had reached the end of any predetermined temporary period but because their European business soured, the court found.

(Hagerty v. Commissioner, T.C. Memo. 1973-162)
8/1/73

◦━━◦

A foreign service officer wins a business deduction for home-leave expenses.

If sustained, the decision may establish a new tax break for the career diplomatic corps. The Ninth Circuit appeals court reversed the Tax Court and allowed the officer to deduct what he spent on travel, food and lodging while on home leave. The Tax Court had considered the leave mainly a vacation and the expenses "primarily personal."

The appeals court noted, however, that the law requires the State Department to slate its employes for home leave after they serve three years abroad. (Congress intended the diplomats "to renew touch with the American way of life.") Thus foreign service personnel are "mandatorily required to take a vacation in the United States," the court declared. That wasn't "a particularly onerous burden," it conceded, "but it still was an unavoidable expense imposed by the employer." But the officer's family's expenses weren't deductible.

The court considered it "important" that the policy came from Congress. If a private employer orders executives to travel on leave, the requirement "becomes more suspect as a device for tax avoidance," the court declared.

(Stratton v. Commissioner, U.S. Ct. of Appeals,
9th Cir., 1971)
9/29/71

❍━━▷

An American can be a foreign resident even if he can't say exactly where.

That's what a U.S. district court decided concerning an oil man, long a resident of Saudi Arabia. The oil man had pulled up stakes there and returned to the U.S. for 10 months, which the IRS argued broke his foreign residence. The oil man protested he had promised to go back and start a business in Lebanon. (He later did so.)

The court considered the promise enough to make him a resident of Lebanon during his U.S. stay. But it also said he needn't "point at every moment to a definite country of residence." That was particularly true when his plans and actions pointed to residence somewhere in "a relatively localized area such as the Middle East."

(Carpenter v. U.S.A., U.S. Dist. Ct., No.
Dist. Texas, 1972)
11/23/72

◦⟨⟩◦

Moving beyond Uncle Sam's reach isn't deductible after all, a circuit court says.

Back in 1970, a divided Tax Court allowed a California couple who moved to Australia to deduct their moving expenses. The Tax Court majority said moving expenses were personal, and it made no difference that the couple's ensuing Australian earnings were exempt from U.S. taxes.

Now the Ninth Circuit has sided with the Tax Court minority in ruling the outlays non-deductible because they led to tax-exempt earnings. Some personal expenses like medical outlays needn't be so allocated, but that's because they have no bearing at all on income. By contrast, the expense of moving to a new job site is "as related to earned income as any expense can be," the Ninth Circuit said in endorsing the Tax Court minority view.

(Hartung v. Commissioner,
U.S. Ct. of Appeals, 9th Cir., 1973)
9/5/73

◦⟨⟩◦

Two Vietnam tours and no tax break: And what of the girl he left behind him?

April 15 hurts less for many Americans who live abroad. In 1967, some 91,000 claimed an exemption from U.S. tax for all or part of income they earned overseas (normally, the first $20,000). One way is to establish bona fide residence abroad for a full taxable year. But "bona fide residence" isn't always clear-cut.

An American signed on with an engineering firm to work in Vietnam. His contract provided that if he lasted

50 weeks, his return fare would be paid. He worked that long at a communications site at Pleiku, then returned to the U.S. He signed a new contract and was sent to Nha Trang. Some 13 months later, he left Vietnam for good. While in Vietnam, he enjoyed American officers' benefits, including commissary and PX. He became friendly with some Vietnamese, but spoke little of their language and read almost none. He acquired a motorcycle, a scooter and a Vietnamese "fiancee." At one point, he bought a house in her name.

The Court decided he had merely served two hitches, not become resident. On arrival, he apparently intended to stay 50 weeks, but not necessarily longer. He shared no "community of interest" with the Vietnamese, the court concluded. Nor was his pay subject to their tax.

(Coyle v. Commissioner, T.C. Memo. 1969-53.)
3/26/69

Americans abroad may avoid most U.S. taxes even though the country they live in doesn't require them to pay its taxes, the Court of Claims rules. The case involved two professors sent to Argentina for the UN. Argentina granted them a tax-exemption and immunity from certain local laws. The court found that they had become "well integrated" in the Argentine community, and that was enough to qualify them as "bona fide foreign residents."

(Scott v. U.S., U.S. Ct. of Claims, 1970.)
11/4/70

A tax break for military officers serving in Vietnam is denied a commercial pilot who flew charters between the U.S. and the war zone. Officers in a combat area don't have to pay taxes on $500 a month in income. The pilot carried a card identifying him as a "civilian non-combatant serving with the Armed Forces of the U.S."

and designating him a colonel for purposes of enemy treatment if captured. But the Tax Court ruled that didn't make him a military officer in the eyes of tax law.

(Reynolds v. Commissioner, T.C. Memo. 1972-84.)
4/19/72

Salting a Little
Something Away

The IRS spells out more detail on when pay can be deferred until retirement.

An employe can sometimes put off pay until later years, when he presumably is in a lower tax bracket. Generally, such an agreement must be made before the pay is earned, and the money can't be put aside in a special trust fund. In addition, the employer's duty to pay must merely be contractual, not covered by a note or otherwise secured.

The IRS outlined two specific circumstances that qualify. In one case, a firm gave annual bonuses to employes designated by a committee of directors. The committee had the sole right to defer any or all of the bonuses, and the employe had no right to the money until the deferral expired (a maximum of 10 years past retirement). In the other case, employes aged 40 or older could defer 5% or 10% of their salary. To take effect, the choice had to be made before a year began. The pay was paid over the 10 years after retirement.

In both instances, the IRS ruled that the pay wasn't taxable until the employe actually received it. Similarly, the company couldn't deduct the sums until actually paid.

(Rev. Ruling 69-649.)
1/14/70

◦⟨⟩◦

Self-employed benefit plans leap in popularity.

IRS approvals of retirement plans set up by self-employed individuals soared to 66,400 in the first nine months of 1968, up from 29,400 for all of 1967 and 7,400 in 1966. The sudden allure: A change, effective in 1968, making annual contributions toward retirement fully deductible.

The law permits the self-employed to invest 10% of earned income, up to $2,500, under a regular retirement program. Interest and gains escape taxation until distributed. Until the deductible portion was boosted to 100% from 50%, applications lagged, largely because the self-employed must make equivalent payments for their own employes.

But some people run into problems with the plans. An osteopath, for example, bought $2,400 in U.S. retirement bonds in 1963, but didn't get around to submitting a plan for IRS approval until 1965. The Tax Court, ruling on his 1963 return, disallowed his deduction for the bonds that year on the ground that a definite written program must be in effect when contributions toward retirement are made.

A key point: Even though an IRS okay isn't essential to initiate a plan, some written program must exist to insure statutory requirements are being met.

2/5/69

∘⟨⟩∘

Inept refunding can erase the tax benefits of pension plans, the IRS warns.

More self-employed persons are taking advantage of a law that lets them deduct 10% of their earned income, up to $2,500, and invest it under a tax-sheltered retirement program. But the law also provides that if the beneficiary taps the funds before he turns 59½, or is disabled, the money is subject to penalty taxes.

One plan-holder was penalized when he cashed in an existing contract to put the proceeds into a new

qualified pension plan. The transfer was a premature
pay-out, the IRS ruled, because he wasn't legally obligated to put the money in the new plan. In other cases,
the IRS noted, beneficiaries had avoided penalties. The
trustee of one plan gave the money directly to the new
plan's custodian. In another case, beneficiaries signed
binding pacts to pay the money to their new pension
trust.

(Rev. Ruling 69-254.)
6/4/69

It isn't enough for a pension plan to look good on
paper, the IRS warns.

To qualify for special tax benefits, a retirement
plan can't discriminate in favor of officers, shareholders
or highly paid employes. But the IRS rejected a plan
even though it treated everyone the same. It covered all
employes, but provided that an employe forfeited his
pension benefits unless he worked at least 15 years and
stayed on until age 65.

Trouble was, the IRS said, except for a few stock-
holder-executives, all the employes were migrant workers, who in the nature of things never stayed around
very long. The retirement plan might appear satisfactory on paper, but in operation it benefited only the
brass.

(Rev. Ruling 71-263.)
6/30/71

Profit-sharing for salaried employes only wins approval by the Treasury.

Tax-sheltered profit-sharing plans aren't required
to cover all employes, but they can't discriminate in
favor of employes who are also officers, stockholders, supervisors or highly-paid. This has been a strict standard, but recently the IRS accepted a profit-sharing
plan that included 40 salaried employes but excluded

110 others who would have qualified except for being paid on an hourly basis.

Those covered by the plan included four officers and 18 supervisors, many of whom were also stockholders. But the Treasury was willing to approve the plan as nondiscriminatory apparently because there was no great disparity between what the two groups were paid. Except for the top four officers, the pay of the salaried people was "substantially the same" as that of those on an hourly scale. One person on salary made less than $5,000, while 18 hourly wage workers made more than $15,000.

Some tax advisers interpret the ruling as a boon for small firms that employ skilled, highly paid craft workers but pay them on an hourly basis.

(Rev. Ruling 70-200.)
5/6/70

○══○

Profit-sharing at one small firm is rejected as stacked to favor its owner.

Company profit-sharing plans are allowed substantial tax benefits, but such plans can't discriminate in favor of employes who are officers, shareholders, supervisors or highly-paid. In one recent case, a small construction firm tied each employe's share of the firm's contributions to the length of his employment with the firm. The Tax Court ruled the plan discriminatory, however, because it resulted in a greater benefit for the firm's president-treasurer, who was also its sole shareholder.

The firm contended the provision served the legitimate end of encouraging employees to stay with the firm. The president happened to have been there longer than anyone else. But the court considered it irrelevant that the plan's objective was reasonable. If "invidious or rank discrimination" were required, that would substantially curtail the scope of the law, the court said.

Two judges dissented. They said the court's decision made it "virtually impossible" for a small, owner-operated business to set up profit-sharing tied to past service.

(McMenamy v. Commissioner, 54 T.C. No. 102.)
6/3/70

o<>o

The pension plan at a small company failed to pass IRS muster.

The corporation had only two employes, the officer-shareholder and someone the IRS refers to as a "rank-and-file" employe. Its pension plan provided that the corporation contribute 20% of each employe's salary for the current year, or for his first year, whichever was higher. That sounds all right, but in practice it favored the boss.

The rank-and-filer earned $5,000, and under the plan, the corporation duly salted away $1,000 toward his or her pension. The officer-shareholder earned $50,000, but the annual contribution to his pension was $14,000, or 28%. That's because his first-year salary had been pegged at $70,000. The IRS ruled that this was discriminatory.

In effect, the plan was exploiting an IRS rule: If someone's pay is cut, there's no requirement that his pension benefits or contributions be cut back, too. But this provision can't be applied with discriminatory effect.

(Rev. Ruling 71-331.)
8/11/71

o<>o

A gambler's choice is coming due for restricted stock granted after last June 30.

Restricted stock is a device to defer pay by allowing an employe to buy stock at a bargain rate, subject to forfeiture if certain conditions are violated (such as quitting his job before a given date). Formerly, no tax was paid until the restrictions lapsed.

The new tax law is much tougher: An employe will incur an income tax when there is no longer "a substantial risk" of forfeiture. That tax would cover the spread between what he paid and the shares' market value when the tax comes due. Any subsequent appreciation is taxed as capital gain when realized.

But the law leaves an out for those who will take a chance. The employe can elect to pay the income tax the same year he receives the stock—even though real restrictions remain. This means that practically all appreciation is taxed at lower capital gains rates. But here's the catch: If the stock is forfeited, there's no refund or deduction for taxes already paid.

Normally an employe must make his choice within 30 days of receiving his stock.

(IRS News Release IR-1006, 1970.)
1/21/70

◦━━▷◦

Sugar Ray wins a belated nod from the IRS on his deferral of income.

Some years ago, when Sugar Ray Robinson arranged to have a purse paid to him over several years, the IRS balked. It claimed the arrangement was a joint venture between Robinson and the boxing club, and Robinson's share was taxable when the club received it. But the Tax Court gave the decision to Robinson. The IRS acquiesced and no longer lists the purse arrangement as an example of a joint venture.

In its place, however, the IRS offers the example of a theatrical performer who contracts with a producer to share the profits or losses from a play. The producer puts up the cash and does the things producers do. The performer takes the leading role, directs the play, and supervises other things. These facts amount to a joint venture, the IRS declares. The actor can't defer taxes on his share of the net, no matter when it is paid to him.

According to Tax Coordinator, an advisory service, the new ruling means that sharing profits in exchange for services may create a joint venture "where the individual also agrees to share losses."

(Rev. Ruling 70-435.)
9/2/70

⊶

No more rulings will be made by the IRS on the acceptability of pension programs set up by the self-employed under master or prototype plans. The service says it has already approved some 3,000 prototypes that the self-employed can adopt, and experience shows it's a waste of time to check each individual's program. The IRS will continue to rule on plans a person draws up himself, however.

(Rev. Procedure 69-24.)
11/12/69

⊶

The IRS eases rules on employe contributions to tax-sheltered company pension plans. An employe has been permitted to add up to 10% of his salary to employer contributions. But it's been assumed that if a full 10% wasn't salted away one year, it couldn't be made up later. Now, the IRS rules, payments may be made in any year, provided their total isn't more than 10% of total pay for all the years the employe takes part in the plan.

(Rev. Ruling 69-217.)
5/14/69

⊶

Pension plans that enjoy tax benefits can't discriminate in favor of officers, shareholders, or highly paid employes. The IRS nevertheless approved a plan under which most of the payout would go to the boss. The retirement pay was pegged at 50% of an employe's average career pay, and in the small corporation, the owner-officer's pay accounted for 80% of the payroll. The IRS didn't object, however, because the 50% rule applied to everyone.

(Rev. Ruling 71-255.)
6/23/71

When Doctors and
Lawyers Incorporate

Doctors Inc. gains ground despite stubborn IRS opposition.

In California, it's estimated that some 30,000 doctors will choose to incorporate under regulations taking effect tomorrow. Lawyers are already eligible, and rules for dentists should follow in several weeks. At least 36 other states specifically permit such professional service corporations. In Oklahoma, a U.S. district court recently upheld an incorporated group of doctors. Federal tax collectors had previously lost all seven similar cases. Several are on appeal, and a Supreme Court test is likely.

"Taxes eat doctors to death," says Professional Financial Services Inc., Los Angeles. But a corporation of doctors can contribute up to 25% of employe salaries to pension and profit-sharing plans and deduct the payments as business expenses. The contributions aren't taxable to the doctors, and ultimate pay-outs are taxed as capital gains. One adviser figures that over 30 years, a doctor making $50,000 annually and saving 25% could accumulate $593,000 through a corporate plan, compared with $191,000 without a plan.

But some doctors object to increased bookkeeping and costs of incorporating. Other objections go deeper: "People are becoming more callous, more businesslike, but some older doctors feel incorporating is a loss of identity," an adviser notes.

4/9/69

Another circuit court blisters the IRS and upholds professional incorporating.

The stubborn IRS refusal to recognize corporations formed by doctors or other professionals as corporations for tax purposes appears battered and reeling. The Fifth Circuit appeals court upheld a Florida medical corporation. The court scored IRS rulings curbing incorporation as "wholly arbitrary and discriminatory . . . the only apparent expediency (they serve) has been the collection of more taxes." Being taxed as a corporation would make substantial tax benefits available to professionals.

The IRS says it hasn't decided whether to appeal the decision. One tax authority believes the taxmen are stymied. "They're gotten clobbered on this, and they're close to giving up," he predicts. To date, the Government has lost in three circuit courts and several district courts. With such agreement among lower courts, the tax authority maintains, the IRS isn't likely to obtain a Supreme Court hearing unless it can win at least one lower court to its side.

"They're finished," the tax expert declares. "The service is running out of circuit courts." (Indeed it was. The IRS abandoned its legal fight in August, 1969.)

(Kurzner v. U.S.A., U.S. Ct. of Appeals, 5th Cir., 1969, and IRS Technical Information Release No. 1019, Aug. 8, 1969.)
6/11/69

◦━━◦

Professional corporations must be corporate in fact as well as form.

Last August, the Treasury dropped its protracted opposition to accepting professional service corporations as corporations for Federal tax purposes. Doctors in particular have been eager to gain tax benefits by incorporating. Now a Tax Court decision makes it clear that such benefits by no means follow automatically:

Such endeavors must "put flesh on the bones of the corporate skeleton."

The case involved four radiologists who set up a corporation under Wisconsin law. The men had separate practices in their own names before they incorporated, and their practices were largely unaffected thereafter—except that all their fees and expenses were paid into or from the corporation's checking accounts. Each doctor was credited with what he earned and docked for what he spent.

The Tax Court said the income couldn't be taxed to the corporation because it did nothing to earn it. It sold no services, owned no equipment, and exerted no real control over its "employes." "A mere set of bookkeeping entries and bank accounts," the court said.

(Roubik v. Commissioner, 53 T.C. No. 36.)
12/10/69

◦⟨⟩◦

The Tax Court rules against a corporation it says was set up to avoid taxes.

Currently many professionals and other proprietors are on the brink of incorporation, attracted by likely tax advantages. But the Tax Court wouldn't permit a proprietor to gain by becoming an employe of his own business. The law provides that "amounts received under an accident or health plan for employes" are deductible by employers but don't count as income for employes.

A Wisconsin plumber incorporated to take advantage of this. Under a plan, the corporation would pay medical bills for full-time employes—of which he was the only one. In 1964, the business paid out $1,100. But the IRS argued the sum was taxable income for the plumber, and the Tax Court agreed. Though its decisions have wavered somewhat, the court has stressed that such medical plans must be "for employes." In this case it ruled the plan wouldn't benefit the plumber, as an employe, but rather as owner and sole stockholder.

"The genesis and the primary purpose of the plan —indeed of the incorporation—(was) the avoidance of Federal income taxation," the court declared.

(Smithback v. Commissioner, T.C. Memo. 1969-136.)
7/23/69

◦──▻

It may still pay for professionals to incorporate, Lybrand contends.

High Treasury officials have indicated that steps are afoot to equalize the retirement benefits permitted corporate employes and the self-employed. Maybe so, says Coopers & Lybrand, the accounting firm, but such reports "shouldn't necessarily deter" doctors or other professionals from incorporating their practices. Lybrand says the Treasury has long discouraged such a move, and the latest reports may merely be "another attempt in the drive."

Lybrand contends it's impossible to predict when, if ever, such changes would become law. As yet, they aren't even formal proposals. Any effort to cut back current corporate benefit provisions will meet strong opposition, it says. If, on the other hand, self-employed benefits are liberalized to match current corporate benefits, incorporating may still be useful.

"Problems and pitfalls" will remain in setting up such corporations, Lybrand says, but these can be overcome. The latest Treasury ideas "don't alter the basic situation," the accounting firm concludes.

4/21/71

Life Is Very Taxing
These Days (IV)

Calls from drunks are the least of Los Angeles tax authorities' problems.

Ever since mid-July, when the courts threw out the city's 5% tax on drinks served in bars, the tax refund office has been plagued with telephone calls from indignant inebriates. "They claim they're entitled to huge refunds," an official says. "From the way they sound, their claims are probably valid." But no refunds of the $10 million the city collected have been made, and no one yet knows what to do. "It's going to be difficult," sighs a deputy city attorney. A bill to allow the tax got nowhere in the state legislature.

Individuals, bar owners, liquor retailers, bar mitzvah hosts, and caterers have claimed more than $2 million in refunds. An "individual tippler" and two retailers have sued to force the city to put the $10 million in a trust fund. Los Angeles bars might tap that fund to buy people drinks, an attorney in the suit suggests.

That wouldn't give the money back to the people who paid the tax, he concedes. But it would achieve "a rough justice."

8/26/70

Some Tax-Exempt Groups

A court denies the University Hill Foundation its tax-exempt status.

The controversial foundation carried out an ingenious plan to raise money for Loyola University of Los Angeles. More than $10 million in taxes are at issue in the current litigation. Over nine years, the foundation bought 25 businesses, largely on credit, and promptly leased them back to their original owners. Subsequent profits went to the foundation as deductible payments of rent. The foundation then used that tax-free rental income to pay off the notes it gave to buy the businesses.

The foundation has donated about $2 million to Loyola and it has said it will give $4 million more if its tax-exempt status is upheld. The Tax Court ruled in its favor, but the Ninth Circuit appeals court reversed that decision. Clearly, it said, the foundation wasn't operated exclusively for charitable ends. It was "in the business of using its claimed tax exemptions to buy used businesses," the court declared. It was "a used-business dealer."

Judge Schnacke dissented. The court was awed by the foundation's success, he said. It apparently saw "something sinister" in the "ingenious, complex and somewhat unorthodox" arrangements.

(University Hill Foundation v. Commissioner,
U.S. Ct. of Appeals, 9th Cir., 1971.)
6/9/71

The sale of a business wasn't really a sale, a split Tax Court rules.

A tax-exempt religious organization in Philadelphia agreed to buy the stock of a women's clothing business for $6 million, roughly twice what a normal buyer would have paid. But there were some catches that explain the high price. The religious group didn't commit any money. Rather, it was to pay the purchase price in installments over a period of years out of the clothier's earnings. The religious organization got to keep a small portion of the profits. The former owners of the business stayed on to manage it.

The sellers reported the installment payments they received on the sale price as capital gains, as a seller of stock normally would. But the Tax Court ruled the money was ordinary income because the transaction wasn't a legitimate sale. What really happened, the court reasoned, was that the clothiers paid the religious group a fee, in the form of a small portion of the business's earnings, in exchange for a tax break on the rest of the earnings, which went to the owners of the business just as before, but were disguised as installment payments on a supposed sale.

The court differentiated the deal from a case several years ago in which the Supreme Court upheld six-to-three a somewhat similar transaction that didn't involve such an excessive purchase price. Seven Tax Court judges (out of 16) dissented in the current ruling.

(Berenson v. Commissioner, 59 T.C. No. 39.)
1/3/73

◁▷

Is it too easy for the IRS to revoke a charitable group's tax-exempt status?

The question is increasingly controversial, and the Supreme Court or Congress ultimately may have to answer it, lawyers say. It's nearly impossible not to stop the IRS from cutting off a tax exemption. The law says a court can't stop assessment of a tax (implied in withdrawal of tax exemption) unless the taxpayer would be irreparably harmed and unless it's readily obvious to the court that revocation of exempt status is illegal. It isn't hard for a charity to show the devastating effect of losing tax exemption. But showing the IRS action on its face is illegal can be very difficult. Often, therefore, a group's only alternative is to accept the revocation and then force a court to hear the merits of its case by suing for a refund if and when it has to pay taxes. By then, it may already have suffered severe financial damage by losing donations from people who can no longer deduct their gifts.

Despite this law, the District of Columbia U.S. appeals court ordered a district court to hear a claim by Americans United for Separation of Church and State that the law underlying revocation of its tax exempt status violates the Constitution by discriminating against small groups. That law says a tax-exempt group can't devote a "substantial" part of its resources to politics. What's substantial and illegal for a little group may be insignificant, and thus legal, for a big group doing the same thing, Americans United argued.

But the Fourth Circuit appeals court reached the opposite conclusion in the somewhat similar case of Bob Jones University. The court said the law against stopping assessment of taxes bars hearing the segregationist school's arguments against revoking its tax-exempt status.

(Americans United v. Walters,
U.S. Ct. of Appeals, D.C. Cir., 1973.)
2/7/73

о⟨⟩o

A private school fails to stop a probe of its tax-exempt status.

The Alabama school refused to desegregate, and the IRS began an investigation as a prelude to possibly cutting off its tax-exemption. The school asked a district court to stop the IRS inquiry.

The court refused. It stated the law generally bars courts from stopping in advance the collection of taxes, unless it's proved the collection would do "irreparable" harm to the taxpayer and the collection is clearly illegal. Even though the Alabama school complained of the investigation rather than actual collection, the court ruled the investigation was an essential preliminary to tax collection and thus subject to the law barring restraint of collection. Furthermore, although some contributors to the school might stop giving because of the threat to tax deductions, the court said this wasn't necessarily "irreparable" harm.

The court also mentioned that ending tax exemption for segregated schools had previously been declared legal by other courts. Finally, the court said, the injunction request wasn't the proper way to proceed in the first place; the school should have waited and sued for a refund if the tax was actually assessed.

(Crenshaw County Private School Foundation v. Connally, U.S. Dist. Ct., Middle Dist., Alabama, 1972.)
7/5/72

◦⟨⟩◦

A segregated university loses a crucial battle over its tax-exempt status.

Bob Jones University in Greenville, S.C., is famous for its unswerving refusal to admit blacks. The school says the policy stems from its belief that God didn't intend for races to mingle. The IRS threatened to revoke Jones's tax-exempt status, but a U.S. district court stopped the IRS from doing so until a trial could be held on the merits of the school's position. The court said the case presented a "substantial" constitutional conflict between freedom of religion and freedom not to be discriminated against.

But the Fourth Circuit appeals court says the district court was wrong. The circuit court pointed out that courts are barred by law from stopping collection of tax unless the collection would do irreparable harm and unless the court finds the collection is clearly illegal. The circuit court said revoking Jones's tax status undoubtedly would harm the school. But it also said it's unlikely the revocation and subsequent tax collection would be found illegal in view of the laws against segregation.

The Fourth Circuit also found Bob Jones hadn't exhausted all its administrative appeal possibilities, as it should have before filing its injunction suit.

(Bob Jones University, v. Connally, U.S. Ct. of
Appeals, 4th Cir., 1973.)
1/30/73

◦━━◦

A tax break is upheld for businesses trying to stave off a city's decay.

The city, Monterey, Calif., isn't one that springs instantly to mind when one thinks of urban problems. But several Monterey businessmen were worried that downtown Monterey's narrow streets, increasing vehicular traffic and lack of off-street parking facilities, together with expanding suburban shopping areas, would hurt business in the central city and thus foster its deterioration. So they formed a corporation to build and operate a large public parking lot to make downtown shopping easier.

The businessmen felt the lot's income shouldn't be taxable because the facility was intended to benefit the city at large rather than a few private businesses. (Income of public interest groups generally is tax-exempt.) But the IRS wanted to tax the parking corporation. It reasoned that the main purpose of those who started the lot was helping their own businesses. A U.S. appeals court, however, has just upheld a district court decision that the parking lot should be exempt from tax.

The effort to prevent decay, while obviously beneficial to the parking lot's backers, also helped the city as a whole, the courts said.

(Monterey Public Parking Corp. v. U.S.A.,
U.S. Ct. of Appeals, 9th Cir., 1973.)
7/25/73

◁▷

A Calcutta: A posh wagering pool wins a close one in a U.S. district court.

"The decision could go either way. I have tergiversated for months," the judge confessed, before ruling for the Augusta Golf Association Inc. The issue, dating from the early 1960s, was whether the group could be a tax-exempt social club when its income then came from calcutta pools—including pools at the Masters tournament. In a calcutta, the tourney players are "sold" to the highest bidder. If a golfer does well in the tournament, his sponsor gets a cut of the pool.

The government contended that members of Augusta Country Club, not Augusta National where the Masters is held, had set up the group just to run calcuttas and to draw wagers from the public. The association took 10% off the top. The court noted, however, that profits went for things like buying golf gear for high school teams. It also noted that the pools were restricted to members and guests—though guests outnumbered members, and in earlier years, the Masters calcuttas were public.

The district court also ruled the pools weren't subject to the 10% tax on wagering: They weren't conducted for profit or by professionals.

(Augusta Golf Association v. U.S.A., U.S.
Dist. Ct., So. Dist. Ga., 1971.)
10/20/71

Rochester Liederkranz, a social club, wins a tax battle with the IRS.

Controversy frequently surrounds the tax treatment of proceeds from lotteries that social clubs hold to raise money. Generally, if the drawings are limited to members and the money goes strictly to the club and not to individuals, the proceeds are tax-exempt. But the IRS interprets the law narrowly and tries to collect the tax wherever it can.

The Rochester, N.Y., club, whose members perform vocal music and have access to a bar, restaurant and bowling alley, got 61% of its total receipts from its lotteries. But only members participated in the drawings and the take went to the club treasury. Nevertheless, the IRS said the individual members benefited directly because the dependence on drawings allowed the club's dues and prices to be low. A circuit appeals court, however, held the lottery was exempt from taxes. It called the IRS's view "grudgingly narrow,"

(Rochester Liederkranz v. U.S.A., U.S. Ct. of Appeals, 2nd Cir., 1972.)
3/15/72

◦⟨⟩◦

Social clubs face new guidelines on nonmember business, the IRS says.

The new requirements take effect July 1, 1971. They concern a perennial tax sorepoint, the use by nonmembers of facilities at tax-exempt country clubs, recreation centers and the like. Too much patronage from the general public may cost a club its exemption. Even if such use isn't excessive, the club may be liable for taxes on such income. The new IRS guidelines don't say flatly how much is too much, but generally if receipts from the general public are less than $2,500, or 5% of the club's total receipts, the exemption won't be in danger.

The "general public" includes anyone who isn't a

member, a member's dependent, or his guest. The IRS says that a group of eight persons or fewer, including a member, will be assumed to be the member's guests, provided he or his employer pays. A similar assumption holds when 75% or more of a group of members, and a member or his employer pays. ("Adequate records" must document this.)

In all other instances involving nonmembers, the club must keep detailed records to IRS specifications, to substantiate the "host-guest" relationship.

(Rev. Procedure 71-17.)
5/19/71

◦⟶

A social club finds it can't use its losses to spare outside income from taxes.

The Adirondack League Club is a nonprofit social club that owns a 50,000-acre hunting and fishing reserve in the Adirondack Forest region. It lost its tax-exempt status years ago because it makes substantial income from timbering on its land. The league charges its members dues and fees for lodging and services, but it doesn't turn a profit on these operations.

The league was in the courts recently, and this time the question was whether it could use its losses on services to members to offset its taxable timbering income and thus escape taxes. The Tax Court ruled that it couldn't. The law provides a deduction for expenses incurred in carrying on a business, it said, but the services to members weren't part of the timbering business. In substance, the court said, the league distributed its timbering profits to its members in the form of lower dues and fees.

Congress didn't intend that a private social club, not taxable, subsidize its activities with outside income without paying taxes on that income, the court declared.

(Adirondack League Club v. Commissioner, 55 T.C. No. 83.)
3/3/71

A big insurance company loses a battle with the IRS in a circuit appeals court.

Nationwide Corp., the insurance holding company, tried to deduct a $175,434 loss it claimed to have taken when it sold a block of stock to Nationwide Foundation. The foundation was founded by the company and the tax question turned on their relationship. Under the law, a company can't deduct a loss for tax purposes on a transaction with another entity it controls. The purpose is to keep members of a corporate group from dealing among themselves to avoid taxes.

In a new ruling, a U.S. appeals court says it agrees with a lower court that Nationwide controls the foundation. The corporation's 12 directors included six who were trustees of the foundation, and the court said the six knew the foundation was buying the stock for less than it was worth.

Essentially, those who sold the stock were the same people who bought it, the court reasoned.

(Nationwide Corp. v. U.S.A., U.S. Ct. of Appeals,
6th Cir., 1972.)
3/28/73

◦━━◦

David G. Baird Sr., the New York financier, wins his long tax battle.

When his troubles began several years ago, Baird was senior trustee of the Winfield Baird Foundation. A congressional committee accused him of flagrantly misusing the foundation as a "multimillion-dollar tax-free securities dealer." And in one case, the Tax Court ruled that a $672,000 gift to the foundation was actually a taxable payment for Baird's alleged role in arranging a merger.

An appeals court rejected the ruling on the ground the IRS had broadened its original allegation without informing Baird. The IRS first said the payment was a finder's fee, then later claimed it also was payment for past and future services. The circuit court said Baird hadn't been given a fair chance to rebut the broader charge, so it returned the matter to the Tax Court and instructed it either to decide the case on the finder's fee theory alone or, if the IRS desired, to reopen the record for evidence on the expanded charge.

The IRS didn't ask for the record to be reopened, but simply maintained it had proved the finder's fee charge. The Tax Court disagreed, thus giving Baird the victory.

(Baird v. Commissioner, T.C. Memo. 1972-75.)
4/12/72

◦⟨⟩◦

A scheme to beat taxes by using a foundation fails to shield a founder.

A few years back, an outfit called Americans Building Constitutionally was advising people they could avoid taxes by setting up a foundation to take over their business and putting other assets in trust. The ABC's of tax avoidance didn't come cheap (membership fees ran up to $10,500), but they drew a lot of attention—including investigations by the IRS and a congressional subcommittee. In 1969, ABC's top official and several local promoters were convicted in California of grand theft or conspiracy to commit grand theft.

Davis E. Keeler, an Illinois lawyer, helped organize ABC, but he says he left the group early and was never charged with anything illegal. But he lost in Tax Court on an ABC matter. Keeler ran the Raintree Foundation, a sister unit that ABC hired to write the "education program" it used to instruct its members. Keeler did the work, and ABC paid Raintree $2,000.

Raintree never paid Keeler anything except "some expense money," the court said, but it ruled Keeler had to pay taxes on the $2,000. It said Raintree was "a passive entity" that performed no business function, and it earned the $2,000 "only in form."

(Keeler v. Commissioner, T.C. Memo. 1971-214.)
9/22/71

A gift to a foundation from a firm it owns is ruled a dividend.

Tax-exempt foundations are under fire in part because many have substantial business holdings. Critics contend such holdings are often managed with a greater eye to profit than to the foundation's charitable goals. They say, for example, that some foundations permit the firms they own to retain their earnings, rather than pay the dividends a normal business would be obliged to pay. A Treasury survey found that where foundations owned 50% or more of a firm, in two cases out of three, the stock had a zero yield.

A U.S. circuit court ruled that a $100,000 payment to the Sid W. Richardson Foundation by the Richardson Carbon & Gasoline Co. was a dividend, rather than a tax-deductible gift. The foundation was willed 75% of the firm by the late Texas oilman. The remaining 25% was held by Percy R. Bass, Richardson's nephew and a director of the foundation.

"The conclusion is inescapable," the court said, "that any action (the firm) took was also an action taken by the persons who had sole control of the foundation."

(Richardson Carbon & Gasoline Co.,
U.S. Ct. of Appeals, 5th Cir., 1969.)
10/8/69

The IRS drops a rule that hospitals serve the poor free to qualify as tax-exempt.

For years it has said that a private, nonprofit hospital must be operated "to the extent of its financial ability for those not able to pay." Hospitals have opposed this, arguing in part that schools, museums and other causes aren't required to provide free programs. The hospitals also say that private and governmental medical insurance now covers most persons.

But the IRS ruled in effect that merely offering medical services to the general public is enough—provided a hospital isn't run by a small clique, or to benefit one, and no emergency patient is turned away. "We're delighted," the American Hospital Association declares. Hospitals say they are glad to have their status clarified, but maintain that the ruling won't reduce the services given the poor. Joe Greathouse, administrator of Vanderbilt University Hospital, cites other factors— such as medical ethics, hospital charters, and licensing and accreditation requirements—that "strongly imply" a hospital must serve all segments of the community.

"The ruling won't affect what we do," says New York's Montefiore Hospital. "We've always considered ourselves a community hospital."

(Rev. Ruling 69-545.)
10/15/69

0◁▷0

A "scientology" church is denied tax-exempt status: Better luck in the next life.

The Court of Claims ducked the question of whether the cult is a legitimate church. Scientology teaches that each person contains an immortal spirit, which at death passes into another body. In the string of its lives, however, this spirit becomes inhibited by "engrams" or "detrimental aberrations," rising from misdeeds or unpleasant experiences. Scientology ministers claim they can ease the burden of these engrams by a certain "processing"—normally offered at $20 an hour for 25 hours.

The Court of Claims ruled that the Founding Church of Scientology, Washington, D.C., failed to prove it was entitled to tax-exempt status during the years at issue (1956, 1958 and 1959). It didn't show its net income didn't benefit private individuals. The court noted that the group had paid its founder more than $100,000 over four years, plus the use of a car and a home. His family had also received payments, some of them never explained. In some cases, the founder was also granted 10% of the gross income of affiliated Scientology havens. "Such an arrangement suggests a franchise network for private profit," the Claims Court declared.

(Founding Church of Scientology v. U.S., U.S. Ct. of Claims, 1969.)
7/30/69

More groups are considered exempt from Federal income taxes.

The Revenue Service held that a nonprofit organization formed to educate the public about an illegal activity and to seek legislation that would legalize the activity can qualify for exemption as a social welfare organization. The IRS said that even though the activity might be controversial, "the education of the public on such a subject is deemed beneficial to the community because society benefits from an informed citizenry."

Also ruled is an organization formed for the multiple purposes of promoting racial integration in housing, lessening neighborhood tensions and preventing the deterioration of a neighborhood.

(Rev. Ruling 68-656 and Rev: Ruling 68-655.)
1/8/69

The "singing doctors," a group of physicians, made some money selling their recordings of popular song parodies they had written. The IRS went after some of the money, but a federal district court ruled it wasn't taxable. The medical association that sponsored the group and received the income was tax-exempt to start with. Furthermore, the court found the singing group wasn't a "trade or business" and the doctors individually weren't paid.

(Greene County Medical Society Foundation v. U.S.A., U.S. Dist. Ct., West Dist. Mo., 1972.)
8/16/72

o⫘o

Open and shut: After the Oak Hill Country Club, Rochester, N.Y., played host to the U.S. Open golf championship in 1968, the IRS challenged its tax-exempt status. The IRS contended the club was making its facilities available to the public too much. (The 1956 Open was also at Oak Hill.) The club protested, and the IRS recently reversed itself and closed the file. It concluded the Open was incidental to the club's general purposes.
10/20/71

o⫘o

A religious sect's practice of its beliefs sometimes involves violating state laws, and the sect's tenets bar its members from defending themselves against prosecution for such violations. So an organization was formed to provide the members with legal defense. The IRS ruled that the defense group, financed through contributions, is tax-exempt. The sect wasn't identified.

(Rev. Rul. 73-285.)
7/18/73

o⫘o

A Seventh Day Adventist couple claimed Social Security taxes abridged their religious freedom because they conscientiously objected to life insurance. The law does permit an exemption for adherents of a sect whose tenets forbid public or private insurance and which makes adequate provision for its members. But the Tax Court found it reasonable to limit the exemption to members of such sects. And the couple relied on the teachings of a prophet, not on a set position of their church.

(Palmer v. Commissioner, 52 T.C. No. 36.)
6/4/69

A drug clinic qualifies as a tax-exempt charity, and thus donations to it are tax-deductible, the IRS rules. The ruling involved a nonprofit group that offers a 24-hour emergency rescue center to deal with bad trips on hallucinatory drugs. The group also gives out literature on drug hazards and sends speakers to local high schools.

(Rev. Ruling 70-590.)
12/2/70

○◁▷○

A businessman's lunch isn't enough to warrant a tax exemption, the IRS rules. A club was organized as a gathering place for businessmen to talk over business affairs. It owned and operated luncheon and bar facilities, but that was as far as it went. And without a more substantial program, the group couldn't qualify as a tax-exempt business league.

(Rev. Ruling 70-244.)
5/27/70

○◁▷○

The IRS ruled that a training school for dogs couldn't qualify for tax exemption as an educational organization (which would make contributions to it deductible). It qualified as an exempt nonprofit club, however.

(Rev. Rul. 71-421.)
9/29/71

○◁▷○

Harvard? Disappear? In an application to the IRS concerning tax-exempt status, the Harvard Club of Washington, D.C., said if it was dissolved, its assets would be turned over to Harvard. What would happen, the IRS replied, if Harvard "disappears" before the club does? The club changed the application to provide that if Harvard wasn't around to receive the club's assets, other tax-exempt organizations would get them.

12/13/72

Small Business Matters

Many small businesses can rest easier because of a new circuit court ruling.

They are those that choose to have their income taxed directly to shareholders instead of to the company. Conflicting court decisions have caused confusion over how a company stays within the strict lines the law draws for such arrangements. The law limits a company choosing the special status to only one class of stock. In some cases, the IRS has contended that "loans" shareholders make to companies beyond their original equity stakes weren't really loans but rather were additional equity contributions amounting to a new class of stock. On that basis, the IRS tried to revoke these concerns' tax status.

The Fifth U.S. Circuit Court of Appeals has decided in two cases that the IRS rule covering such situations is more restrictive than Congress intended; that is, there's nothing in the law that says a new class of stock is created just because a shareholder contributes additional equity. But a three-judge panel of the Seventh Circuit appeals court last year took the opposite view. It said there's no such thing as non-stock equity.

The full Seventh Circuit, however, reversed that ruling and agreed with the Fifth Circuit. The new decision clears the air and could make it easier for shareholders to advance extra capital to small companies without jeopardizing the companies' tax status.

(Portage Plastics Co. v. U.S.A., U.S. Ct. of Appeals, 7th Cir., 1973)
3/21/73

The IRS retreats on a tax question important to many small businesses.

The businesses are those that choose to have their profits taxed directly to shareholders instead of to the companies themselves. To qualify for such treatment, a company must limit itself to only one class of stock. Frequently the original stockholders or others later will advance additional capital to the company, and the IRS sometimes tries to make a case that these subsequent contributions represent a second class of stock, thus disqualifying the company from the special tax treatment.

The IRS position has been that almost any equity contribution beyond the company's original capitalization amounts to another stock class. But two circuit appeals courts have ruled this isn't necessarily so. And the IRS announced it plans to change its policy. It didn't say how, but it won't continue litigating the issue until it decides.

8/8/73

◦⟨⟩◦

A split Tax Court overturns an IRS ruling curbing Subchapter S corporations.

Subchapter S allows a small business to incorporate but be taxed as a partnership. Among other limits, such corporations are restricted to one class of stock. Sometimes, however, shareholders receive not only stock but notes for capital they put into the business. When most of a firm's assets are offset by such debt, the IRS feels the stock doesn't mean a lot, and the "debt" really shows ownership.

A California partnership formed such a corporation to operate a driving range. The new entity issued a total of 100 shares of $1 par stock to the former partners. It also gave them notes, bearing no interest, equal to the capital each had in the firm.

The IRS denied the firm qualified under Subchapter S. It cited a ruling that unless such debt is held "in substantially the same proportion" as the stock—and in this case it wasn't—the debt in effect is a second class of stock: It creates another set of ownership claims.

Over six dissents, the Tax Court held the ruling "invalid as applied to this case." Simple instalment debt, carrying no equity rights such as voting, didn't make another class of stock "merely because it creates disproportionate right . . . to the assets."

(Stinnett v. Commissioner, 54 T.C. No. 20.)
2/18/70

◦⟨⟩◦

A small firm paid medical bills for its owner-operators, and a court approves.

People who run small businesses often aren't aware they can arrange to have their corporation pay their medical bills. Money received under an "accident or health plan for employes" isn't taxable income. A business may have different plans for different classes of employes, or leave out some entirely. It isn't even essential that the plan be in writing. The Tax Court recently upheld a plan limited to employes who were also officers —the couple who owned and ran a small supply house.

In 1965, their corporation paid $3,000 in medical bills for them. The IRS claimed the sum was taxable, but the Tax Court disagreed. By law, a plan must be "for employes," the court said, but employes could also be stockholders. The man and wife did most of the work; no excluded employe had comparable duties. There were a dozen lesser employes, but only one had worked more than four months. Their short tenure was "a natural basis" for exclusion.

And as the $3,000 qualified as a nontaxable benefit, it followed that the corporation could deduct it as a business expense.

(Smith v. Commissioner, T.C. Memo. 1970-243.)
9/2/70

Back home in Indiana, a small-town bank survives an IRS challenge.

In a novel case, the IRS attacked the bank as a personal holding company, which isn't a good thing to be. The law exacts a whopping 70% tax on undistributed personal holding company earnings, to prevent its use as a storehouse for profits. (Uncle Sam prefers profits paid out to shareholders, which gives another crack at taxing them.) Banks are excepted, but the IRS claimed the Indiana bank didn't deal with the public enough to be a bank.

Like much else in Austin, Ind., the bank "was controlled" by the Morgan family, whose packing company was the town's dominant employer. The bank didn't lend much (2% to 4% of deposits), and most loans went to Morgan interests. Morgan people accounted for a big slice of its deposits. The little bank shared a room with another firm, and its president found time for lots of outside interests, like running a Dairy Queen. The Tax Court nevertheless ruled the bank a valid operation. About 65% of its deposits were from non-Morgan sources.

The operation "looked like a bank, conducted business like a bank, and believed it was a bank. We must conclude (it) was a bank," the court declared.

(Austin State Bank v. Commissioner, 57 T.C. No. 17)
11/10/71

0◁▷0

The tax court okays a company's financing policy over IRS objections.

The Revenue Service has authority to impose a stiff penalty when it decides a company is letting its profits pile up beyond its needs. Small companies sometimes do this to eliminate the personal taxes their owners would have to pay if the profits were distributed as dividends. To successfully rebut the IRS, a company must show it needed to retain its earnings for some legitimate business purpose.

A small Muncie, Ind., trucking company found that it's well worth taking the IRS to court. The company contended the main reasons it allowed profits to accumulate were that it expected labor costs to rise sharply and anticipated buying new property.

In upholding the company, the Tax Court wasn't deterred by the fact that it didn't actually spend the money for the new property until years after it was originally set aside.

3/7/73

◦◦◦

Calling stock prices shouldn't be required for a company to avoid tax woes.

That's what a U.S. district court said in ruling for Ivan Allen Co., an Atlanta concern hit with the "accumulated earnings tax." The law imposes the tax as a penalty on any corporation retaining earnings "beyond the reasonable needs of the business." The idea is to prod companies to pay out profits to shareholders, who must pay taxes on them.

The Allen company had invested its retained earnings in marketable securities, and that caused the dispute. The IRS conceded that, valued at cost, the securities weren't an "unreasonable" accumulation. But their market value was much higher, and it boosted the retained earnings into the "unreasonable" bracket, the IRS claimed.

The federal court disagreed and decided to value the securities at cost. The law doesn't require taking unrealized gain into account, it said. Nor should a company be forced to sell a high-valued stock merely because its appreciation on paper might trigger the penalty tax.

Stock-market prices fluctuate with "a wide array of imponderables" beyond a company's control, the court declared. Anticipating them would require "crystal-ball gazing rather than sound business management."

(Allen Co. v. U.S.A., U.S. Dist. Ct., No. Dist. Ga., 1972)
11/23/72

◦───◦

An Olds dealer's bonuses were too big for the IRS but fine with a court.

When Ed Shoff Jr. took over Skyland Oldsmobile in Asheville, N.C., in 1959, it was on the "abyss of failure." Pretax profit for 1958 was $484.71. Sales were lagging. Morale was low. Over the next few years, Ed worked 70-hour weeks and didn't take vacations. He moved the agency to a better location and reorganized every facet of the business. By 1966, sales had more than doubled, profits had skyrocketed, and Skyland had a national reputation.

Ed took a straight salary of $10,773 in 1960. But by 1966, he was paying himself a $60,000 bonus atop a $12,000 salary. The IRS said the excess of Ed's take over $42,500 was unreasonable and therefore couldn't be deducted as business expenses of the agency. But the Tax Court found the full bonuses okay.

The court was influenced by an Olds executive who testified he'd have paid Ed similar bonuses under the circumstances.

(Skyland Oldsmobile v. Commissioner, T.C. Memo. 1972-17)
2/2/72

◦───◦

Tricky business: The Tax Court sets "reasonable" pay for an executive.

The IRS and the courts have that authority under the law if they determine a company owner is paying himself more salary than he's worth in order to keep taxable corporate profits as low as possible. (Salaries are deductible to the companies that pay them.) Charles Schneider, who operated several small companies in Council Bluffs, Iowa, ran afoul of the tax authorities mainly because of a bonus plan which accounted for most of his pay.

Over a three-year period, Schneider was paid an average of $63,000 annually. Roughly two-thirds of that was bonus. The IRS refused to permit Schneider's company to deduct more than $35,000 a year in salary to him. The Tax Court was only slightly less restrictive, raising the figure to $40,000. The court noted Schneider worked only part-time during the years at issue, and in previous years when he worked full-time his salary was only $45,000. The court said the bonus arrangement apparently bore little relation "to the services performed."

Despite having authority to define a reasonable salary, the court is rarely comfortable doing so. "We admit the uncertainties in substituting our business judgment for that of others," the court noted in the Schneider case.

(Chas. Schneider & Co. v. Commissioner, T.C. Memo. 1973-130)
7/18/73

०<>०

Unreasonably high pay is okay, if it makes up for unreasonably low past pay.

That essentially is what the Tax Court said in a ruling involving the salary of a Denver businessman, R. J. Nicoll. In the first few years after Nicoll started his company, he paid himself about $9,000 a year even though his services were worth $15,000 to $18,000. He worked long hours six or seven days a week, but underpaid himself so he could put as much as possible back into the business.

In later years, Nicoll cut back his activity drastically but paid himself about $11,500 a year. His company deducted that salary as a reasonable business expense, but the IRS rejected more than half the deductions. (It has the power to do this if it feels a company is paying high salaries to avoid paying dividends or reporting fat profits.) The IRS said $11,500 was an unreasonably high salary, given the limited amount of work Nicoll did.

Nicoll argued that the amount was justified because he had intentionally underpaid himself in the past. The Tax Court agreed.

(R. J. Nicoll Co. v. Commissioner, 59 T.C. No. 3)
10/18/72

◦━━◦

A corporate string slips through an IRS net.

The Treasury contends it was denied an estimated $235 million last year by some large enterprises that operate as a string of separate corporations to exploit a "surtax exemption" meant for small businesses. Corporations pay 22% on their first $25,000 of income, but 48% on earnings above that. One parent company on record had 516 subsidiaries, each claiming the lower rate on its first $25,000 earnings.

The IRS can bar multiple exemptions when corporations are set up mainly for tax ends. But one IRS effort was rebuffed. A New Yorker agreed to operate soft goods sections in six discount department stores. He created a corporation for each store. He chose that set up, he said, to limit his personal liability and keep the different operations separate. But the IRS scoffed. It noted he assumed unnecessary liability when he himself leased store space and borrowed money for the corporations.

The Tax Court ruled for the businessman. It found his rationale credible, even if not consistently followed. And facts indicated he didn't know of the tax advantages.

(Lake Textile Co. et al. v. Commissioner, T.C. Memo. 1969-44.)
3/19/69

The Much-Criticized Property Tax

Could the states use income taxes as a substitute for property taxes?

Not unless the income levies were set substantially higher than the rates we're accustomed to, a study finds. The Education Commission of the States figured the likely revenue yield if *every* state levied individual and corporate income taxes at least as high as the average rate of states that already have such taxes ($16.89 per $1,000 income for individuals and $4.75 for corporations).

If all states levied both taxes, the additional yield would offset only 23% of current property tax collections. By itself, an average-rate personal income tax in all 50 states would offset only 18%. The impact varies greatly: With a personal income tax, Alabama could cut property taxes 61%. But in many states—Maryland, Virginia, New York, Minnesota, for instance—an average-rate income tax "wouldn't reduce property taxes a jot or tittle."

If, in addition, all 50 states imposed general and selective sales taxes at existing average rates, the total new money could offset only 38% of property taxes, the study says.

2/21/73

०<>०

Onerous as it is, the property tax has some key attributes, Citibank says.

It's a more stable and dependable source of revenue for local governments than other taxes are, contends First National City in its monthly economic letter. A landowner can't move his land away just because he doesn't like the property tax. So the town can count on much of the tax base always being there. (High taxes can, of course, discourage new construction, the bank acknowledges.) Another advantage: Property tax assessments don't swing up and down with business cycles as much as income tax collections do. This means revenue levels from property levies are more predictable, and municipal budget planning easier.

These factors are crucial in financing local governments, which depend on a stable inflow of funds more than the federal government does, the bank says. Many cities are restricted from borrowing as readily as the national government can. And securities markets aren't so receptive to large placements by municipalities as they are to federal financings.

5/10/72

०<⚬>०

Computer software is eyed by county tax men as a property tax gold mine.

All the software in the U.S. is worth well up in the billions of dollars but hasn't been taxed much until recently. (Software is industry shorthand for the programs in a computer.) Intangible property isn't taxed in most states, and there's controversy over whether software is tangible or intangible. Many tax men feel software is just as tangible as the computers themselves; computers can't operate without programs. Some counties in California, Michigan, Kansas and Washington State have begun taxing software, as has the District of Columbia. (Densely populated Orange County in Southern California has done it for several years.) New York, Connecticut, Massachusetts, Ohio,

Wisconsin, Oklahoma and Mississippi could do it soon, according to an American Management Association survey.

Software owners and users gear for a fight. Honeywell Inc. is contesting assessments in 15 California counties, including Los Angeles, Orange and San Francisco. California Computer Products Inc. has filed a refund suit against Orange County. A new California law puts a two-year moratorium on taxing software while the matter is studied. But there are exceptions to the ban which some companies feel will result in more taxation than before.

An analyst for the California legislature says the state's counties could raise $45 million a year if they all taxed all software. Some companies ponder moving their software out of state while assessors are around.

11/15/72

∞

"The sad fact is almost nobody realizes how bad property tax assessments are."

That's the consensus of a panel of municipal, tax and planning experts. Property taxes yield more than $33 billion a year, but the panel sees the levy as too often assessed unevenly and haphazardly by undertrained and underpaid officials. The great disparities in assessment practices cause some cities to pass up as much as 50% of their potential take, the panel says. Most properties are assessed too low.

The panel also charges that too often the tax assessor is still a key fund-raiser in local politics. "The power structure" relies on large property owners, who expect low assessments in return. The panel asks that assessment rolls be publicized, and assessment appeals made easy. "Ninety per cent of today's homeowners mistakenly believe they are getting the best of a bad deal," it says.

Forty experts took part in the panel, sponsored by seven major civic groups along with the Schalkenbach Foundation and Time Inc. The report published in Nation's Cities, represents "broad and general agreement," though not unanimity.

5/20/72

◦━━◦

A Detroit suburb stirs debate on how hefty land taxes affected its boom.

Some urban scholars say American cities stifle new construction by taxing buildings too heavily and land too lightly. Southfield, Mich., has been praised as a sharp exception. By one account, the Detroit suburb became "the boomingest city in the state" after a 1962 survey doubled the assessment—and the taxes—on land, thereby permitting "a substantial reduction in the tax on improvements."

But local opinion is by no means unanimous. Former Mayor S. James Clarkson doesn't doubt the increased assessments were crucial. "If you tax land, you tax it into use," he declares. But others note that assessment at 50% of fair market value is set by Michigan's constitution. They cite other reasons for the city's growth. "Probably most important," says Mayor Norman W. Feder, was a network of expressways that eases access to the city. Another allure was the huge Northland shopping center. And Southfield lies in the path of expansion from Detroit.

"The tax philosophy played no constructive part," one large property owner contends. The heavier land assessments "prevented or delayed improvements we otherwise would have carried out."

4/23/69

◦━━◦

A ceiling on property taxes is proposed by an intergovernmental group.

The Advisory Commission on Intergovernmental Relations estimates that the average U.S. urban family pays about 4% of its household income in local property taxes, either directly or in its rent. Yet about three million households pay 10% or more—"a truly extraordinary tax burden," the commission says. In 1968, Wisconsin granted tax relief to 66,000 low-income elderly. For 22,000 of these people, their property tax would otherwise have taken 20% of family income and often much more.

With state legislatures in session, the commission has revived its proposal for a "circuit-breaker" provision that would in effect refund property taxes above a certain percentage of income. Four states—Wisconsin, Minnesota, Vermont and Kansas—have such laws. All four plans are limited to the low-income elderly. In Wisconsin, when such a taxpayer's property tax exceeds about 11% of his income, he gets a tax credit or a cash refund of the difference, within certain limits, the commission says.

The elderly are the neediest, but the commission recommends that circuit-breakers apply to all low-income families.

3/17/71

Wisconsin helps more low-income elderly persons with local property taxes.

The state offsets part of the property tax bite by giving income tax credits or cash refunds to persons 65 or older whose household incomes are under $3,500. An old person or couple who pays $250 in local property taxes can expect a $23.70 refund from the state if household income was $2,900, and a $122.70 refund if income was $1,500. Renters as well as homeowners are included: 25% of rent is considered payment of taxes.

A Federal advisory commission lauds the Wisconsin

program as effective relief without an unreasonable drain on the state treasury. In fiscal 67-68, some 68,400 elderly claimants got an average of about $90 each. In the fiscal year beginning this July 1, it's expected that claims will grow to 78,300 and average payments to $97.50. Some tax people believe that extending the benefits to all low-income groups is a logical next step.

2/19/69

∘⟨⟩∘

More states enact property tax relief, usually limited to the elderly.

Florida increased its homestead exemption to $10,000 for taxpayers 65 or older. South Carolina passed a homestead exemption for the elderly that's expected to cost $1.5 million next year. Colorado has granted an income tax credit or refund of up to $200 for part of property taxes paid. It's restricted to the elderly with net worth less than $20,000 and with income less than $3,700 if married.

Iowa and Vermont also passed measures for the elderly, but not all relief is for old folks only. Oregon enacted $20 million in tax relief for homestead owners. It comes into play when property taxes exceed a certain percentage of household income (3% for incomes under $1,500, with relief limited to $400 in that bracket). In Washington State, tax relief includes a provision that will reduce property taxes by $43.9 million in the next two years. It requires counties, when revaluing properties, to reduce assessment ratios to the average county ratio.

The value of the U.S. property tax base nearly doubled between 1961 and 1971, a Commerce Department report says. The assessed value of property was $717.8 billion in 1971, up from $367.3 billion 10 years earlier. Locally assessed real estate, which comprised about 80% of the 1971 base, rose 105% in the 10-year period to

$553 billion from $270 billion. However, property tax revenue during the same years fell to 40% of all state-local government revenue from 46%. The report doesn't differentiate between assessments on new property and rising assessments on existing property.

4/25/73

◦───◦

Property taxes are presumably a tax on wealth, but according to a Rand Corp. study of rental housing in New York City, they amount to a 30% tax on consumption of rented shelter. City taxes on real estate add "roughly one-third" to the typical family's rent bill, the study says. It also found that the effective tax rate on market value runs about 30% higher on multiple-family buildings than on one-family and two-family housing.

8/12/70

◦───◦

Rule of thumb—or of thumbs down? Whenever a school district's property tax hits 4% of true market value, you can expect trouble from homeowners. That's the experience of Engelhardt & Engelhardt Inc., a consulting firm that advises school districts on financing. The 4% threshold triggers protests, organized debates and other controversy, the firm says.

12/23/70

◦───◦

Old soldiers: Effective Sept. 9, Oregon will no longer allow a property tax exemption for disabled veterans of the Mexican War, Civil War or Indian Wars.

7/14/71

And in Those Days...

There went out a decree from Caesar Augustus that all the world should be taxed.

So begins Luke's recounting of the birth of Christ, but his account has left Biblical scholars puzzled over exactly what levy Joseph returned to Bethlehem to pay. For centuries, Egypt had required a census of citizens every 14 years. Borrowing the idea, Caesar Augustus made a census mandatory in 6 B.C. (the presumed actual year of Christ's birth). It covered males over 14 years old and females over 12 and listed possessions and sources of income. The elderly were exempt.

Scholars aren't entirely sure, but they believe the taxes were imposed annually. It's clear they were steep. A Roman property tax in the provinces ran up to 25% to 33% of a crop's yield. It's known that the Romans also exacted a "poll tax," which included a uniform head tax, an income tax and other personal taxes. No one knows the exact rates, but they were steep, too. Taxes varied from place to place, often at the tax collector's whim.

The Jews came from well-defined families stemming from certain ancestral areas. To minimize tax evasion, the Romans ordered Jews to return to these places for the census. That's the reason Luke gives for having Mary and Joseph, who was of the House of David, travel some 60 miles by donkey from Nazareth to Bethlehem.

A few scholars question Luke's accuracy. They say the Manger story belongs in the same category as Jonah and the Whale. It should be read for theological, rather than historical, truth, they contend.

12/23/70